Thought F
and
Hallucinations

This book is dedicated with gratitude and appreciation to all those whose painstaking labour and researches have provided the material from which it has been compiled

ADVANCE PRAISE FOR THE BOOK

"Very comprehensive, scholarly and clearly written. I am impressed."

- **Dr. Erlendur Haraldsson Ph.D.,
Professor Emeritus, University of Iceland**

☙❧

".....the book provides a highly inspiring reading experience expanding the confines of world view."

- **Dr. Matti Pitkänen, Ph.D.,
Quantum Theoretical Physicist, Hanko, Finland.**

☙❧

"..[the author] did a good job in mentioning all the cases where our science of today does not have an explanation. Being a great fan of the Holographic principle, I liked very much the chapter 'Holographic Mind'"

- **Dr. Petrus Soons, M.D.,
Holographic Shroud Researcher, Volcan, Panama.**

☙❧

"This book explores subjects that have been neglected by researchers and not grasped by skeptics. It offers much to ponder on"

- **Michael E. Tymn, Editor,
Journal for Spirituality and Consciousness Studies.**

☙❧

Praise for the Book

"it looks interesting indeed. The idea of intense thoughts or mental images becoming reality is quite akin to my view of the mind as a three-dimensional imaging system capable of generating images of any object imaginable. Where we diverse is our ontology of mind...."

- Dr. Steven Lehar, Ph.D.,
Research Fellow in Ophthalmology,
Harvard University, and an independent researcher.

ഴ‍ര

"At a glance, it looks wonderful."

- Rev.Karen E.Herrick, Ph.D.,
President of the Academy for Spiritual
and Consciousness Studies, Inc., USA.

ഴ‍ര

"I agree that the numerous examples of human and animal behaviors make an impressive case for the existence of a universal quantum hologram that allows for complex and diverse observed phenomena not explained by current understanding of functioning within the brain. And an impressive list of scholastic researchers have contributed to a growing awareness that an external field which all brains interact with must be the origin of the phenomena. I particularly liked the conclusion that "the brain is a hologram enfolded in holographic universe." I especially liked the pen-ultimate chapter that traces the development of thought and experiment that brings us to this conclusion, and the very considerable bibliography that allows us to individually explore further."

- Dr. Rudolph E. Schild, Ph.D.,
Harvard-Smithsonian Center for Astrophysics,
Cambridge

DISCLAIMER AND WARNING

This book is intended to provide explanations to many mind-related phenomena like thought-forms, mental hallucinations, stigmata, etc. If the explanation offered in the book hurts in any way the religious sentiments of the readers directly or indirectly, I, as the author, apologize to the readers. The reproduction of illustrations or citations does not necessarily mean that the respective authors agree with the ideas contained in this book.

Prospective and expectant mothers are highly dissuaded from reading the chapter on Maternal Impressions as it may cause undesirable psychological fears in their mind and is likely to prove counter-productive.

FOREWORD

Dr. Matti Pitkänen Ph.D.,
Founder of the Topological Geometro-dynamics (TGD)
inspired Theory of Consciousness

The book *'Thought-Forms and Hallucinations'* by Chidambaram Ramesh represents a comprehensive amount of anecdotal evidence challenging the standard view about consciousness dominating still in neuroscience, although new visions inspired by quantum physics are evolving and quantum biology has emerged as a new branch of science. As a theorist I find this kind of book fascinating because it serves as a reminder about the anomalies.

What is human mind? This is the question motivating also this book. The view inspired by classical physics assumes that consciousness is a mere epiphenomenon: contents of consciousness are in principle known once the state of brain is known in every detail. This implies that the destruction of brain means the end of consciousness. Consciousness emerges in some mystical manner in sufficiently complex systems and has no causal powers in the materialistic framework. This view often accompanied by the belief inspired by the locality of classical physics: minds are completely isolated inside brains. Locality is however in conflict with the quantum physics but it seems that the needed macroscopic quantum coherence is not possible in standard quantum physics. The materialistic vision has practically no explanatory power since there is no idea about the coding of physical state to conscious experience and no idea why brain should be the sole seat of consciousness.

One could of course uncritically accept the classical view or adopt some of the quantum views about consciousness which also tend to force the mind to the format of an existing theory rather than bravely asking what consciousness could give to the quantum physics. A more difficult alternative is to start from mind itself by making questions about the basic ontology. Do matter and mind represent different levels of existence? Are mind and consciousness one and same thing? How to define these notions more precisely? In Einstein's theory and in its predecessors' matter has space-time geometry as its correlate; could also thoughts (cognition) and intentions possess such geometric correlates? What happens when intention transforms into action or sensory percepts create thought?

This approach might look hopeless but the condition of internal coherence is surprisingly powerful once one has at least some key idea. As a matter of fact, the existing view about consciousness is full of internal incoherencies and also quantum consciousness theory suffers from a deep internal conflict (measurement problem). Mere armchair theorizing is however not enough and can lead to highly lopsided thought constructs as anyone studied philosophies of mind has found. Empirical approach is needed too, and here anomalies challenging both the dominating and alternative belief systems provide further strong guidelines. There indeed exists a rich spectrum of empirical facts which do not conform to the materialistic view and this book contains a comprehensive discussion of this kind of empirical facts and is therefore a precious gift to anyone who wants to challenge and develop personal beliefs about consciousness.

Contrary to the materialistic dogmas, practically everyone describes episodes of personal life in terms of acts of free will and has no doubts about having a possession over own body. These actions over personal body can of course be also non-volitional; emotional expression is the basic example about this. The common belief is however that psycho-kinesis is impossible; intentional actions cannot affect other biological bodies or non-living matter. The biological body is thus distinguished as a very special part of the Universe. This might be indeed the case in excellent approximation but there is however no real justification for this in the framework of standard physics.

Hypnosis represents a basic example about a well-established phenomenon, which could also have interpretation as a remote mental interaction and thus in conflict with the dogma of isolated minds. There is also laboratory evidence for remote mental interactions such as telepathy, remote viewing, and remote healing, especially so between emotionally bonded persons. The relationship between mother and child represents perhaps the strongest bonding of this kind and the ability of the mother to wake up to even slightest sound produced by her child challenges the assumption about isolated minds.

The ability of imagination to induce bodily effects – say change in skin conductance, *placebo* effect, the power of visualization – all these suggest that imagination is a powerful tool to change the world, perhaps even the external world. This motivates the author to introduce the notion of thought-form identified as a kind of mind-like entity. Maybe one could understand this notion as the ability of volition to transform intentions to actions – mind to matter, one might say. Not only inside personal biological body as in emotional expression and in *placebo* healing but in some cases outside it as in psycho-kinesis and in some strange cases discussed in the book. Examples are thought-photographs and the texts of Khuran appearing on the skin of child whose mother, during her pregnancy, had read Khuran with high spiritual devotion. Certainly, the ability to transform thoughts into matter would require profound modifications in the existing ontology of physics.

When one speaks about consciousness, one cannot avoid mentioning time. The relationship between experienced time and the rather well understood time of physicist – geometric time – is poorly understood. There are strong correlations but also big differences between these notions so that their identification is not justified. It also seems that the assumption that our contents of consciousness is about single 3-D snapshot of space-time is too strong a simplification. Already the ability to remember and anticipate suggests temporal non-locality. The examples of this book about memories of previous lives and about birthmarks representing injuries associated with incidents of previous life support temporal non-locality in long time scales. Similar temporal non-locality manifests itself in sensory perception in the scale of about 0.1 second defining the duration of moment of sensory perception.

The fundamental question is how mind affects matter. Of course, if mind is equated with consciousness rather than only its correlate, already this question contains an implicit ontological assumption boiling down to the assumption about existence of conscious entities. It might well be that only the conscious experiences are what exist and conscious entity – experiencer – is a figment defined by the contents of emotionally loaded part of conscious experience. If so, Descartes would have been wrong! In any case, it is very practical to talk about conscious entities as something real, and this is the approach adopted in the book.

Accepting this, the question is "Who am I?" This biological body or something more as the visions of mystics suggest? Author chooses the latter option and introduces the notion of subtle field body. An interesting question is whether one can formulate this notion using the language and concepts of recent day physics. It has become clear that the role of long range electromagnetic (at least) fields is central in living matter; especially bio-photons, EEG, magnetic fields, and strong electric fields seem to have an important role in biology. It is however questionable whether the expressive power of quantum mechanics and Maxwell's theory is enough to formulate the notion of subtle field body.

Another basic theoretical proposal of the book relies on the notion of bio-holography. It states that parts of the biological body can represent biological body itself. This is of course realized at abstract level via DNA but there is evidence that body parts such as ear quite concretely provide holograms of other body parts. Holography is also realized at the level of brain as experiments with salamander brain dramatically demonstrate. The challenge of theorists is to formulate what the notion of bio-hologram actually means. Holography is one of the guiding ideas for those trying to build the theory of everything; but holography has several widely different interpretations. Bio-holography need not, of course correspond such to holography in this sense. Summarizing, besides providing an extensive commentary of various fascinating anomalies, the author introduces three basic propositions in the attempt to understand the empirical evidence in a coherent manner. There are entities, which could be called 'thought-forms' and their exteriorizations outside the body are possible. There is continuity of thoughts after destruction of brain. Thought-forms, to some extent, can have autonomous existence. The attempt to imagine physical realizations for these propositions is an exciting challenge. Also for the reader not building a theory of consciousness based on new physics, the book provides a highly inspiring reading experience expanding the confines of world view.

Matti Pitkanen
Hanko, Finland.
14.12.2013

PREFACE

It is no proof of wisdom to refuse to examine certain phenomena because we think it certain that they are impossible, as if our knowledge of the universe were already completed.

- **Prof. Lodge**

The fundamental question in brain sciences today is the mind-brain-body relation. Classical and molecular biologists imagine that man is nothing but a bundle of molecules so curiously organized by the genetic mechanism combined with biochemical interactions. Such belief, though based on several aspects of research in genetics, conveys only a part of the message. Biology is not simply genetics. There are many psychological and quantum state phenomena that have an undeniable bearing on biological phenomenon, including the expression of genes. Yet again, genetics has failed to explain many fundamental characteristics of an organism, its development and inheritance of characters intimately connected with the morphological and physiological properties of the organism. So there must be something more than genetics at play in orchestrating the physical constitution of biological organisms. But what it is… is a deep mystery, unfathomable by the conventional scientific concepts and ideas.

In recent times, the subject of consciousness has emerged as an important paradigm of scientific investigation and research, despite most of its concerns having roots in philosophy, religion and occultism.

What is consciousness? What is the substance of consciousness? Is it material or immaterial, mortal or immortal? How is it connected with a body? Has it a particular seat in any particular body as the brain does? Is consciousness synonymous with mind? Is it eternal and non-local? These questions have interested thinkers for many centuries.

First, let me say how the questions present themselves to us here. How the brain generates thoughts remains one of the major mysteries of neuroscience. Nonetheless, it would not be easy to expatiate on the boundless realms of 'human mind' and its feelings, and also treat the theme adequately, unless introspection into the observational records of their outward manifestations is used as our chief instrument of scientific exploration.

All bodily manifestations have their root in the mind. The interpretations we get by observing the simple bodily manifestations can help us to unravel complex mind-related mysteries.

One remarkable incident that occurred four years ago in the Russian Republic of Dagestan has also a bearing on this question. A nine-month old baby boy, Ali Yakubov, left doctors baffled after phrases from the holy Quran began appearing on his skin. These sayings from the Islamic holy book were said to appear on his back, arms, legs and stomach, before fading away and being replaced with new sayings. Medical specialists have denied that the lettering is from someone writing on the boy's skin. Would it have had any connection with the mental thinking of the baby's mother who used to read the Quran with emotion and devotion?

Similar incredible cases of birthmarks have widely been reported in many countries at various times and have been vouched by many authorities. There are various instances on record in which individuals have been said to have *words* (generally a name) marked on their skin, or even upon the *iris*.

Impressed by these incidents, I started collecting similar clinical cases of curious mind-related bodily manifestations, of which I have many written in my note-book; but they became so numerous that they could only be compiled in the form of a book.

Some readers may regard it as a waste of time and energy except as a diverting curiosity. However, a sincere motive underlies it. I did not want to make a mere reproduction of such material facts in a story-telling pattern. Rather, I have attempted to make a comparative and analytical study of these phenomena. By doing this, I could perhaps lift the veil to find that the various threads of these diverse phenomenological features are basically woven together into a fabric of scientific unity.

The various phenomena reported in this volume are peculiar and interesting effects of nature and are merely the links in a chain of causes and effects. We cannot dismiss these natural phenomena as superstitious or foolishness simply because today's science cannot explain them. Nothing in nature falls outside the domain of science. Rather, these wondrous phenomena of nature signal the inadequacy of the contemporary scientific theories as a total explanation of the world and its happenings and remind us of the task of understanding and explaining phenomena such as these. Surely something is not quite right with our present understanding of the faculties of the mind and we shall hardly make progress towards mental science if we are sticking to the classical theories of mind and body.

It is the object of the present work to demonstrate, through a series of cases reported across the world at various times relating to the creation of mental entities, the imprints of indelible images on the human body, thought photographs, and similar curious manifestations of mind on the physical body.

Again, the book does not stop with the mere reproduction of recorded cases and just messaging the dimension of the problem, but extends over to solve it by suggesting a bio-holographic theory of body and mind.

The light which the bio-holographic theory is capable of throwing on the deeper problems of human thought and developmental biology is only beginning to be appreciated. The field over which it can be applied is almost indefinitely wide and deep. The parts touched in the present volume constitute of course of only a selection; yet they are sufficiently diverse to include the following– the creation of mental entities or thought forms, hallucinations, birthmarks and bodily deformities corresponding to injuries sustained in the previous births, imprint of mental images on photographic plates, maternal impressions, and so on.

Preface

The reader may, sometimes, tire of the lengthy list of cases narrated in the book; but in the interest of providing strong and sufficient evidences, I wish to give extensive (not exhaustive) information which may instruct us in the field of mind processing.

Last but not least, I must mention I am but a layman, a humble student of the scientific labour of others, not an original investigator myself. In writing this volume, I have consulted numerous works of historical credibility and my scheme is to use only those cases which, I believe, have the stamp of truth.

To add credibility to the cases referred to in this volume, I decided not to alter the language of their original authentic records. I have no other aim than to state, as simply as possible, what I have learned in the course of some years that were spent in these rather discredited and unfrequented regions of science. Many of the facts and analyses presented in the book will be of interest to medical experts as well as general readers.

I hope the subject is alike novel, fun-filled, profound and useful, thus affording that blend of interest and instruction which cannot fail to render it interesting to the inquisitive and candid mind. Whether my investigation of the process of mind has at all furthered the understanding of it, I must leave it to my readers.

Chidambaram Ramesh
Vellore, India.
Write to: c.ramesh@yahoo.com

ACKNOWLEDGEMENTS

There are many people who played a valuable role in getting this book out into the world. I hereby express my gratitude to Kathleen E. Erickson, Managing Editor of the *Journal of Scientific Exploration* for granting me special permission to make use of copyrighted works of Dr. Ian Stevenson and Dr. Satwant K. Pasricha. My acknowledgements are due to Dr. Matti Pitkänen, Finnish theoretical physicist and founder of the Topological Geometro-dynamics (TGD) theory, for enlightening me on various issues relating to the holographic nature of mind and body.

I am thankful to Dr. Erlendur Haraldosson, Professor Emeritus, University of Iceland; Alfredo Pereira Jr., Institute of Biosciences, São Paulo State University, Brazil; Peter Rowland's, Department of Physics, University of Liverpool, Michael E Tymn of Association for Evaluation and Communication for Evidence for Survival (AECES), Martinsburg, Dr. Bokkon Istvan, Ph.D., Professor at Vision Research Institute (USA) and Dr. Jonathan D Cowan, Ph.D., the founder and President of NeuroTek, USA, Dr. Jacob D Bekenstein, Polak Professor of Theoretical Physics, Hebrew University of Jerusalam, Dr. Spyros Papageorgiou, Institute of Biology, Demokritos, Athens, Greece, for having graciously consented to allow me to make use of their papers. It must not be inferred, however, that these scientists endorse all the views expressed in the book. My special thanks are due to Christine Lynch for sharing with me her reflections on *the Cottingley Fairies* that appeared in a series of photographers taken by her mother Frances Griffiths and Elsie Wright between 1917 and 1920 which were considered by scientists, including Sir Arthur Conan Doyle, as 'thought forms.'

In the preparation of this volume, I have made careful research in the literature, touching on every phase of the many subjects considered. For this purpose, I have had recourse not only to my own library, but to various other libraries, particularly the library in the Madras Institute of Developmental Studies, Chennai. Many public domain reference works are available in the internet thanks to *Project Gutenberg* and the *Internet Archive*.

I am grateful to the hundreds of authors whose work I depend on. After all, this book is a compilation of what they have achieved.

CONTENTS

1. INTRODUCTION	1
General Scheme of the Book	6
2. THOUGHT FORMS	12
General Appearance of Thought-Forms	13
'Thought Forms' in History	14
1. Creation of Thought-entities by Voluntary Mind Force	17
David Neel's Unwanted Companion	18
Conjuring up Philip	19
Family Gods and Angel Guides	22
Imaginary Companions	24
2. The Manifestation of Thought-Forms due to Yearning Desire	25
Apparition of the Virgin Mary that Caused the Train to Stop	25
Seeing One's Own Thought Body	27
Double's Yearning Desire	27
Punctuality of the Mental Body	29
Thought Body that Came for a Book	31
3. Psychic Characters and the Writer's Psyche due to Intensive Thinking	32
The Writer's & Composer's Psyche and Psychic Characters	33
Thought Form That Haunted Shelley	34
Johannes Brahms' Mental Images	34
Balzac identified Himself with his Characters	35
Mozart – Miraculous Compositions	35
Saint-Saeans and Stevenson	36
Charles Dickens Characters	36
Samuel Taylor Coleridge's Kuble Khan	37
Giuseppe Tartini	37
4. Dream Reasoning	37
Discovery of the ring of Benzene Molecule	39
Deciphering Fossil Imprints in Dream	39
Professor Hilprecht	41

	Figures in Imagination	42
	The Dream Detective	44
	Experience outside the Body	45
	Bodily Manifestations of Mental Images during Dreams	47
	Photographic (Eidetic) Memory	50
	Painters' Mental Images	51
	Phillis Atwater' Imaginary House	52
	Dream-thought Transmissions	53
3.	**HALLUCINATIONS**	**55**
	The Hallucinated Afterimage Obeys Optical Laws	59
	Self-Hypnotic Pet Polar Bear	61
	Astral Wolf	61
	Great Cat Hallucination	62
	Haunted by Himself	64
	A Spirit Story	64
	Apparition of the Deceased	65
	Skeleton Spectators	66
	Hypnotism and Auto-suggestion	67
4.	**THOUGHT-PHOTOGRAPHY**	**70**
	Roger's Thought Experiments	72
	Dr Hyppolyte Baraduc	73
	Commandant Louis Darget	75
	Eusapia Palladino	76
	Fukurai's Experiments	77
	The Thoughtographic Man: Serios	78
	Spirit-Photography – A Kind of 'Thought-Photography'	81
	Thought Photograph of Abraham Lincoln	83
	Other Examples	83
	Another Instance of a Thought Photograph	84
	Thoughts Projected into Water	85
5.	**IDEOPLASTY AND MATERIALIZATION**	**88**
	Little Stasia	90
	Eva Materialization Case	93
	Franek Kluski	97
	The Bird	97

Contents

	'Ape-man' Materialized in Experimental Physical Séance in Warsaw!	98
	Paraffin moulds of the materialized Hands	100
	Ethel Post-Parrish and her 'Silver Belle'	101
	Goligher's Table Levitation	103
	Hamlin Garland's Observations	104
6.	**PAST LIFE MEMORIES**	**109**
	Birthmarks/Birth Defects in Cases of Alleged Re-births	111
	The Case of Thiang San Kla – Fatal Wound on the Head	115
	The Case of Krishnan Chaudhri – Sutured Wound on the Face	118
	The Case of Chatura Karunaratne –	120
	Reminiscence of an accident	120
	The Case of Ranbir Singh – Missing Hand Mangled in a Machine	123
	The Case of Semih Tutusmus – Rebirth of a Man who came in the dream	124
	The Case of Hanumant Sexena – Impressions of an accidental gunshot	125
	The Case of Rajani – Indelible Scars of self-immolation	127
	The Case of Yashbir Yadav – Birthmark of Bullet Wound	128
	The Case of Khin Mar Htoo – Congenital absence of lower leg	130
	The Case of Lekh Pal – Amputated fingers	131
	Bio-Holographic Model	133
7.	**MATERNAL IMPRESSIONS**	**137**
	Resemblance to Animals due to Fright caused by them	141
	Monstrous Births due to Maternal Mental Influence	144
	Fright by Opossum	145
	A Child Half-Fish	146
	A Snake Man	147
	A Monstrous Cat-headed Child	148
	The Monkey Girl	149
	Children Resembling a Frog	150
	Frightened by a Cow	151
	Turtle Man	152
	Resembling a Rabbit	152
	Birthmarks due to Mother's Craving and Fantasy	154
	Dated Kitten	154

	Contents	
	The 'Napoleon Eyed' Child	155
	Alleged Father's Name Appears in Infant's Eyes	156
	The 'Elohim Eyed Boy'	157
	Ace of Spades in the Eye	157
	Verses from the Quran on an Infant's Body	157
	Paternal Effects Transmitted to Foetus through Mother	160
	Impact of Dreams	164
	Impact of Paintings	164
8.	**MENTAL STIGMATA AND BODILY IMPRINTS**	**168**
	Cross Mark on a Girl's Arm	170
	Therese Neumann's Stigmatization	171
	Girl with Stigmatic Biting	172
	Reproduction of Target Images on Skin	172
9.	**HOLOGRAPHIC MIND**	**178**
	Holographic Nature of Brain, Mind and Consciousness	179
	What is a Hologram?	181
	Holographic Brain	184
	Memories are Disbursed Throughout the Brain	184
	Karl H Pribram's Holonomic Mind Process	185
	Shuffle Brain Theory of Paul Pietsch	187
	Bohm's Implicate and Explicate Orders	188
	Other Theories that Suggest Holographic Brain Mechanism	189
	Philip R Westlake's Analogy	189
	Schempp's Quantum Holographic Neuro-Dynamics	189
	Universal Holographic Principle – Raphael Bousso	190
	The World as a Hologram – Leonard Susskind	190
	Nikolai Bernstein: Movements are Waveforms	191
	Pieter van Heerden's concept of 'Recognition Holography'	192
	John Eccles – Not Energy but Information	192
	Collective Consciousness Theory of Carl Jung	193
	Holographic Projection of Mental Images	193
	Some Other Holographic Models of Mind and Consciousness	195
	Pitkanen's TGD inspired Theory of Consciousness	195
	Max Velman's 'Reflexive Model'	196

Rupert Sheldrake's Model of Visual Perception	196
Lehar's model of Gestalt Isomorphism	198
Cowan's Mentaholomorphic field	199
Francisco Di Biase' Quantum-Informational Holographic Model	200
10. CONCLUSION	**202**
Bibliography	

ILLUSTRATIONS

Figure 1	Opera House in Central City, Calorado (Left)	80
Figure 2	Ted Serios' Thought photograph (Right)	80
Figure 3	Mary Todd Lincoln's portrait with the thought-form of her husband, President Abraham Lincoln, photo taken by William H.Mumler	81
Figure 4	The phogograph of a mind projected capital letter "G" caught emerging up out of water viewed through a microscope	85
Figure 5	Medium Eva.C Photograph taken in 1912, apparently showing a light manifestation between her hands and a materialization on her head.	94
Figure 6	Materialization obtained from the medium Eva C. during an experimental session performed with Prof. Schrenck-Notzing	95
Figure 7	Gustave Geley: Materialization of a Woman's Face Produced by the Medium Eva.C, February 26, 1918.	96
Figure 8	Photography of the materialization of a bird obtained at the session of the Paris Institute of Metaphysics by Franek Kluski	97
Figure 9	The Materialized "Ape-man"(veiled human form) standing behind Franek Kluski on his right side	99
Figure 10	Photograph of the plaster casting of the materialization hand made from the paraffin molding in a séance with Franek Kluski	101
Figure 11	The white smoky ectoplasm is being drawn from the medium- Ethel Post-Parrish, sitting inside the cabinet (the curtained enclosure)	102
Figure 12	The ectoplasm coming from the medium's body forms a 'pillar of cloud' from the ground upwards	102
Figure 13	Slowly, Silver Belle, the spirit guide of the medium, sculpts her features into the column of ectoplasm	103
Figure 14	The fully materialized 'Silver Belle'	103
Figure 15	Kathleen Goligher ectoplasm rod is levitating table	104

Illustrations

Figure 16 Large verrucous epidermal nevus on Thiang San Kla's head, who as a child remembered the life of his paternal uncle Phoh, who was killed with a blow on the head from a heavy knife. 116

Figure 17 Congenital malformation of nail on right great toe of Thiang. 117

Figure 18 Birthmark on the right cheek of Krishnan Chaudhri as it appeared in March 1997 when he was 13 years old. 119

Figure 19 Chatura's birthmarks on the rear of his jaw and on his throat, both close to the left ear, are close to the location of the internal head injury that brought Dayananda to death. 122

Figure 20 Ranbir Singh at his home in February 1994. His right hand and distal fourth of his right forearm was missing. His left hand was normal. 123

Figure 21 Severely malformed ear (microtia) in a Turkish boy who said that he remembered the life of a man who was fatally wounded on the right side of the head by a shotgun discharged at close range. 124

Figure 22 Hypopigmented macule on the chest of Hanumant Saxena's chest as it appeared in 1971 when he was 16 years old. 126

Figure 23 Sketch showing location of fatal wounds on Maha Ram Singh, Dr. S.C.Pandeya (Civil Surgeon, Fatehgarh, UP., India) 126

Figure 24 Birthmark on Rajani Singh's head as it appeared in November 1995 when she was 4 years old. 128

Figure 25 Birthmark on the neck of Yashbir Yadav as it appeared in March 1997 when he was 9 ½ years old. 129

Figure 26 Khin Mar Htoo's right leg as it appeared in 1980 when she was 12 years old. It shows congenital absence of the lower right leg (unilateral hemimelia). 130

Figure 27 Almost absent fingers (*brachydactyly*) of one hand in a boy of India who said he remembered the life of a boy of another village who had put his hand into the blades of a fodder-chopping machine and had his fingers amputated 131

Figure 28 Birthmarks in form of Arabic scripts have been appearing on the baby's body since his birth. 158

Figure 29 Therese Neumann with stigmata 171

Figure 30 Mentaholomorphic Field Formation according to Dr. Cowan's Model 200

1
INTRODUCTION

Thoughts are things. Thoughts are forces, the most vital and powerful in the universe. They have form and substance and power, the quality of the power determined as it is by the quality of the life in whose organism the thoughts are engendered; and so, when a thought is given birth to, it does not end there, but takes form, and on a force it goes out and has its effect upon other minds and lives, the effect being determined by its intensity and the quality of the prevailing emotions, and also by the emotions dominating the person at the time the thoughts are engendered and given form.

-Ralph Waldo Trine (1866-1958)

The real nature of human mind is still a mystery, ironically to the human mind itself. From the earliest record of intelligent beings, we learn that the mystery has been inconceivably powerful and unable to easily yield up its secrets to human understanding. Contemporary sciences, which occupy themselves with inquiries concerning the mind as an isolated abstraction, throw little light upon the real mental interactions and workings of human nature. Nevertheless Nature, the great teacher who taught scientists like Newton by making an apple fall on his head, has been unstintingly using the most efficient yet simple strategies, to reveal its mysteries to the world. The problem is that Nature's code is sometimes too simplistic to invite the attention of the scientists; and in other cases, too fascinating to believe!

So where does the problem of understanding the human mind lie? It is in the way we approach it. The study of human mind cannot be reduced to purely objective, mathematical formulations. Nature has produced the variety of life without recourse to a laboratory. Certain sciences will always remain sciences of observation, because the phenomenon under study cannot be reproduced by human efforts, as in the case of astronomy, seismology, geology and many areas of organismal and developmental biology. An astronomer cannot have the whole universe at his disposal, nor can a seismologist cause an earthquake at his will. They can only make observations. All sciences begin as sciences of pure observation.

A better understanding of the human mind can also be made by observation and significant generalizations. All attempts to understand human behavior and mental thoughts were studies, not by scientists, but by philosophers, until well into the 19th century. Indeed, such observational studies laid the very foundation for the deduction of general laws of mind. They can well be called 'experimental' as they rest on experience and observation, not upon self-evident propositions.

These theories offer explanations based on the deep knowledge and minute observations of the investigators of the period. Although we should not consider them final, we should appreciate rather than scorn these ideas.

Surely it is time we put seriously to ourselves the question whether the inductive method, which has proved its worth by its abundant fruitfulness whenever it has been faithfully applied, should not be as rigidly used in the investigation of mind as in the investigation of other natural phenomena. If so, we should certainly begin our inquiry with the observation of the simplest instances—with its physiological manifestations in children, in animals, in the surroundings, mounting by degrees to the highest and most recondite facts of thought forms and consciousness. The logical inferences which we get by observing these simple phenomena of nature may help disentangle the complex mechanism operative behind the human mind.

Such observational science has many times been so strong as to convince many experimenters to have a relook and even modify their theory because they know that this is the only way to go forward and to make progress in science. These different styles of scientific inquiries reinforce and correct each other. Thus, both observational science and experimental science are not only complementary and supplementary to each other but also absolutely indispensable for each other for the full growth and establishment of science.

The central theme of the present book is to make use of such deep and sincere observational records which have portrayed frozen instants of mental reality and provide many vital insights into our understanding of the mind.

Let us come back to our subject. The classical approach to cognitive science treats the mental processes like vision, thought, perception, imagination, etc., solely as products of electrical and chemical changes taking place within the physical organ called the brain. According to this view, one person's mental thoughts cannot affect another's. It is body-dependent. When death occurs, all thought and consciousness abruptly comes to an end. Such a view is concomitant with the known laws of classical physics.

But what Nature teaches us is rather different. There are many sophisticated and complex activities of the brain which classical brain science cannot explain. A mother who sleeps by the side of her baby will not wake up at the sound of thunder; but the moan of her child will awaken her. So also, a nurse will sleep through all kinds of noise which do not concern her patient; but he cannot exhibit an unusual respiration without attracting her attention.

According to the classical physics, only the decibel of the sound produced could have had an effect and not the person who caused it. Then, what is the state of the mind in sleep? Is the mind always consciously active? Or, is it unconsciously active? Is there a source of thought and emotion that is separate from the physiological brain? Classical science fails to answer this sort of questions.

There are many mind-related phenomena which, in the present state of our understanding, we are unable to reconcile, but this inability is solely due to our ignorance.

When we gaze upon an architectural marvel like the Taj Mahal, or look at a beautiful girl or a handsome man, or when we witness a tragedy like the death of a friend, the emotions which any of these instances excite in our mind derive their power from mysterious origins. Human behavior cannot be simply limited to chemical behavior. There is something more. It is a mind-versus-body (psycho-somatic) problem rather than one of brain-versus-hormone, though emotions, of course, create hormonal responses.

Seeing the Taj Mahal while being in front of it, is perception; whereas making a visual picture of it while being in our house is memory or imagination. The mental imagination of the Taj Mahal, the remembrance of it and the perception of it are all one, and differ only in the degree of vivacity.

In other words, imagination has the same effect on the human mind as perception does. If a person is connected to a brain-wave analyzer and is asked to close his eyes and imagine an object, the same area of his brain lights up, as if he were actually looking at that object. Recent researches in the field of neuro-imaging have revealed that at least two-thirds of the same brain areas are activated during visual imagery and visual perception. Mental images of objects and events can engage much of the same processing that occurs during the perceptual experience.

Visual imagery of aversive stimuli (like burnt bodies or the face of a battered person) causes skin conductance changes and changes in heart-rate (Centre for Educational Research and Innovation, 2007). Hence *mental images affect the body.*

The mental influence on curing bodily disorders has long been recognized by administering a make-believe medicine like sugar-coated tablets or saline solutions to the patients who respond to such medication on the sole mental belief that they are being given best-quality medical treatment. This effect is referred to as *placebo effect* in medical phraseology.

The influence of faith in the cure of disease is well illustrated by a fact mentioned in John Ayrton Paris's book, *'The Life of Sir Humphry Davy'*. In the early period of his scientific career, Davy was assisting Dr. Beddoes in his experiments on the inhalation of nitrous oxide. Dr. Beddoes, thinking the oxide must be a specific for paralysis, selected a patient for trial and placed him under the care of Sir Humphry Davy.

Before administering the gas, a small thermometer was inserted under the patient's tongue to ascertain his body temperature. The paralytic, wholly ignorant of the process to which he was to be subjected, but deeply impressed by Dr. Beddoes with the certainty of its success, no sooner felt the thermometer between his teeth that he concluded that the magical medicinal influence was at work. In a burst of enthusiasm, he declared that he felt its healing power through his whole body.

Here was an opportunity to test the influence of the mind in the cure of palsy. The gas was not used, but on the days that followed, the thermometer was again employed, with equally marked effects. At the end of two weeks, the patient was discharged cured, no remedy of any kind having been used, except the thermometer! His faith cured him, not by accident, nor by a miracle, but by an invariable law of our being – *mental influence on body*.

Like this, there are many anomalous mind-related phenomena that we can see in our daily lives. These phenomena, the authenticity of which has been attested by various persons, cannot be ignored on the lame excuse that science has no concern with fables, myths and superstitions.

As said earlier, many of these mental events can hardly be experimented upon in laboratory-controlled circumstances; they can only be experienced. It is one of the major concerns of official science to analyze, dissect and comprehend Nature. Science cannot rest quiet until she understands what it is. This warrants a novel approach to uncoil the mysteries surrounding mind and mind-related phenomena.

The basic scheme of this book is to draw the attention of biologists and others to the bio-holographic activities which constitute the very basis of biological organisms. For this, a series of observational records relating to 'mental events' are systematically provided, facilitating the readers to understand for themselves the underlying scientific principles of these curious and hitherto unexplained mental phenomena.

General Scheme of the Book

The book contains many chapters, each with a different emphasis on the theme. Introductory quotations have been provided at the beginning of each chapter to introduce some important points discussed in the chapter and to lend credibility to them.

Chapter 1 gives an overview of the book to gain a basic understanding of the subject.

Chapter 2 deals with one of the axiomatic truths of metaphysics - *thoughts are things*. The mind of man is so powerful as to bring thoughts into being and literally make into living entities the ideas that it entertains.

When thoughts take form, they become thought-forms. According to Annie Besant and Leadbeater, the chief exponents of this concept, when a person is thinking of another person, a miniature image of the second person may float in front of the first person. In a like manner, if a person thinks of a creature, place, or thing, the object of her thoughts may appear in miniature in front of her. This phenomenon applies even to objects of the imagination. Many classic examples of manifestations of thought-forms are going to be discussed in this chapter.

Chapter 3 narrates cases of hypnopompic hallucinations and other kinds of mental hallucinations. According to the '*Dictionary of Hallucinations,*' hypnopompic hallucinations are perceptual phenomena taking place in the intermediate state between wakefulness and sleep. These hallucinations are visual, tactile, auditory, or other sensory events, usually brief but sometimes prolonged, that occur at the transition from wakefulness to sleep (hypnagogic) or from sleep to wakefulness (hypnopompic).

The affected individual usually suffers from combinations of auditory and visual hallucinations. These visual and auditory illusions are very vivid and may be bizarre or very disturbing to the subject (Kompanje, 2008). We are going to study many cases relating to mental hallucinations of similar kind in this chapter.

Chapter 4 picks up the theme of *thought-photography*. Mind can create images directly on the photographic film. The cases reported in this chapter are not only interesting but suggestive enough to induce us to keep an open mind towards the subject we have undertaken here. Dr. Hyppolyte Baraduc, Commandant Darget and Ted Serios are remarkable persons who captured a large number of authentic thought-photographs on films.

Chapter 5 discusses cases of ideoplasty– that is, materialization of an intense thought or idea. Ideoplasty moulds the matter itself, gives it its shape and attributes. Dr. Charles Richet, who won the Nobel Prize for medicine in the year 1913, experimentally observed the materialization of human forms and faces produced by mediums from the portraits of deceased persons that were presented to them.

The process involved externalization of a kind of polymorphic or gelatinous substance that exudes from the body of the medium, formless at first, and takes form later according to the mind force of the medium. Cases of materialization experiments with photographic evidences demonstrate beyond doubt that mind can mould the subtle fields and thereby the matter.

Chapter 6 deals with very fascinating and curious cases of children who claimed to have remembered their previous life. Cases in which the subjects had birthmarks/bodily deformities corresponding to the injuries or physical characteristics they bore in the previous life form the main theme of this chapter.

Many of the case-histories discussed in this chapter are borrowed from the works of Dr. Ian Stevenson who in the year 1997 published a monograph about 3000 cases of rebirths– out of which 225 cases were with birth defects/unusual physical deformities connected with incidents in previous births. Dr. Stevenson took pains to obtain the medical records, including postmortem reports, in respect of about 43 cases, where a close correspondence between the wounds on the previous personality and the birthmarks (or birth defects) on the subjects were evidently found.

In 1998, Dr. Satwant K. Pasricha (India) published a report of ten additional cases with the feature of birthmarks or birth defects.

In seven of them, medical documents, such as a postmortem report of the previous personality, showed a close correspondence between the birthmark or birth defects and wounds on the previous personality.

Chapter 7 discusses cases of maternal impressions. It has been by-and-large acknowledged that there is a communication of thought– a kind of thought-transference, between the mother and the foetus. The child in *utero* receives the same impressions of the objects, and is moved by the same passions as her mother. In such a case, since the mind and the body occupy different realms of being, an intermediary agent is needed to communicate the mother's mentality to the malleable body of the foetus. It is theorized that the thought or imagination of the mother is able to create a force-field that correspond to in shape and size (which may sometimes vary) to the object thought of, or imagined, and this force-field is capable of affecting the subtle body of the child. "The imagination, which according to Aristotelian tradition, is an inward sense whose objects differed from others only in their lack of materiality, occupies a limbo zone on the lower level of the mental world and thus is able to relay messages between it and the material one, in both directions." (Bakewell, 1998)

Chapter 8 discusses some of the curious cases relating to the appearance of bodily marks due to intensive thinking. Commonly, the word *stigmata*, is used to refer to the cases of bodily manifestations of the wounds of Christ, in the form of bleeding hands, feet, and side. Yet, the term *stigmata*, is used here to mean not just these markings, and includes any other bodily manifestations of intensive mental thoughts and ideas fixed in the subconscious mind. These phenomena also demonstrate the power of mind over the body.

Chapter 9 is significant insofar as it unveils the underlying, organizing principle governing all these psychosomatic (mind-body) phenomena. The human being is a compound of body and mind. Many scientists now believe the brain and body operate on holographic principles on the cellular, molecular, and neural levels.

In '*Space-Time and Beyond*,' Bob Toben (1975, p. 130) describes how DNA contains the coding for orderly growth. "Nonlinearity in electrochemical reaction pathways of biological processes provides feedback patterns that are responsible for self-organization. On a deeper level, there may be self-organizing bio-gravitational fields whose structure determines the shape of biological molecules, cellular differentiation, and the overall shape of living systems".

Likewise, the mind also functions on the *holographic principle*. Many mind-related phenomena, including memory, recognition, remote mental interactions like telepathy, remote-viewing, etc., could be best explained by the holographic model of mind process. This chapter narrates some of the modern theories which support the holographic nature of mind process.

Chapter 10 is the concluding part and gives a brief account of the various mind-related phenomena discussed in the previous chapters, the intricate connection among them, and the underlying holographic concept of the mind process.

Before leaping into the holographic process of the mind, it is expedient to know the holographic properties of the human body. Many of the phenomena discussed in this volume demonstrate mind-body interaction, in other words, how the mind controls the *body holographic*. But by what instrumentality does mind fashion and control matter? It is theorized that it is through a *bio-holographic* field.

Then what is the exact relationship between the conscious process and the holographic process?

Light (part of the electromagnetic spectrum) enables us to see the objects around us. Everything we see needs particles (or waves) of light to be bouncing off it. This passes through the pupil, an adjustable opening which controls the amount of light entering the eyes. The light carrying the information regarding the object we perceive passes through a clear jelly-like substance called vitreous humor to strike the retina at the back of the eye. At this point the information carried by the light is converted into an 'image' that is presented to consciousness.

This process in itself is shrouded in mystery inasmuch as how does a small, inverted image on the back of the eye create the lifelike, vibrant, colorful field of vision? Who is it in the brain that experiences these signals as sound, smell and sensation? Or, as Arthur Koestler puts it, who is the *'Ghost in the Machine'*? Darwinist-materialists who believe that everything consist of matter cannot answer these questions.

However, with the advent of the holographic paradigm, the mind science has entered a new era. Holographic theory considers Universe as a single, gigantic hologram where everything is connected to the rest, including our minds. Everything we observe in our daily life is only a holographic projection – projection from another level of reality transcending space and time.

Bell's Theorem has proved that the universe is a 'stupendous multi-dimensional hologram' where each part is 'infinitely interconnected' with the rest of the universe. Following the conclusions of Bell's Theorem, David Bohm believes that such 'inter-connectedness' might even shed light on the phenomenon of consciousness itself. Even in dreams, man sometimes dreams the experiences belonging to other persons. These are, according to Carl. G. Jung, the archetypal experiences. It leads to the idea of 'a sort of group mind'. Sankhya philosophy calls this 'cosmic mind' (Mahat). (Jitatmananda 1993)

Thus the theory of holographic universe proves to be intrinsically connected with the theory of holographic brain and mind. Not only the brain, but the body and even the whole universe appear to be a hologram– one participating in another, forming a universal fabric of interaction and communication. It is a hierarchical system of 'hologram within a hologram', like a Chinese nesting doll (*matryoshka* doll).

These are not mere theoretical abstractions or philosophical speculations; but something flowing out of pure science based on the empirical observations of natural phenomena.

Thus, in the forthcoming chapters we will be discussing each one of these themes in their entirety. The specialty is each one of these themes builds upon the other and if added together we have convincing proof for the holograph-like function of body and mind.

I have written the chapters in such a way that the theme of each chapter is easily discernible and the intrinsic similarity of the phenomena studied is reflected in their contents. But, the themes, like thought-photography, hallucination and materialization, etc., may seem to be unconnected to one another, at least initially. The reader, during the course of an assiduous reading of the narrations of cases in this volume, can himself realize and understand that these phenomena of nature are closely connected to some great underlying scientific principle.

If it is asked, why is this book written, the answer is two-fold. First, to collect together in one volume, authentic illustrations relating to the power of the mind to create thought-forms, scattered through various medical and other works. Second, to give these cases fresh interest and value in the light of the contemporary developments in quantum science.

For the convenience of the readers, I will briefly recapitulate here the several propositions which I have covered in the following pages, and hope these will receive their serious consideration.

- Human mind can bring into being thought-forms and can exteriorize them, giving them some objective consistency.
- There can be continuity of thoughts even after the destruction of the physical brain.
- These psychic entities are sometimes given a kind of autonomy so that they may act and seemingly think without the consent or even knowledge of their creator.

2
THOUGHT FORMS

Every thought we think images itself in the mind and every image that is persistently held in mind is bound to materialize. This is the law. I cannot feel why it is so, any more than I can tell why from a few seeds sown in fertile soil, we reap an abundant crop. I only know that the law of thought-externalization is as definite and as sure in results as are the laws of seed-time and harvest.

- **Jean Porter Rudd**

A thought form is an energy manifestation, to say, a subtle energy matrix, created by intensive thinking and often takes the shape of the object perceived or thought of. According to Besant and Leadbeater, a thought-form begins as a vibration in the mental body. The initial impulse of any thought is the intention behind the thought. This initial intention and its accompanying spray of colors leads to the vibration of the mental body. This intention creates a resonance in the surrounding mental body which then transfers to the surrounding medium of the mental plane. To a non-clairvoyant, this series of processes is not perceived as such and one would simply seem to be thinking a thought.

In other words, what we perceive as the subjective experience of thinking a thought, the clairvoyant perceives as a series of complex processes beginning with the appearance of an intention in the mental body (as indicated by the 'spray' of colours) and the resulting resonances of the mental body and surrounding mental space.

The resonance set up in the mental plane attracts to it material of the mental plane, which Besant and Leadbeater call *elemental essence*, and this elemental essence 'clothes' the vibration, or assumes it shape. That is, the elemental essence ensouls the vibrational pattern in the mental space surrounding the mental body, and at this point we have a functioning thought-form.

So then, according to Beasant and Leadbeater, the thought-form consists of two main ingredients: the vibrational pattern set up in the mental environment that originated in the subject's mental body (mind), and the elemental essence that essentially precipitates or nucleates around the vibrational pattern. This elemental essence is the actual matter of the mental plane (or astral plane depending on the nature of the thought), and is like a glue that holds the vibrational pattern in place after we are done with a thought. And, according to Besant and Leadbeater, it is this elemental essence that gives the thought-form.

General Appearance of Thought-Forms

According to Besant and Leadbeater, these thought-forms differ very materially from one another in form and general appearance. The most common form is that of a tiny series of waves, similar to those caused by the dropping of a pebble in a pond of water. Sometimes the thought-form takes on the appearance of a whirlpool, rotating around a centre, and moving through space as well. Another form is like that of the pin-wheel fireworks, swirling away from its centre as it moves through space. Still another form is that of a whirling ring, like that emitted from a smokestack of a locomotive, or the mouth of a smoker– the familiar 'ring' of the smoker. Others have the form and appearance of semi-luminous globes, glowing like a giant opal.

When a man thinks of a concrete object– a book, house, landscape, etc., he builds a tiny image of the object in the matter of his mental body. This image floats in the upper part of that body, usually in front of the face of the man, and at about the level of the eyes. It remains there as long as the man is contemplating the object, and usually for a little time afterwards.

Swami Panchadasi, in his book, '*Clairvoyance and Occult Powers*,' quotes from an English investigator of astral phenomenon:

"All students are aware that thought takes form, at any rate upon its own plane, and in the majority of cases upon the astral plane also; but it may not be so generally known that if a man thinks strongly of himself as present at any given place, the form as assumed by that particular thought will be likeness of the thinker himself, which will appear at the place in question. Essentially this form must be composed of the matter of the mental plane, but in very many cases it would draw round itself matter of the astral plane also, and so would approach much nearer to visibility. There are, in fact, many instances in which it has been seen by the person thought of, most probably by means of the unconscious influence emanating from the original thinker. None of the consciousness of the thinker would, however, be included within this thought-form. When once sent out from him, it would normally be a quite separate entity – not indeed absolutely unconnected with its maker, but practically so as far as the possibility of receiving any impression through it is concerned." (Panchadasi, 1915)

Eliphas Levi, more than whom no modern writer on the subject of magic is better informed, or more honest in the expression of his real conviction, gives utterance to the following:

"Human thought creates what it imagines; the phantoms of superstition project their real deformity in the Astral Light, and live by the very terrors they produce. They owe their being to the delusions of imagination and to the aberration of the senses, and are never produced in the presence of anyone who knows and can expose the mystery of their monstrous birth."

'Thought Forms' in History

The ability to project thought and manifest it, is a well documented phenomenon throughout the world. In Tibetan Shaman traditions, the act of meditation is often used to 'visualise' and thereby commune with the student's tutelary god. After a time, the Yidam does materialize, and gradually takes on a similar quasi-reality as the spirit monk. The tantric mystics of Tibet referred to the 'stuff' of thoughts as *shugs* or *tsal* and held that every mental action produced waves of mysterious energy. That energy, they believe, is produced every time a mental action takes place.

The twelfth century Persian sufis also stressed the importance of visualization in altering and reshaping one's destiny and called the subtle matter of thought *Alam almithal*.

The term *thought-form* was used as early as 1927 in Evan-Wentz' translation of the *'Tibetan Book of the Dead,'* described as "giving palpable being to a visualization, in very much the same manner as an architect gives concrete expressions in three-dimensions to [.....] his blue-print."

Nearly three hundred years ago, the great Swedish mystic Emanuel Swedenborg reported that he could see a *wave-substance* around people, and in the wave-substance a person's thoughts were visible as images he called *portrayals*. Swedenborg could also see portrayals in his own energy fields. He said, "When I think about someone I knew, then his image appeared as he looked when he was named in human presence; but all around, like something flowing in waves, was everything I had known and thought about him from boyhood. So, that whole man, as he existed in my thought and affection, was instantly visible among the spirits." (Emanuel Swedenborg, 1985)

Michael Talbot, in a paper, *'Swedenborg and the Holographic Paradigm,'* stated that the Swedenborg's concept of *portrayals* and his assertion that the inhabitants of spiritual regions communicate through elaborate sequences of images or pictures – could be explained in terms of the holographic paradigm.

"If the apparent concreteness of objective reality is only a partial and fragmental translation of *All That Is*, it may be that the various spiritual kingdoms Swedenborg witnessed were only deeper levels of the super-holographic domain. If this is the case, it may be that the deeper our 'frequency receivers' travel into the super-hologram, the more freely such frequencies are translated into images. In other words, here in the so-called physical world the holograms of our brains have learned to translate frequencies in a rigid and highly structured manner, and this has caused us to view reality as solid and objective." (Talbot, Swedenborg and the Holographic Paradigm, 1988)

Edgar Cayce, the great American mystic (whom Jess Stearn called the 'sleeping prophet') spoke of thoughts as *tangible things*, a finer form of matter and, when he was in trance, repeatedly told his clients that their thoughts created their destiny and that 'thought is the builder'. In his view, the thinking process is like a spider constantly spinning, constantly adding to its web. Cayce said that every moment of our lives we are creating the images and patterns that give our future energy and shape. According to him, it is a form created by concentrated thought yet lacking the solidarity of mundane matters.

Captain Walter Carey in his *'Master Keys of Life and Death,'* (Rider & Co. Ltd.) said, "Thoughts are things. Given a good brain in combination with a developed mental body, the act of thinking creates thought-forms, which take shape and colour according to the type of thought. These, like the aura, are visible to a comparatively small number of people, but they are just as real or perhaps more so, than physical objects."

'The Betty Book,' by Steward Edward White (Psychic Book Club, 1943) said, "We are broadcasting even with our most secret thoughts and desires. We are accountable for what we send out."

Mrs. Eileen J. Garrett found that 'thoughts are things possessing their own vitality, their own destiny, for ill or good'. In her book *'Adventures in the Supernormal,'* she tells us how she began to feel and sense the thoughts of people as forms of light that moved to their destinies, impacting and dissipating according to their natures and the force with which they had been projected. She came to know that thoughts are dimensional things which become clothed with form and life as they are born. (Garrett, 1949)

The eminent scientist, Edgar Mitchell, states, "…the omnipresent and omni-directional transfer of influence (including thought, emotion and interaction) at the quantum level instantly, simultaneously and ubiquitously, through a wave-like or field-like resonance wherein spatial and temporal factors are inconsequential…"

Thus, the phenomenon of thought-forms has long been known and many explanatory theories have also been proposed. Interestingly, many of the ideas relating to thought-forms are compatible with contemporary scientific concepts under the quantum realm.

In this chapter, we will discuss some of the interesting cases where thought-entities were created by intensive thoughts.

1. Creation of Thought-entities by Voluntary Mind Force

Thought forms are generally considered to be complexes of energy or consciousness manifested from a blend of mental force and bio-energy. Like the *Tulpa* of Tibetan Buddhism and mysticism, thought-forms are brought into existence merely through power of will and strength of mind. A *Tulpa* is defined as 'a humanoid thought-form' and likened to a personal 'genie' that you create using thought energy. Once created, the *Tulpa* acts as a sort of robot, as it can be controlled by the creator according to his wish, but sometimes, the *Tulpas* manage to acquire some kind of autonomous personality (David-Néel, 1967).

In Evans-Wentz's book, *'The Tibetan Book of the Dead,'* he summarizes the Tibetan belief concerning the yogic power of domination over bodily form as follows: "Through transcendal direction of that subtle mental faculty, or psychic power, whereby all forms, animate and inanimate, including man's own form, are created, the human body can either be dissolved, and thereby made visible, by *yogically* inhibiting the faculty, or be made mentally imperceptible to others, and thus equally invisible to them, by changing the body's rate of vibration. When the mind inhibits emanation of its radioactivity, it ceases to be the source of mental stimuli to others, so that they become unconscious of invisible beings living in a rate of vibration unlike their own. Inasmuch as the mind creates the world of appearances, it can create any particular object desired. The process consists of giving palpable being to a particular object desired. The process consists of giving palpable being to a visualization, in very much the same manner as an architect gives concrete expression in three dimensions to his abstract concepts after first having given them expression in the two-dimensions of his blue-print. The Tibetans call the One Mind's concretized visualization the *Khorva* (*Hkhorva*), equivalent to the Sanskrit *Sangsara*; that of an incarnate deity, like the Dalai or Tashi Lama, they call a *Tul-ku* (*Sprul-sku*), and that of a magician a *Tul-pa* (*Sprul-pa*), meaning a magically produced illusion or creation. A master of yoga can dissolve a *Tul-pa* as readily as he can create it; and his own illusory human body, or *Tul-ku*, he can likewise dissolve, and thus outwit death. Sometimes, by means of this magic, one human form can be amalgamated with another, as in the instance of the wife of *Marpa*, guru of *Milarepa*, who ended her life by incorporating herself in the body of *Marpa*." (Evans-Wentz, 2000)

Geoffrey Ashe says in his book, *'The Ancient Wisdom'*:

"If the concentration of thought and will is powerful enough - perhaps a joint effort by many people - a human *tulpa* [thought form] can be more than a phantasm. It can come into being by normal birth, as a stable physical form with personality. It is then called a *tulku* or *phantom body*."

Madame Alexandra David-Neel, who investigated these magical matters among the Tibetans, states that, "a phantom horse trots and neighs. The phantom rider who rides it can get off his beast, speak with travelers on the road, and behave in every way like a real person. A phantom house will shelter real travelers, and so on." (Evans-Wentz, 2000)

David Neel's Unwanted Companion

In Alexandra David-Neel's book on Tibet, she claims to have imaginatively created a projection of a monk that took on a solid form and looked and behaved so real that other individuals, who also observed him, thought he was a real Lama. He shared her apartment like a guest and when she departed for a journey, he accompanied her entourage. At first, the phantom-monk put an appearance only when his creator thought of him.

But after a time, this thought-form developed an independent personality of its own, and began to behave in a very independent manner and to perform various actions not directed by his creator. The psychic entity even exhibited hostility and was completely beyond the control of its creator. So real did he become in time, that on one occasion, when a herdsman came to Neel's encampment to bring her some butter, he mistook the chimerical monk for a living Lama. It took several months on concentrated effort to dematerialize him. Such is the incredible power of the human mind and its ability to physically manifest thought-forms.

"Professor H.H.Price, the Oxford philosopher and parapsychologist, suggests that once an idea has been created, it 'is no longer wholly under the control of the consciousness which gave it birth' but may operate independently on the minds of other people or on physical objects."

This is what Leadbeater described, above a century ago.

"The effect produced is of the most striking nature. The thought seizes upon the plastic essence, and moulds it instantly into a living being of appropriate form, a being which when once thus created is in no way under the control of its creator, but lives out a life of its own, the length of which is proportionate to the intensity of the thought or wish which called it into existence. It lasts, in fact, just as long as the thought-force holds it together. Most people's thoughts are so fleeting and indecisive that the elements created by them last only a few minutes or a few hours, but an often repeated thought of an earnest wish will form an elemental whose existence may extend to many days." (C.W.Leadbeater, The Astral Plane, 1895)

Conjuring up Philip

During the later part of the 20th century, a theory began to take form stating that most of the manifestations in the séance-room were a result of a person's subconscious mind sending signals into the environment, or a kind of *thought-form*.

In the year 1972, a team of eight persons led by Dr. A.R.G. Owen from the *Toronto Society of Psychical Research* purposed to attempt to create, through intense and prolonged concentration, a collective thought-form and conducted an exceptionally interesting and intriguing piece of research, which was documented in the 1976 book, '*Conjuring Up Philip.*' None of the team members was known to have any special abilities in Extrasensory Perception (ESP), psychic, channelling or other psychical or mental specialties. They mentally concentrated on visualizing an imaginary aristocratic Englishman named Philip Aylesford. The team created Philip's entire life story. Everyone in the group memorized Philip's fictional history, and discussed various details until all were in a basic agreement on his appearance, character, and the events in his life.

The original intent of the group was to produce a visual hallucination that would be perceived by members of the group. They met faithfully every week for a year, meditating together and concentrating on seeing Philip, but without success. At the end of the year, they decided to change their methods to imitate the techniques reported by some English parapsychologists, especially K. J. Batcheldor who described the achievement of paranormal effects, within a few weeks, by groups without special psychic ability.

It worked. During one evening's séance, the group received its first communication from Philip in the form of a distinct rap on the table. Soon Philip was answering questions asked by the group– one rap for yes, two for no. They knew it was Philip because, well, they asked him. Within a few weeks, the Toronto team found that the table was starting to move on its own. On one occasion, the table rose into the air with all four of its legs clear of the floor (Owen. I, 1976). Had Philip, just a composite psychokinetic phenomenon, become a separate and independent entity? The Philip Experiment showed that conscious thought could be translated paranormally into actual physical force, or a thought-form.

That Philip was a creation of the group's collective imagination was evident in his limitations. Although he could accurately answer questions about events and people of his time period, it did not appear to be information that the group was unaware of.

In other words, Philip's responses were coming from their subconscious— their own minds. Some members thought they heard whispers in response to questions, but no voice was ever captured on tape. Philip's psychokinetic powers, however, were amazing and completely unexplained. If the group asked Philip to dim the lights, they would dim instantly. When asked to restore the lights, he would oblige. The table around which the group sat was almost always the focal point of peculiar phenomena. After feeling a cool breeze blow across the table, they asked Philip if he could cause it to start and stop at will. He could and he did.

The group noticed that the table itself felt different to the touch whenever Philip was present, having a subtle electric or 'alive' quality. On a few occasions, a fine mist formed over the center of the table. Most astonishing, the group reported that the table would sometimes be so animated that it would rush over to meet latecomers to the session, or even trap members in the corner of the room.

Although the Philip experiment gave the Owen group far more than they ever imagined possible, it was never able to attain one of their original goals— to have the spirit of Philip actually materialize. The Philip experiment was so successful that the Toronto organization decided to try it again with a completely different group of people and a new fictional character.

After just five weeks, the new group established 'contact' with their new 'ghost' called Lilith, a French-Canadian spy. Other similar experiments conjured up such entities as Sebastian, a medieval alchemist and even Axel, a man from the future. All of them were completely fictional, yet all produced unexplained communication through their unique raps.

Thereafter, a Sydney, Australia group attempted a similar test with 'The Skippy Experiment'. The six participants created the story of Skippy Cartman, a fourteen year old Australian girl. The group reported that Skippy communicated with them through raps and scratching sounds.

The experiment proved the connection between the mind and psychokinetic effects during séances, essentially demonstrating the theory of British psychologist Kenneth J. Batcheldor, who stated that the atmosphere of belief and expectation that permeates a séance in effect creates the phenomena that spiritualists attribute to spirits. It was proved that the human will can produce spirits through expectation, imagination and visualization.

Family Gods and Angel Guides

Swamy Panchadasi, in his work, *'The Astral World: Its Scenes, Dwellers, and Phenomena,'* says:

"Another, and quite a large, class of these artificial astral entities consists of thought-forms of supernatural beings, sent out by the strong mental pictures, oft repeated, of the persons creating them– the creator usually being unconscious of the result. For instance, a strongly religious mother, who prays for the protective influence of the angels around and about her children, and whose strong religious imagination pictures these heavenly visitors as present by the side of the children, frequently actually creates thought-form of such angel guardians around her children, who are given a degree of life and mind vibrations from the soul of the mother." (Panchadasi, 1915)

In a similar way, many 'family ghosts' have been created and kept in being in the same way, by the constantly repeated tale and belief in their reality, on the part of generation after generation. In this class belong the celebrated historic ghosts who warn royal or noble families of approaching death or sorrow.

Panchadasi says, "The ghosts may be *laid* by anyone familiar with the laws of thought-forms. It must be remembered that these artificial entities are of purely human creation, and obtain all their apparent and mind from the action of the thought-force of their creators. Repeated thought and repeated belief, will serve to keep alive and to strengthen these entities– otherwise they will disappear in time."

Many are the stories of a murderer being haunted by the ghost of his victim. These are, in most of the cases, nothing but the objective manifestation of the fear of being haunted. There are also a great number of cases on record where, in consequence of a sudden and intense emotion, for instance, the desire to see a certain person, the thought-form projecting itself from the physical body has become conscious and visible at a distance.

Leadbeater says that the apparitions of birds frequently making their appearance in families as harbingers of death are a kind of thought-form. When the Oxenhams of Devonshire were visited by the apparition of a white bird they knew that one of the family was doomed. The well-known story is told by James Oxenham in a tract titled, "*A True relation of an Apparition in the likenesse of a Bird with a white breast that appeared hovering over the death-beds of some of the children of Mr. James Oxenham, of Sale Monachorum, Devon, Gent.*"

One of the first members of the family to see the apparition was the famous John Oxenham, a young man of twenty-two, who was taken ill in the vigour of his youth, a great strapping fellow six foot and a half in height, well built, of comely countenance and of great intellectual gifts. He died on the fifth day of September, 1635, and two days before his death the bird with the white breast hovered over his bed.

No sooner was John Oxenham in his grave than the apparition showed itself to Thomasine, wife of James Oxenham, who died on the seventh of September, 1635. She was quite a young woman and, according to the witnesses, Elizabeth Frost and Joan Tooker, the strange phantom was seen clearly fluttering above her sick-bed. The next member of the Oxenhams to whom the warning appeared was Thomasine's little sister, Rebecca, a child of eight, who breathed her last on September the ninth, following. And no sooner had the little girl been laid in her grave than Thomasine, infant of the above-mentioned Thomasine and James Oxenham, was taken sick and died on the 15th of September, 1635, the bird appearing also in this case.

Imaginary Companions

Children, at a certain early stage, create 'imaginary companions' and exhibit activities such as fantasy, make-believe gestures, interacting with imaginary persons, characters in films or books, etc. Recent research has revealed most of the patients suffering from the Multiple-Personality Disorder (MPD) have had 'imaginary companions' as children.

In his classical book *'Play, Dreams and Imitation in Childhood,'* Jean Piaget carefully documented a series of imaginary companions created by his daughter Jacqueline. At 3:11, she invented an *"aseau,"* a strange birdlike creature whose physical characteristics changed often – a dog, an insect, or any other animal according to Jacqueline's fancy. (Piaget, 1999).

Church J and L.J.Stone write, "It is during the preschool years, especially at ages four and five, that imaginary companions most often appear.... Most imaginary companions seem to have vanished by age ten, although it is not unheard of for adults to have imaginary companions." They further state that: "Imaginary companions are often experienced with all the vividness and solidity of real material objects." (Church J, 1968)

The imaginary companions are created by chidlren in situation of high stress or of a traumatic character. Murphy describes the stress situation during which Sam, 3 years and 3 months, created his imaginary companion "Woody." When at the doctor's office for removal of finger stiches, Sam was forcibly taken away from his mother, and says Murthy, "as an outgrowth of this separation situation, a little elf named "Woody" appeared in Sam's fantasy.... Woody turned up in many different situations and served many different purposes – sometimes a companion, sometimes a helper, sometimes a scapegoat..." L.B.Murphy, 1962)

In 1954, the psychiatrist O.E.Sperling, in his *"An Imaginary Companion,"* reported the fascinating case of a child named Rudy who had a particularly vivid hallucinatory companion whom he called 'Rudyman.' He demanded a chair for him to sit on and would ask permission from Rudyman to do certain things. If he was asked to eat his soup, he would report that he first had to consult rudyman on the topic and then he would say, "Rudyman said I should eat the soup." Sperling observed that the child's father name was Herman and that Rudyman was a combination of Rudy and his father's name and further believed the companion to be an indirect form of identification with Rudy's father.

2. The Manifestation of Thought-Forms due to Yearning Desire

As we have seen in the previous pages, a thought-form is really but a strongly manifested thought or feeling which has taken form in the astral substance. Its power and duration depend upon the degree of force of the thought or feeling manifesting it. It is a specialized grouping of astral substance, crystallized by the strong thought impulses or vibrations of a person thinking, or manifesting strong emotional excitement. It is generated in the aura of the person, in the first place, but is then thrown off or emitted from the atmosphere of the person, and is sent off into space.

The thought-forms are commonly not perceptible to human sense. A kind of *coercive force* is required to transcend the threshold of consciousness and this can be done by deliberate and strong exercise of will, or during the exalted state of mine (like one at or near the moment of death).

Here we will see some of the curious instances where the thought-form of persons manifested due to a yearning desire, or an exalted state of mind.

Apparition of the Virgin Mary that Caused the Train to Stop

The *'Mattino'* of Naples published on April 22, 1906, the item given below, sent in by its Beggio (Calabria) Correspondent:

"The other day, at the central station at Reggio, a young seminarist boarded the Reggio-Battipaglia-Naples express, which leaves here at 5:55, and took his seat in a compartment in which was the comptroller-in-chief of the road, Signore Dominic Fischetti.

When the train had started, Signore Fischetti asked the seminarist what his destination might be. The latter answered that he had to go to Catena, to be present at the Festival of Saint Francis. The comptroller then gave the future priest to understand that he had made a great mistake, for the train in which he was did not stop at Catena, and in order to get off at that place he should have taken the other train, which leaves Reggio at 6:17.

One may imagine the grief and disappointment of the seminarist! He began to work himself up, to ask help, to pray to the Holy Virgin, with tears in his eyes; when his traveling companion confirmed what he had already said, he threatened to throw himself out of the door if the train did not stop at Catena.

All this time the train continued on its way. When they had got to the bridge, which is reached before the Catena station, they heard the repeated whistling of the locomotive and, immediately afterward, the emergency whistle. The train began to slacken speed, then finally stopped.

What, then, had happened? The seminarist, full of joy, triumphant almost, threw himself from the railway carriage, crying out that Saint Francis had just worked a miracle in his favor, and the travelers on the train learned from the engineer, a certain Signore Trieepi, that the halt was due to the presence of a nun, clothed in white, and two other women, in the middle of the track; despite the whistling of the locomotive they had not stirred.

The passengers got off to see them, but saw no one, save the seminarist, running towards the station as fast as his legs could carry him. Signore Fischetti, astounded, told what the young man had said, to the stupefaction of those who heard him; the engineer, in the most explicit way, gave assurance of having seen the three women on the track, motionless, immovable. Then, since no explanation of this strange fact could be given, talk of a miracle began.

Such is the highly veracious account furnished by a young employee of the railroad, in the presence of several persons; he added, as documentary proof, that the train's extraordinary stop upon the Catena Bridge is entered, according to regulations, on the daily record.

How can we explain the engineer's act? May we assume a telepathic influence, leaving seminarist's brain, and producing a visual hallucination on the part of the engineer! (Flammarion, 1922)

Seeing One's Own Thought Body

In his *'Footfalls on the Boundary of Another World: With Narrative Illustrations,'* Robert Dale Owen records a still more remarkable case of duplication of the body. A gentleman in Ohio, in 1833, had built a new house, seventy or eighty yards distant from his old residence on the other side of a small ravine.

One afternoon, about five o'clock, his wife saw his eldest daughter, Rhoda, aged sixteen, holding the youngest Lucy, aged four, in her arm, sitting in a rocking-chair, just within the kitchen door of the new residence. She called the attention of another sister to what she saw, and was startled to hear that Rhoda and Lucy were upstairs in the old house. They were at once sent for, and on coming downstairs they saw, to their amazement, their exact doubles sitting on the doorstep of the new house. All the family collected – twelve in all – and they all saw the phantasmal Rhoda and Lucy; the real Rhoda and Lucy standing beside them. The figures seated at the hall door, and the two children now actually in their midst, were absolutely identical in appearance, even to each minute particular of dress. After watching them for five minutes, the father started to cross the ravine and solve the mystery. Hardly had he descended the ravine when the phantasmal Rhoda rose from the rocking chair, with the child in her arms, and lay down on the threshold. There she remained a moment or two, and then apparently sank into the earth. When the father reached the house no trace could be found of any human being." (Stead, 1921)

Double's Yearning Desire

A correspondent, writing from a Yorkshire village, sent William Thomas Stead, the author of 'Real Ghost Stories', the following account of an apparition of a thought-body in circumstances when there was nothing more serious than a yearning desire on the part of a person whose phantasm appeared to occupy his old bed. The correspondent stated that he took it down from the lips of one of the most truthful men he ever knew, and a sensible person to boot. The story is as follows:

"Sixty years ago I was a farm servant at a place in Pembrokeshire (I can give the name, but don't wish it to be published). I was about fifteen years old. I, along with three other men-servants, slept in a granary in the yard. Our bedchamber was reached by means of ten broad stone steps. It was soon after Allhallows time, when all farm servants change places in that part of the country.

A good and faithful foreman, who had been years on the farm, had this time desired a change, and had engaged to service some fifteen miles off, a change which he afterwards much regretted.

One night I woke up in my bed some time during the small hours of the morning, and obedient to the call of nature, I got up, opened the door, and stood on the upper step of the stairs. It was a beautiful moonlight night. I surveyed the yard and the fields about. To my surprise, but without the least apprehension, I noticed a man coming down a field, jump over a low wall, and walk straight towards me. He stepped the three first steps one by one, then he took two or three steps at a stride. I knew the man well and recognised him perfectly. I knew all the clothes he wore, particularly a light waistcoat which he put on on great occasions. As he drew near me I receded to the doorway, and as he lifted up his two hands, as in the act of opening the door, which was open already, I fled in screaming, and passing my own bed jumped in between two older men in the next bed. And neither time nor the sympathy of my comrades could pacify me for hours.

I told my tale, which, after searching and seeing nobody, they disbelieved and put down to my timidity.

Next morning, however, just as we were coming out from breakfast, in the presence of all of us the discharged foreman was seen coming down the same field, jumping the wall, walking toward the sleeping chamber, ascending the steps, lifting up his two hands to open the door in the self-same manner in every particular as I had described, and went straight to the same bed as I got into.

I asked him, 'Were you here last night, John?'

'No, my boy,' was the answer; 'my body was not here, but my mind was. I have run away from that horrid place, travelled most of the night, and every step I took my mind was fixed on this old bed, where my weary bones might be at rest." (Stead, 1921)

The Correspondent had further stated that he could supply the names and all particulars of the persons concerned, but he did not wish them to be published.

Punctuality of the Mental Body

William Thomas Stead, in his book '*Real Ghost Stories*,' recounts the following case communicated to him by Mr. Robert Kidd of Gray Street, Broughty Ferry, who, according to Stead, had filled many important offices during his lifetime.

"Mr. Alexander Drummond was a painter, who had a big business and a large staff of men. His clerk was Walter Souter, his brother-in-law. His business was to be at the shop (in Northgate, Dundee) sharp at six o'clock in the morning to take an account of where the men were going, quantity of material, etc. In this he was assisted by Miss Drummond. One morning he did not turn up at the hour, but at twenty minutes past six he came in at the door and appeared very much excited; but instead of stepping to the desk, where Mr. and Miss Drummond were awaiting him, he went through the front shop and out at the side door. This, in sight of Mr. and Miss D, and also in sight of a whole squad of workmen.

Well, exactly in another twenty minutes he came in, also very much excited, and explained that it was twenty minutes past six when he awakened, and that he had run all the way from his house (he lived a mile from the place of business). He was a very exemplary, punctual man, and when Mr. Drummond asked him where he went to when he came first, he was dumbfounded, and could not comprehend what was meant. To test his truthfulness, Mr. D went out to his wife that afternoon, when she told him the same story; that it was twenty past six o'clock when he awoke, and that he was very much excited about it, as it was the first time he had slept in (i.e., overslept).

A similar narrative, supplied by Mr. R. P. Roberts, 10, Exchange Street, Manchester, appeared in the *'Proceedings of the Psychical Research Society.'*

"When I was an apprentice in a drapery establishment, I used to go to dinner at 12 and return at 12.30. My employer was very strict and hot-tempered, which made me anxious to avoid his displeasure. The shop stood at the corner of Castle Street and Rating Row, Beaumaris, and I lived in the latter street. One day I went home to dinner at the usual hour. When I had partly finished I looked at the clock. To my astonishment it appeared that the time by the clock was 12.30. I have an unusual start. I certainly thought that it was most extraordinary. I had only half-finished my dinner, and it was time for me to be at the shop. I felt dubious, so in a few seconds had another look, when to my agreeable surprise I found that I had been mistaken. It was only just turned 12.15. I could never explain how it was I made the mistake. The error gave me such a shock for a few minutes as if something had happened, and I had to make an effort to shake off the sensation. I finished my dinner, and returned to business at 12.30. On entering the shop I was accosted by Mrs. Owen, my employer's wife, who used to assist in the business. She asked me rather sternly where I had been since my return from dinner. I replied that I had come straight from dinner. A long discussion followed, which brought out the following facts. About a quarter of an hour previous to my actual entering the shop (i.e., about 12.15), I was seen by Mr. and Mrs. Owen and well-known customer, Mrs. Jones, to walk into the shop, go behind the counter, and place my hat upon the peg. As I was going behind the counter, Mrs. Owen remarked, with the intention that I should hear, 'that I had arrived now that I was not wanted.' This remark was prompted by the fact that a few minutes previous a customer was in the shop in want of an article which belonged to the stock under my charge, and which could not be found in my absence. As soon as this customer left I was seen to enter the shop.

It was observed by Mr. and Mrs. Owen and Mrs. Jones that I did not appear to notice the remark made. In fact, I looked quite absent-minded and vague. Immediately after putting my hat on the peg I returned to the same spot, put my hat on again, and walked out of the shop, still looking in a mysterious manner, which induced one of the parties, I think Mrs. Owen, to say that my behaviour was very odd, and she wondered where I was off to.

I, of course, contradicted these statements, and endeavoured to prove that I could not have eaten my dinner and returned in a quarter of an hour. This, however, availed nothing, and during our discussion the above-mentioned Mrs. Jones came into the shop again, and was appealed to at once by Mr. and Mrs. Owen. She corroborated every word of their account, and added that she saw me coming down Rating Row when within a few yards of the shop; that she was only a step or two behind me, and entered the shop in time to hear Mrs. Owen's remarks about my coming too late. These three persons gave their statement of the affair quite independently of each other. There was no other person near my age in the Owen's establishment, and there could be no reasonable doubt that my form had been seen by them and by Mrs. Jones. They would not believe my story until my aunt, who had dined with me, said positively that I had not left the table before my time was up. You will, no doubt, notice the coincidence. At the moment when I felt, with a startling sensation, that I ought to be at the shop, and when Mr. and Mrs. Owen were extremely anxious that I should be there, I appeared to them looking, as they said, 'as if in a dream or in a state of somnambulism.'" (Stead, 1921)

Thought Body that Came for a Book

The Landrichter, or Sheriff F., in Frankfurt, sent his secretary on an errand; presently afterwards, the secretary re-entered the room, and laid hold of a book. His master asked him what had brought him back, whereupon the figure vanished, and the book fell to the ground, it was a volume of Linnaeus. In the evening, when the secretary returned, and was interrogated with regard to his expedition, he said that he had fallen into an eager dispute with an acquaintance, as he went along, about some botanical question, and had ardently wished he had had his Linnaeus with him to refer to. (Crowe, 1850)

A President of the Supreme Court, in Ulm, named Pfizer, attested the truth of the following case:

"A gentleman, holding an official situation, had a son at Gottingen, who wrote home to his father, requesting him to send him, without delay, a certain book, which he required to aid him in preparing a dissertation he was engaged in. The father answered, that he had sought but could not find the work, in question. Shortly afterwards, the latter had been taking a book from his shelves, when, on turning round, be beheld, to his amazement, his son just in the act of stretching up his hand towards one of a high shelf in another part of the room. "Hallo!" he exclaimed, supposing it to be the young man himself; but the figure disappeared; and, on examining the shelf, the father found there the book that was required, which he immediately forwarded to Gottingen; but before it could arrive there, he received a letter from his son, describing the exact spot where it was to be found." (Crowe, 1850)

3. Psychic Characters and the Writer's Psyche due to Intensive Thinking

We have already seen that when a man thinks of his friend he forms within his mental body a minute image of that friend, which often passes outward and usually floats suspended in the air before him. In the same way if he thinks of a room, a house, a landscape, tiny images of these things are formed within the mental body and afterwards externalized. This is equally true when he is exercising his imagination; the painter who forms a conception of his future picture builds it up out of the matter of his mental body, and then projects it into space in front of him, keeps it before his mind's eye, and copies it.

The novelist in the same way builds images of his characters in mental matter, and by the exercise of his will moves these puppets from one position or grouping to another, so that the plot of his story is literally executed before his mind's eyes. With our curiously inverted conceptions of reality it is hard for us to understand that these mental images actually exist, and are so entirely objective that they may readily be seen by the clairvoyant, and can even be rearranged by someone other than their creator.

Thus, there may be mental or thought-bodies created entirely by the mind and will of the experimenter. In a case, cited in '*Your Psychic Powers and How to Develop Them*,' a clairvoyant was sent on a trip to the house of a person (who was a writer) and asked to describe the individual whom she found there through her psychic powers. She described a certain person in detail – hair, eyes, features, etc., given at great length. When the psychic had finished and recovered full consciousness, she was told that her description was entirely wrong, and that no such person existed in the house in question, and that her description was erroneous throughout.

When the facts were stated to the person (whose house was examined by the psychic), he replied that although he himself did not in any way resemble the clairvoyant description, it corresponded exactly and in minute detail to a character he was creating and writing about in his book! In other words, his thought had actually lived for the time being as an objective entity and was seen as such by the entranced clairvoyant.(Carrington 1920)

The Writer's & Composer's Psyche and Psychic Characters

'*The Hope Booklets*' explains that the writer who creates a character or characters (with the entire narration and the whole of the environment in which it takes place), whenever he starts doing this in a succession of inspired moments, gives to himself and to his own subconscious something that in a wider sense can certainly be defined as an authentic form of suggestion.

The character or the characters therefore begin to exist as thought-forms in the psyche of the writer. They are thought-forms destined to acquire even greater concreteness to the extent to which they receive sustenance from other thought-forms, from ever-new characterizations that complete the characters as such.

Sown in the submerged and unconscious part of the writer's psyche and left there to sleep, these thought-forms draw nourishment from this psychic *humus* not only to strengthen themselves and attain ever greater consistency, but also to grow and develop in an autonomous manner.

Their mode of growth is undoubtedly autonomous, just as the reactions by these characters and their way of speaking and acting are autonomous. As a general rule, however, all this takes place within the framework that has been traced right from the beginning, ever since the character began to take shape and to define itself in the profound psyche of its author. And it is indeed in the author's psyche that the character comes to life.

Thought Form That Haunted Shelley

"On the 23rd June," says one of Shelley's biographers, "he was heard screaming at midnight in the saloon. The Willamses ran in and found him staring on vacancy. He had had a vision of a cloaked figure which came to his bedside and beckoned him to follow. He did so, and when they had reached the sitting-room, the figure lifted the hood of his cloak and disclosed Shelly's own features, and saying, '*Siete soddisfatto?*' vanished. This vision is accounted for on the ground that Shelley had been reading a drama attributed to Calderon, named '*El Embozado o El Encapotado*,' in which a mysterious personage who had been haunting and thwarting the hero all his life, and is at last about to give him satisfaction in a duel, finally unmasks and proves to be the hero's own wraith. He also asks, 'Art thou satisfied?' and the haunted man dies of horror." (Stead, 1921)

Johannes Brahms' Mental Images

In his book '*Talks with Great Composers*', Arthur Abell writes of an evening spent with Johannes Brahmns in 1896, when Brahms confided his special creative process, on the promise that Abell would not publish it until fifty years after his death, a promise Abell kept.

Brahms seemed to deliberately seek a special state of consciousness.

"To realize that we are one with the Creator, as Beethoven did, is a wonderful and awe-inspiring experience... I always contemplate this when I begin to compose. This is the first step. [Then] I feel vibrations that thrill my whole being, those vibrations assume the form of distinct mental images... Straightaway the ideas flow in upon me. And not only do I see distinct themes in my mind's eye, but they are clothed in the right forms, harmonies and orchestrations." (Hudson, 1969)

Balzac identified Himself with his Characters

Honoré de Balzac represents a parallel case. The great French novelist and playwright identified himself with his characters to the point of living alternatively his own life, the life of Honore de Balzac and that of the character whose story he was writing at that time.

According to a precise testimony of Rene Benjamin, while he was writing *Papa Goriot*, he would at times speak like this character, pronounce his phrases and, just like him, handle and "see" the other characters enter the room, conversing with them, wholly identified with story that he lived in the first person, immersed in a hallucination that seemed full and perfect. (Liverziani)

Mozart – Miraculous Compositions

Wolfgang Amadeus Mozart, the great musician, confessed that at certain moments, thoughts crowded into his mind without his being able to say where they came from. Indeed, he said that he knew nothing about it, played no part in it at all. And added that once he had a motif clearly in his mind, another motif quickly comes to join the first according to the needs of the composition, the counterpoint, the instrumental part, and all these ingredients ended up by forming the bulk of the work. As Mozart goes on, the work then grows, he hears it all the time, perceives it even more clearly. Lastly, no matter how long it may be, the composition becomes completely formed and concluded in his mind. He then embraces it with a single overall look, just as if it were a fine painting, not in succession, not in the detail of its parts, as he would do later on, but as a whole, just as his imagination had made him hear it. (Liverziani)

Saint-Saeans and Stevenson

Saint-Saens, as Myers notes, had only to listen to his demon, just like Socrates. Passing on to literature, Myers recalls a testimony by De Musset: "One doesn't work, one simply listens; it is as if someone unknown were whispering into your ear." He also cites Lamartine, who says, "It is not I who thinks, it is my ideas that thinks for me."

Myers recalls Robert Louis Stevenson's Brownies, his 'Little People.'(described in *'A Chapter on Dreams'* in his volume *"Across the Plains"*). "His dreams had always (he tells us) been of great vividness, and often of markedly recurrent type. They populated and agitated his interior theatre. In a certain way they told him about themselves, little by little, a kind of novel in installments, and yet kept him wholly ignorant of their intentions and of how the story was going to end."

Likewise, a dramatist, indicated only by the initials M. S., says: "When I wrote these dramas, it seemed to me to be a spectator in the theatre: I kept looking at what was happening on the stage in anxious, surprised and curious expectation of what was about to happen. And yet I felt that it all came from the very depth of my being."

Charles Dickens' Characters

Charles Dickens was so absorbed in his characters that they appeared to him and followed him around and he used to complain that they literally haunted him. James T.Field said, "He (Charles Dickens) told me that when he was writing *'The Old Curiosity Shop,'* the creatures of his imagination haunted him so much that they would neither let him sleep or eat in peace." When Charles Dickens was engrossed in the writing of *'Martin Chuzzlewit'* (1843-44), one of his fictional characters, Mrs.Gamp, would accompany him to Church and whisper into his ear so that he was unable to control himself and would burst out laughing.

Samuel Taylor Coleridge's Kuble Khan

Samuel Taylor Coleridge's account of his own poetical composition *'Kuble Khan'* – a poem set in a strange, exotic landscape, replete with images, is very curious. He had been reading 'Purchas his Pilgrimage' and fell asleep at the moment he was reading this sentence– "Here the Khan Kubla commanded a palace to be built, and a stately garden thereunto." He continued in profound sleep about three hours, during which he had a vivid confidence that he composed from two to three hundred lines; if, as he says, that can be called composition in which all the images rose up before him as things with a parallel production of correspondent expressions. On awaking he appeared to have a distinct recollection of the whole, and proceeded to write down the wonderful lines that are preserved when he was interrupted, and could never afterwards recall the rest.

Giuseppe Tartini

Giuseppe Tartini, a celebrated Italian Baroque composer and violinist composed his famous *Sonate de Diable* (Devil's Sonate), while he dreamed that the devil challenged him to a trial of skill on his own violin. His *Sonate de Diable* is somehow a plagiarism from the violin played by the dream-devil!

4. Dream Reasoning

There are many such examples of artistic, literary and scientific work executed in the course of dream. In a curious essay *"A Chapter on Dreams,"* Robert Louis Stevenson informs us that many of his stories, and those most original, were composed, or at least sketched, in dream. It may be noted that during part of his life he lived in a psychical condition in which it was very hard to know whether he was asleep or awake. Explaining the cause of these images, Ernesto Bozzano states that whenever a sensation is frequently repeated, it acquires an exceptional vivacity, and this in such a way as at times to persist for a long time even when the cause that produced them no longer exists. These are the ones that he calls *"consecutive images."*

Professor W. R. Newbold narrated cases described as 'Dream Reasoning,' which had occurred in the experience of two of his colleagues.

Dr. W. A. Lamberton, Professor of Greek in the University of Pennsylvania, when a young man, after giving up as insoluble a problem in description geometry upon which he had been working for weeks by the analytical method, awoke one morning several days later to find a hallucinatory figure projected upon a blackboard in his room with all the lines necessary to a geometrical solution of the problem clearly drawn. He had never had any other visual hallucination.

He wrote, "On opening my eyes on the morning in question, I saw projected upon this blackboard surface a complete figure, containing not only the lines given by the problem, but also a number of auxiliary lines, and just such lines as without further thought solved the problem at once." (Newbold, 1897)

The other case was this:

Carl Jung revealed that he was advised by an inner teacher (whom he called Philemon and who seemed to him to have an independent existence) who arose unbidden from the depths of the psyche. Reflecting on his experience of the psyche's autonomy in his autobiography, *'Memories, Dreams, Reflections,'* (1962/1963), Jung writes:

"Philemon and other figures of my fantasies brought home to me the crucial insight that there are things in the psyche which I do not produce, but which produce themselves and have their own life. Philemon represented a force which was not myself. In my fantasies I held conversations with him, and he said things which I had not consciously thought. For I observed clearly that it was he who spoke, not I. He said I treated thoughts as if I generated them myself, but in his view thoughts were like animals in the forest, or people in a room, or birds in the air, and added, "If you should see people in a room, you would not think that you had made those people, or that you were responsible for them." It was he who taught me psychic objectivity, the reality of the psyche.

Through him the distinction was clarified between myself and the object of my thought. He confronted me in an objective manner, and I understood that there is something in me which can say things that I do not know and do not intend, things which may even be directed against me.

Jung continues, "Psychologically, Philemon represented superior insight. He was a mysterious figure to me. At times he seemed to me quite real, as if he were a living personality. I went walking up and down the garden with him, and to me he was what Indians call a guru.... the fact was that he conveyed to me many an illuminating idea."

Discovery of the ring of Benzene Molecule

August Kekule von Stradonitz, the famous German chemist who established the foundation for the structural theory in organic chemistry, recounted how one evening he dozed on a London bus and saw atoms gamboling before his eyes and spent part of that night making sketches of these forms. Some years later a similar event led to the discovery of the ring of the benzene molecule. Here is Kekule's reminiscence:

"I was sitting, writing at my text-book; but the work did not progress; my thoughts were elsewhere. I turned my chair to the fire and dozed. Again the atoms were gamboling before my eyes. This time the smaller groups kept modestly in the background. My mental eyes, rendered more acute by repeated visions of the kind, could now distinguish larger structures, of manifold conformation: long rows, sometimes more closely fitted together; all twining and twisting in snakelike motion. But look! What was that? One of the snakes had seized hold of its own tail, and the form whirled mockingly before my eyes. As if by a flash of lightning I awoke; and this time also I spent the rest of the night working out the consequences of the hypothesis."

Deciphering Fossil Imprints in Dream

Jean Louis Rodolphe Agassiz was a Swiss-American paleontologist, zoologist, and geomorphologist, a renowned natural scientist, and quite influential during his time. His first major scientific work was the description of a collection of Brazilian fish, on which basis he was awarded a Ph.D. degree by the University of Munich in 1829.

The following story is told by Mrs. Agassiz in the life of her husband:

"He had been for two weeks striving to decipher the somewhat obscure impressions of a fossil fish on the stone slab in which it was preserved. Weary and perplexed, he put his work aside at last, and tried to dismiss it from his mind. Shortly after he awoke, persuaded that while asleep he had seen his fish with all the missing features perfectly restored. But when he tried to hold and make fast the image, it escaped him. Nevertheless he went early to the Jardin des Plantes, thinking that, on looking anew at the impression, he should see something which would put him on the track of his vision. In vain – the blurred record was as blank as ever. The next night he saw the fish again, but with no satisfactory result; when he awoke it disappeared from his memory as before. Hoping that the same experience might be repeated on the third night, he placed a pencil and paper beside his bed before going to sleep. Accordingly, towards morning the fish reappeared in his dream, confusedly at first, but, at last, with such distinctness that he had no longer any doubt as to its zoological characters. Still half dreaming, in perfect darkness, he traced these characters on the sheet of paper at the bedside. In the morning he was surprised to see, in his nocturnal sketch, features which he thought it impossible the fossil itself should reveal. He hastened to the Jardin des Plantes and, with his drawing as a guide, succeeded in chiseling away the surface of the stone, under which portions of the fish proved to be hidden. When wholly exposed, it corresponded with his dream and his drawing, and he succeeded in classifying it with ease. He often spoke of this as a good illustration of the well-known fact that when the body is at rest the tired brain will do the work it refused before." (Activity of the Brain during Dream, 1885)

Professor Hilprecht

A remarkable instance of psychometrical dream-vision, bearing relation to articles held and studied during a prior time, is related in the *'Proceedings of the Society for Psychical Research'* (August 1900).

Herr H.V.Hilprecht was a professor of Assyriology in the University of Pennsylvania. The University dispatched an expedition to explore the ruins of Babylon and sketches of the objects discovered there had been sent home. Among these were drawings of two small fragments of agate, inscribed with characters. One Saturday night, in March 1893, Professor Hilprecht had wearied himself with puzzling over the two fragments, which were supposed to be broken pieces of finger-rings. He was inclined, from the nature of the characters, to date them about 1700-1140 B.C; and on the first character of the third line of the first fragment seemed to read 'KU,' he guessed that it might stand for 'Kurigalzu,' a king of that name.

Tired, and without success, he retired and went to sleep. He says: "Then I dreamed the following remarkable dream. A tall, thin priest of the old pre-Christian Nippur, about forty years of age, and clad in a simple abba, led me to the treasure-chamber of the temple on its south-side. He went with me into a small low-ceilinged room without windows, in which there was a large wooden chest, while scraps of agate and lapis-lazuli lay scattered on the floor. Here he addressed me as follows: 'The two fragments which you have published separately... belong together, and their history is as follows: King Kurigalzu (ca.1300 B.C) once sent to the temple of Bel, among other articles of agate and lapis-lazuli, an inscribed votive cylinder of agate. Then we priests suddenly received the command to make for the statue of the god Nidib a pair of earrings of agate. We were in great dismay, since there was no agate as raw material at hand. In order for us to execute the command, there was nothing for us to do but cut the votive cylinder into three parts, thus making three rings, each of which contained a portion of the original inscription. The first two rings served as ear-rings for the statue of the god; the two fragments which have given you so much trouble are portions of them. If you will put the two together you will have confirmation of my words.'"

Mrs. Hilprecht says: "I was awakened from sleep by a sigh, immediately thereafter heard a spring from the bed, and at the same moment saw Professor Hilprecht hurrying into his study. Thence came the cry, 'It is so, it is so.' Grasping the situation, I followed him, and satisfied myself in the midnight hour as to the outcome of his most interesting dream." (Newbold, 1897)

Figures in Imagination

Colborn, a young arithmetical prodigy, told Taine that he saw his calculations clearly before him and 'another' that he saw the figures as though they were written on a slate.

Similarly, Sir Issac Newton is stated to have solved a subtle mathematical problem whilst sleeping, and Condorcet recognized in his dreams the final steps in a difficult calculation which had puzzled him during the day. In this way, Newton, we are told, succeeded in 'seeing' the disk of the sun in such a live manner even many weeks after he had interrupted his astronomical observations. Binet cites the case of Professor Pouchet, a microscopist, who, while he was walking in Paris, saw these real life images suddenly give way to superposed consecutive images of his microbes that were particularly clear and intense. Such images were so clear and precise that they could even be projected onto a white sheet to make their outline with a pencil.

Condorcet told Cabanis that while he was engaged in some abstruse and profound calculations, he was frequently obliged to leave them in an incomplete state, in order to retire to rest; and that the remaining steps, and the conclusion of his calculations, have more than once presented themselves in his dreams. According to Cabanis, Dr. Franklin's ideas respecting the perfection of the mental power during dreams, were still more extraordinary than those of Condorcet; for that Franklin disclosed him that the bearings and issue of political events, which had puzzled him while awake, were not infrequently unfolded to him in his dream (Cabanis, *Rupporte du physique*, et du Moral de l'Home, tom.ii p.547).

Thus, many mathematicians, scientists and statesmen have, in their sleep, solved problems which challenged them when awake. And to the same point is the following anecdote, which Abercrombie tells us.

An eminent lawyer in Scotland was consulted regarding a case of great important and much difficulty. And the lawyer had been studying it with intense anxiety and attention. After several days had been occupied in this manner, he was observed by his wife to rise from his bed in the night and got to a writing-desk, which stood in the bed-room. He then sat down and wrote a long paper, which he put carefully by in the desk, and returned to bed. The following morning he told his wife that he had had a most interesting dream; that he had dreamt of delivering a clear and luminous opinion respective a case which had exceedingly perplexed him, and he would give anything to recover the train of thought which had passed before him in his dream. She then directed him to the writing-desk, where he found the opinion clearly and fully written out and which was afterwards found to be perfectly correct. (Carlyon, 1836)

George William Russell, an Irish writer and artistic painter, in his renowned book *'The Candle of Vision: Have Imaginations Body?'* shares his experience of visualizing thought images. He writes, "…the dream figure or the figure of imagination will walk about with authentic motions and undistorted anatomies."

"I imagine," he continues, "a group of white-robed Arabs standing on a sandy hillock, and they seem of such a noble dignity that I desire to paint them…I say to myself, 'I wish they would raise their arms above their heads,' and at the suggestion all the figures in my vision raise their hands as if in salutation of the dawn…My brain does not by any swift action foresee in detail the pictorial consequences involved by the lifting of arms but yet by a single wish, a simple mental suggestion, the intricate changes are made in the figures of imagination as they would be real Arabs stood before me and raised their hands at my call." (Russell, 1920)

The Dream Detective

Moris Klaw was a 'detective character' created by Sax Rohmer and in a collection of stories, *'The Dream Detective'* (1920). Moris Klaw was capable of recalling the last thoughts of a person–victim or perpetrator. In order to receive such a mental 'negative' of a thought, Klaw used to sleep in the room where a crime took place. None but him was allowed to stay there overnight and he only had 'an odically sterilized cushion' for comfort.

During a conversation with the police detective Coram, Klaw explained:

"Thoughts are things, Mr. Coram. If I might spend a night here [….] I could from the surrounding atmosphere (it is a sensitive plate) recover a picture of the thing in his [the victim's] mind," [….] "what is it," continued the weird old man, "but the odic force, the ether – say it how you please – which carries the wireless message, the lightning? It is a huge, subtle [sic] sensitive plate. Inspiration, what you call bad luck or good luck – all are but reflections from it. The supreme thought preceding death is imprinted on the surrounding atmosphere like a photograph. I have trained this" – he tapped his brow – "to reproduce those photographs!" (Walter J. Black, 1928)

This power of the detective to see the mental thoughts of the victims and perpetrators is not a mere story. There are other cases on record which seem to demonstrate that certain persons are so naturally constructed that their minds are extraordinarily responsive to the thoughts in others' minds. They seem to read the thoughts of others as if they were written in an open book.

There was a Parish priest of Ars, who died in the early seventies of the 19th century. He, it was said, saw with infallible precision, the thoughts of those who came to consult him, disconcerted all skeptics by revealing their own mind, and terrified penitents who feared to confess to him because of his acknowledged power. Similarly, there were the Ursula Nuns, universally dreaded because they were said to be able to reveal the most secret thoughts. There was the case of Sister Claire, an ignorant nun, who answered visitors in the very language of their nation, although she knew but her own.

Vern Cameron, one of the foremost dowsers of his day, could detect thought-forms with his dowsing instruments with consistent accuracy under controlled conditions. A subject would project a thought-form (say, to think of a cat) and Cameron would always locate its exact position and outline (Cater, 1984).

Madame Blavatsky, in her renowned book, 'Isis Unveiled,' refers to the examples cited by Professor Denton demonstrating the psychometrical power of Mrs. Denton. A fragment of Cicero's house at Tusculum enabled her to describe without the slightest intimation as to the nature of the object placed on her forehead, not only the great orator's surroundings, but also the previous owner of the building, Cornelius Sulla Felix, or as he is usually called, Sulla the Dictator. A fragment of marble from the ancient Christian Church of Smyrna, brought before her, its congregation and officiating priests. Specimens from Nineveh, China, Jerusalem, Greece, Ararat, and other places all over the world brought up scenes in the life of various personages, whose ashes had been scattered thousands of years ago. In many cases Professor Denton verified the statements by reference to historical records. More than this, a bit of the skeleton, or a fragment of the tooth of some antediluvian animal, caused the seeress to perceive the creature as it was when alive, and even live for a few brief moments its life, and experience its sensations." (Blavatsky, 2012)

Experience outside the Body

Sometimes the thoughts or desires on the part of the dreamer are so intensive as to propel them out of the ordinary dream state into a full-flown out of body experience (OBE). In other words, the dream body is able to disassociate itself from the material body and can travel elsewhere according to the desire of the dreamer (as in the case of astral travel).

A classic example of a dream-OBE was reported in 1863 by Wilmot of Bridgeport, Connecticut:

"On October 3rd, 1863, I sailed from Liverpool for New York, on the steamer 'City of Limerick', of the Inman line, Captain Jones commanding. On the evening of the second day out, soon after leaving Kinsale Head, a severe storm began, which lasted for nine days. During this time we saw neither sun nor stars nor any vessel; the bulwarks on the weather bow were carried away, one of the anchors broke loose from its lashings, and did considerable damage before it could be secured, and several stout storm sails, though closely reefed, were carried away, and the booms broken.

Upon the night following the eighth day of the storm the tempest moderated a little, and for the first time since leaving port I enjoyed refreshing sleep. Toward morning I dreamed that I saw my wife, whom I had left in the United States, come to the door of my stateroom, clad in her night-dress. At the door she seemed to discover that I was not the only occupant of the room, hesitated a little, then advanced to my side, stooped down and kissed me, and after gently caressing me for a few moments, quietly withdrew.

Upon waking I was surprised to see my fellow-passenger, whose berth was above mine – but not directly over it, owing to the fact that our room was at the stern of the vessel – leaning upon his elbow, and looking fixedly at me. 'You're a pretty fellow', said he at length, 'to have a lady come and visit you in this way.' I pressed him for an explanation, which he at first declined to give, but at length related what he had seen while wide awake, lying in his berth. It exactly corresponded with my dream.

This gentleman's name was William J. Tait, and he had been my room-mate in the passage out, in the preceding July, on the Cunard steamer 'Olympus'. A native of England, and son of a clergyman of the Established Church, he had for a number of years lived in Cleveland, in the State of Ohio, where he held the position of librarian of the Associated Library. He was at this time perhaps fifty years of age, by no means in the habit of practical joking, but a sedate and very religious man, whose testimony upon any subject could be taken unhesitatingly.

The incident seemed so strange to me that I questioned him about it and upon three separate occasions the last one shortly before reaching port, Mr. Tait repeated to me the same account of what he had witnessed. On reaching New York we parted, and I never saw him afterward, but I understand that he died a number of years ago in Cleveland.

The day after landing I went by rail to Watertown, Conn, where my children and my wife had been for some time, visiting her parents. Almost her first question when we were alone together was, 'Did you receive a visit from me a week ago Tuesday?' 'A visit from you?' said I, 'we were more than a thousand miles at sea.' 'I know it,' she replied, 'but it seemed to me that I visited you.' 'It would be impossible,' said I. 'Tell me what makes you think so.'

My wife then told me that on account of the severity of the weather and the reported loss of the 'Africa', which sailed for Boston on the same day that we left Liverpool for New York, and had gone ashore at Cape Race, she had been extremely anxious about me. On the night previous, the same night when, as mentioned above, the storm had just begun to abate, she had lain awake for a long time thinking of me, and about four o'clock in the morning it seemed to her that she went out to seek me. Crossing the wide and stormy sea, she came at length to a low, black steamship, whose side she went up, and then descending into the cabin, passed through it to the stern until she came to my stateroom. 'Tell me,' said she, 'do they ever have staterooms like the one I saw, where the upper berth extends further back than the under one? A man was in the upper berth looking right at me, and for a moment I was afraid to go in but soon I went up to the side of your berth, bent down and kissed you, and embraced you, and then went away.'

The description given by my wife of the steamship was correct in all particulars, though she had never seen it." (1892)

Bodily Manifestations of Mental Images during Dreams

Edward Kelly and his co-authors in their book, *'Irreducible Mind,'* refer to a couple of incidents. The first story was reported in the nineteenth century in the book, '*Influence of the Mind on the Body,*' written by an English physician, Daniel Hack Tuke. It concerns a man who dreamed that he had been hit on the chest by a stone and woke up to find a bruise on his chest. Here is the account from Tuke's book:

In the *Bibliotheque choisie de Medecine*, by Planque, tome vi. p. 103, is the following case: A man, thirty years of age, healthy and robust, saw in a dream a Pole with a stone in his hand, which he threw at his breast. The vivid shock awoke him, and then he found that there was on his chest (dans le même endroit) a round mark, having the appearance of a bruise. Next day there was so much swelling, etc., that a surgeon was requested to see it, who, fearing a slough, scarified the part, and relieved it. The wound healed in a short time. Without more definite information, it would not be safe to build a theory upon this case, but looking at the previous one of the spectre, and others equally well authenticated, there appears no reason to doubt that the dream and the inflammatory action of the skin stood in the relation of cause and effect. (Tuke, Illustrations of the influence of the mind upon the body in health and disease, 1873)

In the recent past, Dr. Ian Stevenson remarked that a rare type of physical change corresponding to a mental image sometimes occurs in the experience of persons in India who come close to death and survive. After regaining consciousness, some of them say that they were mistakenly seized by messengers of the King of the Dead (*Lord Yama*) and taken to the 'realm of the dead'. With discovery of the mistake, they were sent back. Upon recovery, some of these subjects stated that they were burned while in the realm of the dead, and they show areas of inflammation or scarring at the sites of the burning.

Ian Stevenson reported the case of an Indian man, Durga Jatav, who, while seriously ill with typhoid fever, had a vivid dream in which he thought he had died and discovered that his legs had been cut off by some people in the 'other realm'. After recovering, he was found to have scars on his knees which persisted for many years.

These scars were photographed by Stevenson and appear in his book. This is the strange account of that man:

Durga Jatav, a man approximately 50 years old, was interviewed in November, 1979, and again 3 months later. About 30 years before, he had been ill for several weeks, suffering from what had been diagnosed as typhoid. When his body "became cold" for a couple of hours, his family thought he had died. He revived, however, and on the third day following this he told his family he had been taken to another place by 10 people. He had tried to escape, but they had then cut off his legs at the knees to prevent his escape. He was taken to a place where there were tables and chairs and 40 or 50 people sitting. He recognized no one. They looked at his "papers," saw that his name was not on their list, and said, "Why have you brought him here? Take him back." To this Durga had replied, "How can I go back? I don't have feet." He was then shown several pairs of legs, he recognized his own, and they were somehow reattached. He was then sent back with the instructions not to "stretch" (bend?) his knees so that they could mend. (Durga's older sister, who was also interviewed, corroborated his account of his apparent death and revival.) (Stevenson, Where Reincarnation and Biology Intersect, 1997)

Claude de Tisserant, who in the year 1775 wrote a book ,*'De Prodiggis,'* relates the following:

"The wife of a member of the Parliament of Provence in a dream saw her husband beheaded, which also really took place at the same time at Paris. Awaking in a passion of terror at the cruel spectacle, she found her hand convulsively shut, so that she was unable to open it; and when it was with main force opened by her maids, there was found on the palm the perfect image of her husband, with his head cut off, and this bled like the wounds of the stigmatized." (*Of the Nightmare*, 1845)

A very similar instance of the 'bodily imprint of mental images' is related by one Von Meyer:

"Madame V., of N, saw one night, in a very lively dream, a person who offered her a white and a red rose, bidding her choose one of them. She chose the red. When she awoke she felt a vehement burning in one arm, and by degrees there formed itself on the spot so affected, the perfect picture of a red rose, which appeared embossed on the skin, like a mole. On the eighth day this rose was in its most perfect state, both as to drawing and colour; it became thenceforth daily paler, and less defined, and after fourteen days no trace of it remained. This well authenticated fact forms an important contribution to the history of the *stigmata*." (*Of The Nightmare*, 1845)

As early as the 13th century, Jacobus de Voragine assigned of the causes of these phenomena to mind and body interactions, thus taking them out of the category of the supernatural. And Joseph Ennemoser (1787-1854), a South Tyrolean physician said, in reference to all such cases, "these appearances are not artificially produced deceptions, nor yet are they to be explained by the mere physical circumstances of the body. To spirits, or to any immediate divine operation, we will hardly ascribe them. Far from being miraculous, it is in every case a purely physiological process, grounded in a psychic cause."

Photographic (Eidetic) Memory

Photographic memory is the ability to form sharp and detailed visual images on briefly 'scanning' a picture or a page for a short period of time and to recall the entire image at a later stage. For instance, if a photograph of a building is shown, for 30 seconds or so, to a person with eidetic memory, he can subsequently recollect the number of the windows, doors, columns, etc.

Dr. Carpenter tells of a Member of Parliament who could repeat long legal documents and acts of Parliament after one reading. When he was congratulated on his remarkable gift, he replied that, instead of being an advantage to him it was often a source of great inconvenience, because when he wished to recollect anything in a document he had read, he could do it only by repeating the whole from the beginning up to the point which he wished to recall. (Betts, 1914)

Similarly, a distinguished theatrical performer, in consequent of a sudden illness of another actor, had to prepare himself in a very short span of time a part which was entirely new to him, and rather long and difficult. He acquired it in a very short time, and went through it with perfect accuracy, but immediately after the performance, forgot it to such a degree that though he performed the character for several days in succession, he was obliged every day to study it anew. When questioned respecting the mental process which he employed the first time he performed this part, he said that he lost sight entirely of the audience, and seemed to have nothing before him but the pages of the book from which he had learnt it, and that if anything had occurred to interrupt this illusion, he should have stopped instantly. (Abercrombie, 1875)

And, Sir James Mackintosh, who could repeat whole pages of a book on the Brownonian System which he had read thirty years before, always acknowledged that he was guided by a recollection of the actual appearance of the pages of the book itself.

Painters' Mental Images

Certain painters objectified the images of their conception of the painting to such an extent that later they were able to reproduce them on canvas without having the model in front of them. It is reported in the review *Luce e Ombra* (1935, pp.38-40):

In the throes of inspiration, the painter Montevecchi of Bologna saw, for example, the Madonna to be painted already designed in every detail and projected onto the canvas as if the canvas had become transparent. He then felt an impulse to reproduce her on the canvas with the greatest rapidity, as if he feared that he might not be in time to follow the evanescent image (Cfr.B., 1967 pp.14-15).

Dr. Wigan relates the history of one of a renowned English painter of his time, who required only one sitting from his subject to form a perfect portrait. His own account of the subsequent process was as follows:

"When a model was presented, I looked at it attentively for half an hour, sketching occasionally on the canvas. I had no need of a longer sitting. I put aside the drawing, and passed to another person. When I wished to continue the first portrait, I took the subject of it into my mind, I put him in the chair, where I perceived him as distinctly as if he had been there in reality; I may even add, with form and color more defined and lively than in the original. I contemplated, from time to time, the imaginary figure, and set myself to paint; I suspend my work to examine the pose, exactly as if the original had been before me; every time that I cast my eye on the chair I saw the man." (Elam, 1869)

Phillis Atwater' Imaginary House

Phyllis Atwater, a noted writer and an international authority on near-death states, believes in the power of mind to create thought-forms. She says, 'thoughts really are things. They were powerful. All the old stories are true. Thoughts are pre-matter itself for they have substance and mass and thus can be shaped into form at will. It can be done and I did it. I really did it.'

Reproduced here is Phyllis Atwater's mental creation experiment.

Phyllis Atwater commenced her mental creation experiments. She decided to create and give form to a house. In her mind, she established the details and the exact measurements, carefully examining each part observing every proportion, and then focusing everything she saw in order to keep it firm while she projected it into a defined place in front of herself. She maintained her idea in focus and an image formed in front of her... with astonishment she found that the house was there. It was a house! She stepped forward and knocked at a window. It seemed glass. Then she opened and closed all the doors and windows, walked with a heavy step on the green pavement of the porch, gripped the great brass knob of the entrance door, inspected the foundations, the roof and the fireplace, and gave a sharp blow to each of the three white posts of the porch. This white and quadrangular house with its steeply pitched roof was more solid and massive than any other house she had ever seen. It seemed really true!

At this point, Phyllis' mental creativity got itself further objectives. And also, new challenges. The house was inanimate. But now she wanted to try her hand with something animate, live. She decided to create a powerful oak. She repeated the procedure she had used before, designing every detail of the tree in her mind and then projecting the images in front of her, to a particular point to the right of the house, using her mind like a laser beam. There soon appeared the tree complete with bark, all its grains, holes made by insects and its beautiful and brilliant leaves.

It had happened, it was possible, it could be done, said Phillis to herself. A human being like herself could create from nothing. Could put together the tiniest parts of pre-matter, think of energy and command it to form specific animate or inanimate objects. Thoughts are truly things. (Liverziani).

Dream-thought Transmissions

Albert Alberg, a naturalist and author of many books including *'The Floral King; A Life of Linnaeus,'* has recorded a similar instance where the structural pattern of a house that came in the dream of a person got imprinted on the ice tracings in the window pane. His account of the incident as recorded in his book, *"Frost Flowers on the Windows,"* is reproduced below:

"Returning to my friend, the spiritualist, to recount my frosted window investigations, I again quite unexpectedly lit upon another curious experience of ice tracings. I observed that on the small upper side-pane of the bay window of the room in which his son slept, there was a most beautiful design of a wooded hill, at the bottom of which lay a small craft at anchor. A little way up the hill was a flat-roofed house and still higher another building and a fine church with a tower. The architecture of each was very distinct. Two steeples and a flag staff were seen in the distance. Some ravines intersected the lower part, and trees and shrubs, rich in foliage, were scattered about. Above appeared an arch of clouds. It was a most exquisitely beautiful ice tracings, of which I drew a faint delineation on paper. I requested the family to ask the son on his return in the evening what he had dreamt the night previously, for I thought that possibly we might have be on the track of thought-photography, with which Boston has surprised the world, but the young man could remember nothing. However, the family intended shortly to remove to their old home in a rural place near Cleveland, Ohio, which the father declared somewhat resembled the exquisite ice-tracing. When I saw the son (a young gentleman about thirty-two years old) a week later, he admitted that he frequently dreamt of their old home in Ohio, although he could not recollect having done so on the night in question. So that the inference of dream-thought transmission may thus still be left open." (Alberg, 1899)

We have thus far instanced various circumstances that were supposed to give rise to thought forms. They are authentic cases of externalization of thoughts convincing us that thoughts have actual material substance, even though it may be impalpable and invisible in most of the times. However, to concretise the idea of thought-forms, on requires additional evidence which can be perceived and experimented upon. In the forthcoming chapters, we are going to explore some peculiar aspects of these thought-forms and experimental evidences to support it.

3
HALLUCINATIONS

This is the very coinage of your brain; this bodiless creation ecstasy is very cunning.

-Shakespeare in *Hamlet*

What are mental hallucinations? Are they real entities? Are they objective or subjective? Do they have a physical cause to make the sensory experience? Or, are they mere delusions?

William James in *'Principles of Psychology'* observes that 'one often speaks of hallucinations as mental images that a subject projects outside himself by mistake. But when a hallucination is complete, it is far more than a mental image. A hallucination is a form of strictly sensitive consciousness, a fine and true sensation as if it were a real object.'

The psychological paradigm re-created the world of the imagination as haunted. The mind itself could be subject to phantoms and apparitions, an alienating force within subjectivity itself. Castle makes the analogy that: "One could now be 'possessed' by the phantoms of one's own thought—terrorized, entranced, taken over by mental images, just as in earlier centuries people had suffered the visitations of real spirits and demon."

Dr. Brewster remarks that "when the eye is not exposed to the impressions of external objects, or when it is insensible to these objects, in consequence of being engrossed with its own operations, any object of mental contemplation, which has either been called up in the memory or created by the imagination, will be seen as distinctly as if it had been formed from the vision of the real object." (Sir Daniel Keyte Sandford, 1836).

For example: A young woman, having once been frightened by the sudden presentation to her of a white mouse, had been troubled for years by seeing this mouse running about her, upon her clothing, upon anything she was handling, and even upon her food; and, as a result, she was in a state of constant agitation and perplexity, though at times convinced that this was the product of her mind. She washed her hands and her clothing frequently because she was convinced that this animal had made them dirty; and she could not divest herself of the belief that it was real.

In hypnotic cases, it would seem that the vividly externalized hallucinating object produced by suggestion tend to appear more real that the actual object when placed alongside them. Edmund Parish explains: "Y.being in the hypnotic trance, I say to him, 'When you awake, X. will be sitting on this chair; you will be wide awake and have all your senses about you.' Y., on awakening, in fact thinks he sees X. on the chair, converses with this imaginary person, etc. I then point out to him the real X. with the words, 'Now, which is the real X.? You see one on the chair, the other you see standing here.' Y. feels the chair and the real X., in order to convince himself which is X. and which empty air. After trying for some time, he finally comes to the conclusion, "He is sitting here on the chair."'" (Parish, Hallucinations and Illusions: A Study of the Fallacies and Perception, 1897)

MM.Binet and Fere conducted the best-known series of experiments on 'hypnotic hallucinations' and found that the hallucinatory percept behaves under various conditions precisely as 'if it were a real percept'. Thus, if the subject is told to see a picture on a blank card, he will not only see the picture at the time, but he will be able subsequently to pick up the card, recognizing it by means of the hallucinatory picture impressed on it, from a number of similar cards. If the card is inverted, he will see the picture upside-down; if a magnifying glass is interposed, he will see the picture enlarged; viewed through a prism, it will appear doubled; it will be reflected in a mirror; and if the hallucinatory image consists of written or printed words, he will see the writing in the mirror inverted.

There are many other examples.

Dr. Brierre de Boismont, in his curious treatise, '*Trate des hallucinations*,' tells us that a man, perfectly sane, who had never had visions, was tormented one morning by a terrible nightmare; he saw in his room a mysterious ape horrible to behold, who gnashed his teeth upon him, and gave himself over to the most hideous contortions. He woke with a start, it was already day; he jumped from his bed, and was frozen with terror on seeing, really present, the frightful object of his dream. The monkey was there, the exact image of the monkey of the nightmare, equally absurd, equally terrible, even making the same grievances. He could not believe his eyes; he remained nearly half an hour motionless, observing this singular phenomenon, and asking himself whether he was delirious or mad. Ultimately, he approached the phantasm to touch it, and it vanished.

Abercrombie, whose work on cerebral diseases acquired an extraordinary reputation in England, quotes the following fact:

"A distinguished physician, harassed with fatigue, and worn out with anxiety in consequence of the illness of one of his children, slept in his chair, where he dreamed that he saw a gigantic baboon. He awoke much agitated, arose and went towards a table that was in the middle of the room. He was perfectly awake, and recognized the objects around him. At the end of the room, against the wall, he distinctly saw the baboon making the same grimaces as in his dream. This apparition lasted for half a minute." (Boismont A. B., 1855)

The author of "*Phantasms of the Living*," Edmund Gurney, has recorded what an Oxford undergraduate shared with him. Having had a very vivid dream of being chased by a figure in green, he woke and saw the green figure in the middle of his room. "I had no doubt that I was awake, for I saw the light from the street lamp shining on my door. The figure was not in this light but nearer the bed, and the green tinge was very perceptible."

Similarly, Rev. E. H. Sugden of Bradford wrote to Edmund Gurney the following:

"Once I had a most vivid dream about a man whom I knew well. On suddenly awaking I saw him, in the light of early morning, standing at my bedside in the very attitude of the dream. I looked at him for a second or two, and then putting my foot out. I kicked at him; as my foot reached him, he vanished."

Pitres and Regis quote the case of a patient of Seglas, "overcome, at the sight of a rabid dog, with an obsessing fear of rabies. When the crisis overtook him, during his sleepless nights, he used to see dogs in his room. One day, overcome by his crisis in the street, he even began to fly before an imaginary mad dog which he believed he saw at his heels; he cried out, to the astonishment of passers-by, who for their part could see nothing."

We read in Abercombie's work, the case of a man 'who has been all his life affected by the appearance of spectral figures. This peculiarity existed to such an extent that if he met a friend in the street, he could not at first satisfy himself whether he really saw the individual or a spectral figure. By close attention, he could make a distinction between them, in the outline of the real figure being more distinctly defined than that of the spectral; but in general he took means for correcting his visual impression by touching the figure, or by listening to the sound of his footsteps. He also had the power of calling up spectral figures at his will.'

Most of these illusions are associated with the previous occupations, ideas, habits and passions of the subjects. Dr. Boismont, in his *"On Hallucinations,"* describes the case of a young lady who told her that she was unable to rest because all the persons around her wore masks, and she was in the midst of a perpetual carnival. This illusion, like many others, remained quite inexplicable, until the doctor learnt that it originated in a visit she had paid to a *bal masque* (an event which the participants attend in costume wearing a mask) at the opera. (Boismont A.-J.-F. B., On hallucinations, 1859)

We had already seen the case of a painter who, after carefully studying a sitter's appearance, could project it visibly into space, and paint the portrait not from the original but from the phantasm.

He ended by confounding the phantasmal figures with real ones, and became insane. Baillarger reports another painter, Martin, as having similarly projected pictures, which so interested him that he requested anyone who took up a position in front of them to move. And Edmund Gurney in his book, *'Phantasms of the Living'*, had added that in one of the cases of persistent dream images, his informant, Lieut.-Colonel Hartley, of Hartley, near Dartford, remarked, "I can always produce this phenomenon, if I know that I am dreaming, by opening my eye, which wakes me, but the dream-image persists." Professor Ball explicitly claimed such cases as hallucinations provoked by an 'abnormal sensation.' He does not tell us what the abnormal sensation is, or what causes it.

The percipient does not behave towards the apparition exactly as he would do with regard to the objective reality. An example given by Kandinsky may illustrate this point. He reported the case of a person who perceived the hallucinatory figure of a lion (or, according to Kandinsky, "vividly imagined" a lion), and yet manifested no particular excitement, apprehension, or terror. Now, it is true that if the man in question had met in the street a lion escaped from some menagerie, he would have been seized by the above emotion (Parish, 1897).

No wonder, then, that the belief in ghosts and apparitions has prevailed amongst all religions in all times across the latitudes and longitudes, and still prevails widely among many. Any sincere scientific inquirer is now bound to acknowledge such appearances of coinages of mental faculties.

The Hallucinated Afterimage Obeys Optical Laws

In *'Hypnotisme et Suggestion'* (1893), the German physiologist Wilhelm Wundt describes the positive and negative hallucinations experienced by subjects under hypnotic suggestion. In a positive hallucination, one sees what is not there, Wundt describes, for example, a man who recoils in fear when told that a rabid dog is approaching. Correspondingly, a negative hallucination involves blindness to what is present; a subject in a room full of observers, for example, perceives only his or her hypnotist – suggestor. Obviously, such hallucinations must be determined by the mind, which bypasses the eye by either projecting or blocking visual percepts.

And yet, positive hallucinations apparently behave as thought subject to the same optical laws as real images. "For example, we suggest to the hypnotic that, on the white wall in front of him, there is a red cross; he replies that he sees it. If we then order him to look at the ground, he declares that he sees the portrait of this cross, in green." Here, we have an afterimage that shifts with the directions of the eyesight and that appears in the color complementary to that of the original image.

Dr. Albert Moll, in his book *Hypnotism*, mentions similar results obtained by Jendrassik: "If a *d* is drawn with the finger on a sheet of white paper, and it is suggested that the *d* is real, the subject sees the *d*. If the paper is turned upside down, he sees *p*, and in the looking-glass *q*." (Moll, 1890)

In his 1910 book on hypnotism and spiritism, Cesare Lombroso recalls a series of empirical studies that similarly proved that "the suggested image behaves as a real image would." In one such experiment, sixty-three of sixty-five hallucinated images provoke pupil dilation and are susceptible to distortion by optical lenses. "It should be noted," writes Lombroso, "that the hallucination behaves, in almost all subjects, like a real image. It enlarges under a magnifying lens; the pupil dilates when the image of a distant object is suggested; in the opposite case, it contracts." (Goulet, 2011)

MM. Fere, Binet and Parinaud have also conducted experiments to show that the hallucinated images act like a real image, obeying the laws of optics. For example, they contend that a prism doubles it, or again, if cards are colored red and green by suggestion, and these colors are superposed by one of the known methods, the patient sees gray as the resulting color produced by the mixture of these two complementary colors.

Self-Hypnotic Pet Polar Bear

Dr. George H. Estabrooks of Cornell University, in his book *'Hypnotism'* (1943), writes of his attempts to conjure up a self-hypnotic pet polar bear. He writes, "the technique of auto-suggestion is difficult, but it can be mastered. Once the subject has obtained this mastery he will find that not only can be produced, say, hallucinations in the trance itself but can actually suggest posthypnotic hallucinations to himself. It does sound weird but it can be done... Auto suggestion gives us an excellent device with which to study many strange things. The writer had a 'pet' polar bear which he was able to call up merely by counting to five. His pet was as real and as solid-appearing as if it were actually alive and present. This animal would parade around the hospital ward in most convincing fashion, over and under the beds, kiss the nurses and bite the doctors. It was very curious to note how obedient he was to 'mental' commands, even jumping off a three story window on demand. But auto suggestion has a certain menace which this phantom bear illustrated. He became so familiar that he refused to go away. He would turn up in the most unexpected places and without being sent for. The writer was playing bridge one evening and almost threw his hosts into hysterics by suddenly remarking, 'There's that damn bear again. I wish someone would shoot the beast.' He also had a nasty habit of turning up in dark corners at night, all very well when one realized he was just made of ghost stuff but rather hard on ones' nerves for all that. So he was banished and told never to return. It was fully a month before the writer felt quite sure that his ghostly form would not be grinning at him over the foot of his bed during a thunderstorm" (Over, 1972)

Astral Wolf

Something similar happened to the British occultist and psychic Violet Penry Evans, better known by her pen name, Dion Fortune, when she discovered what she called an 'astral wolf' lying on the bottom of her bed. Although she saw the creature as objectively real (it even had a degree of weight) her psychoanalytic training convinced her it was actually a projected thought form that had arisen in her own unconscious mind. When she tried to push the creature out off the bed, it turned and growled at her – another thought form had shown itself to be out of its creator's control. (Dolores Ashcroft-Nowicki, 2001)

Great Cat Hallucination

The following narrative from DeBoismont is illustrative of the nature of mental hallucinations. As regards the authenticity of the case, the author says, "We owe to a very eminent physician of acknowledged reputation, and intimate with Sir Walter Scott, the recital of a fact, that once occurred to a well known personage, which is, without contradiction, one of the most curious examples, that can be offered in the history of hallucinations."

The physician was once called on to attend a man whose external symptoms announced no acute or alarming illness; but he had an unceasing sadness. The physician who attended him wanted him to divulge the reasons of his grief which was dragging him to the grave. After some conversation, he expressed his desire to disclose all the facts frankly to the doctor.

"I assure you," replied the patient, "that my situation is not unique, for there is a similar example in the celebrated romance of Le Sage. Without doubt, you remember by what disease the Duke of Olivares died? He was overcome by the idea that he was followed by an apparition, in whose existence he did not believe; and he died because the presence of this vision conquered his strength, and broke his heart. Well, my dear doctor, mine is similar case; and the vision that persecutes me is so painful and so frightful, that my reason is quite inadequate to combat the effects of a frenzied imagination, and I feel that I shall die, the victim of an imaginary malady."

The patient continued that the attack had been gradual, and that, in the commencement, it was neither terrible nor very unpleasant; and the progress of his sufferings was as follows:

"My visions," he said, "began two or three years ago. I was then annoyed by the presence of a great cat, which came and disappeared, I knew not how; but I did not continue long in doubt, for I perceived that this domestic animal was the result of a vision produced by a derangement in the organs of sight, or of the imagination. However, I have not the same antipathy to these animals as that brave mountain-chief, now dead, whose face turned all the colors of his plaid, if in a room with a cat, even though he did not see it. On the contrary, I rather like them, and I endured the presence of my imaginary companion with a degree of patience that almost amounted to indifference. But, at the end of a few months, the cat disappeared, and was succeeded by a phantom of a higher grade, and whose exterior was at least more imposing. It was no other than a gentleman-usher, dressed as though he were in the service of the Lord-Lieutenant of Ireland, or of a great functionary of the church, or of any other person of rank or dignity.

"This character, in a court-dress, with bag wig, a sword by his side, a vest worked in tambour, and a chapeau-bras, glided by my side like the shade of Beau Nash. Whether in my own house, or elsewhere, he mounted the stairs before me, as if to announce me. Sometimes he mixed in with the company, although it was evident that no one remarked his presence, and that I alone witnessed the chimerical honors he paid me. This caprice of Imagination did not make a strong impression on me; but it raised a question as to the nature of the disease, and I began to fear the effect it might have on my senses. This apparition also had its term. After a few months, my gentleman-usher was no more seen, but was replaced by a phantom horrible to the sight, and distressing to the mind – a skeleton. Alone, or in society," added the unfortunate man, "this apparition never leaves me. It is in vain that I repeat to myself that it has no reality, that it is but an illusion caused by the derangement of my sight, or a disordered imagination. Of what use are such reflections, when the presage and the emblem of death is constantly before my eyes? When I see myself, although only in imagination, forever the companion of a phantom representing the gloomy inhabitant of the tomb, whilst I am still upon earth?

Neither science, philosophy, nor even religion has a remedy for such a disease; and I too truly feel that I shall die this cruel death, although I have no faith in the reality of the spectre that is always present." (Boismont A.-J.-F. B., Hallucinations, 1853)

Haunted by Himself

"I knew," says Arthur Ladbroke Wigan (d.1847), "a very intelligent and amiable man, who had the power of thus placing before his own eyes *himself*, and often laughed heartily at *his double*, who always seemed to laugh in turn. This was long a subject of amusement and joke; but the ultimate result was lamentable. He became gradually convinced that he was haunted by himself (or to say by his self). This other self would argue with him pertinaciously, and, to his great mortification, sometimes refute him, which, as he was very proud of his logical powers, humiliated him exceedingly." (Maudsley, 1878)

A Spirit Story

In the following story in T.P.'s *Weekly*, the editor vouches for the facts, but suppresses the names. I think it best to give it in the words of the writer:

"Here is a spirit story whose truth I can guarantee – so far at least as I can guarantee the truthfulness of the friend who told it me. A young girl on her way to Cambridge to meet her fiancé started up at every station where the train stopped, and looked so wildly out of the window that an old gentleman in the carriage at last asked her what was the matter. 'Oh,' she answered, in great agitation, 'I have seen at every station the friend I am going to meet at Cambridge on the platform, beckoning me to get out, in a kind of terror.' 'Then take my advice,' said the old gentleman, 'and if you see him at the next station still beckoning to you, get out at once.' At the next station there was still the spectre beckoning to her in even wilder excitement than ever. She hesitated no longer, got out at once – as indeed did the old gentleman – and waited for the next train to take her to Cambridge. On her arrival she learned that an accident had happened to the preceding train, and especially to the carriage in which she had been seated, and from which, indeed, she had only and barely escaped with her life. The odd thing was that her fiancé, when his spirit was appearing to warn her, was himself so sound asleep in the waiting-room at Cambridge that he had not even dreamed of anything of the sort." (Coates, 1906)

Apparition of the Deceased

James Coats, the author of *Seeing the Invisible,* vouches the following experience told by Mrs.Coats (who was a widow before marrying Mr.Coats) and the author calls this 'a collective hallucination.'

"About three months after the death of her husband she had the following experience, which might, perhaps be called "a collective hallucination." She had been left with three little ones alive, and for comfort, and because these little ones would feel the loss of their father, she had arranged that they should all sleep in her bedroom. A little daughter about four years of age slept with her mother, and the two boys in little cribs close at hand. There was plenty of room in the house, but this suited all best. On this particular night the children were sound asleep when she retired. She was awakened suddenly from a sound sleep as if by an electric shock, and found herself looking upon a hand which rested on her little daughter's breast. She instantly recognised the hand, which was natural as in life, as that of her late husband. The child was a great favourite of his. Mrs. S. was greatly startled to see the hand and to recognise, and the hand started too, as if conscious of the recognition. Her eyes followed the hand to the arm, and then she saw the whole figure, which, while distinct, was shadowy except the head and face, which were almost as fully defined and as opaque as the hand. The body was between the bed and the wall, which the bed touched. She could see the wall, as it were, through the body, and the veridical hallucination lasted sufficiently long for her to distinctly recognise her husband's face and every movement. She was much terrified and as the hand was lifted the little girl became restless and murmured in her sleep, "Papa is away; he is in heaven," and smiled and fell into sound sleep again. Mrs. S fell asleep too, and about three o'clock she was awakened by the elder boy saying, "Mamma, I saw papa at the foot of the bed." "When?" she asked. "Just now," he replied. "I woke up and saw papa come into the room and stand at the foot of the bed, and he said to me, 'Be good to your mother, John.'" The bedroom door was shut and locked. (Coates, 1906)

Skeleton Spectators

Hyacinthe Zanglois, a distinguished artist of Rouen had told M.Brierre de Boismont, the author of *'On hallucinations: A history and explanation of apparitions, visions, dreams, ecstasy, magnetism, and somnambulism'* (1859), that when he entered on the stage he was able, by the power of his will to banish from his sight the dress of his numerous and brilliant audience, and to substitute in the place of these living persons so many skeletons. When his imagination had thus filled the theatre with these singular spectators, the emotions which he experienced gave such an impulse to his acting as to produce the most startling effects (Tuke, Illustrations of the influence of the mind upon the body in health and disease, 1873).

On this case, M. Brierre remarked that the hallucinations in some cases were under the control of the will, and would seem to be excited instantaneously.

Robert Macnish, a renowned physician of his time and a member of the faculty of Physicians and Surgeons of Glasgow, in his book *'The Philosophy of Sleep,'* remarked that some of the most vivid instances of spectral illusion were those induced by opium. Several of the English Opium-Eater's visions were doubtless of this nature. He borrowed a striking example which Dr. Abercrombic related and which occurred to the late Dr. Gregory. He had gone to the north country by sea to visit a lady, a near relation, in whom he felt deeply interested, and who was in an advanced state of consumption. In returning from the visit, he had taken a moderate dose of laudanum with the view of preventing sea-sickness and was lying on a couch in the cabin when the figure of the lady appeared before him in so distinct a manner that her actual presence could not have been move vivid. He was quite awake, and fully sensible that it was a phantasm produced by the opiate, along with his intense mental feeling; but he was unable by any effort to banish the vision. (Macnish, 1835)

Robert Macnish concludes that anything in which the mind dwells excessively may, by exciting the perceptive organ, give rise to spectral illusions. He adds, it is to this circumstance, that the bereaved husband sees the image of a departed wife, to whom he was fondly attached, that the murderer is haunted by the apparition of his victim, etc. Dr. Conolly related the case of a gentleman who, in danger of being wrecked near the Eddystone lighthouse, saw the images of his whole family.

A long list of eminent persons who had reported similar experiences was given by Dr. Brierre de Boismont and later by Edmund Parish in his *'Hallucinations and Illusions'* (1897). Socrates had auditory hallucinations and was said to have stood all night in a rigid attitude communicating with the voices. He was often restrained and admonished by an inner voice. Savonarola saw visions even in his early youth. Luther was subject to numerous auditory and visual hallucinations. Cardan had a guardian spirit, and the philosopher Hobbes was haunted in the dark by faces of the dead. During one part of his adulthood, Descartes was followed by an invisible being who urged him not to abandon his search for truth. Ben Jonson confided to a friend that he had passed a whole night sitting in his armchair watching Tartars, Turks, and Roman Catholics rise up and fight. Goethe asserted that on one occasion he saw the counterpart of himself coming toward him. Oliver Cromwell was stretched sleepless on his bed when suddenly the curtains opened and a woman of gigantic size appeared and told him that he would be the greatest man in England. (Bliss, 1986)

Hypnotism and Auto-suggestion

George H. Estabrooks discovered that everything we get in the hypnotic trance can also be obtained by means of the post-hypnotic suggestion. And, that anything we find in either can be found in auto-suggestion; and finally, that everything we obtain in any of the three will be encountered in everyday life. In this latter case, we refer to the subject as hysteric, neurotic, or even insane.

Estabrooks cited a typical case of post-hypnotic suggestion by which the hallucinatory figure appeared to the subject as if in reality.

In this case, the operator said to the subject in somnambulism, "Now listen carefully. After you wake up, I will show you the ace of spades from a pack of cards. When I do this, you will see a black dog come in through the door. He is very friendly dog, so you will pet him, then you will give him a bone. He belongs to Professor Fowler so, after you have fed him, you will call Fowler on the telephone and ask him to come get the dog."

The operator repeated these instructions and asked the subject if he understood them thoroughly. Then the subject was awakened. Five minutes later, the hypnotic picked up a deck of cards, selected the ace of spades, and laid it on the table in front of the subject. The latter seemed wide awaken in every sense of the word. He glanced at the door and said, "Why, here is Fowler's dog. He looks hungry. Come on in, fellow, and have a bone." He patted the phantom dog, took a plate from the table and put on it an imaginary bone, and continued to fondle the dog as he ate it. Then he suddenly said, "You know, I don't believe Fowler knows where that dog is. I think I'll call him on the telephone and let him know."

So he went to the phone and put through his call, all the time talking in a perfectly normal manner about his garden, his auto or any other topic of conversation in which he might have been engaged. Fowler, who knew what is happening, came over for a cup of tea. All the time the subject was in the room and kept playing with the dog and finally said good day to the professor and his phantom pet in quite normal fashion. (Estabrooks, 1943).

Similarly, Betty Shin, in her book entitled *'Mind Waves,'* affirms that she has actually seen thought-forms when giving trance healing. She remembers her first experience as follows:

"I was sitting by the side of the healing couch with my hands on the head of a little boy and his mother was sitting opposite me in an armchair. Whilst in trance, I was aware of small clouds of energy emanating from around her head. The image of a little girl was formed from one of the clouds. It was quite distinct.

When I came out of trance, I noticed that the woman was half-asleep. I touched her arm and told her that I had finished healing.

Then I asked her whether she had been dreaming. 'No,' she replied, 'I wasn't really asleep, just day-dreaming, and wondering whether my friend had picked my daughter up from school on time.' She continued, 'I always worry myself sick when I can't pick her up myself because I never really trust other people to drive carefully.'"

Our discussion thus far has focused on cases of veridical and other kinds of hallucinations. These hallucinations are so vivid and real that it is hardly possible to distinguish them and perception proper. In many cases, the hallucinating subjects experience a matching voice, smell, etc., which give them the sense of 'being aware of.' The persons or objects seen by the hallucinating subjects move, changes their form and dimension.

Prof.Paul Greguss, in his *"Biological Signal-Processing Model,"* theorize that the visual system uses neural matrixes functioning as spatial filters in a holographic form, and the Central Nervous System (CNS) acts as a Fourier analyzer. Thus, it can be assumed, according to Greguss that, if this model is a functionary one indeed, non-specific stimuli (e.g., electric or magnetic stimulation, etc.) when acting on such a function group, may result in a visual pattern the CNS used in its signal processing. Such so-called "subjective light patterns of the second kind," are not unknown in physiology (Phosphenes) and in psychiatry (hallucinations).

4
THOUGHT-PHOTOGRAPHY

The capital phenomenon consists in how the sensitive plate, which is thought not to receive any impression in the dark, is impressed. The silver salts are converted, not only by what we call exterior solar light and by electric fulguration, but also by the intimate light of the soul.

–Dr. H. Baraduc

We have thus far seen that our mental thinking objectifies itself. Such mental images possess not only the form, but also force and power and occupy space in the mental realm. If, in spite of all the evidences in its support, and of their reasonableness, we are doubtful of the existence of mind's power to create thought-forms, it is mainly because of the fact that it is totally against our known sensory perceptions. As Sperry, the Nobel Laureate, righty said, 'we were having problem with understanding consciousness because the inner sensations, feelings, concepts, mental images and the like cannot be weighted, measured, photographed or spectrographed or chromatographed or otherwise recorded or dealt with objectively by any known scientific methodology. So, we need proof – proof that our own eyes can see and sense.' Thoughts are substantial in so much as they are susceptible to the impression of the photographic plate. If so, can thoughts be photographed? Certainly. It may sound absurd to say so. But we have a clear proof based on genuine photographs that thought is a substantial form, and in its transference, there is more than merely a mental process involved. Now let us see in this chapter how the thought-forms can be captured on photographic plates.

There are people who could transfer to a photographic plate whatever they had in their mind, without any physical contact with the film or the camera, by a vital force emanating from their mind. These thought images acquire a capability of externalization, and thus produce objective pictures.

For instance, Teen Psychic Joey Lain is able to transmit mental images and memories to photographic film with the power of his mind alone! Parapsychologist Dr. Stefan Bolling, who tested and retested the 15-year-old boy under rigorous scientific conditions, concluded that he can literally create a photograph of anything that he has ever seen just by looking at a camera, that has been loaded with unexposed film. Joey said he found out about his ability to project mental images to film, when he picked up his father's camera and thought about shooting pictures of his girlfriend – but didn't. When his father got prints back from a photo lab after taking pictures of his sister's birthday a few weeks later, the film had been double exposed with the images of the party – and Joey's girlfriend! (Cunninghm, 1999)

Another noteworthy experiment carried out by Miss Scatcherd is that of a photograph that Archdeacon Colley one day took of her in the garden of the presbytery. 'We are in July 1910. At the moment of the snapshot Miss Scatcherd thought that, having to leave home very hastily, she had forgotten to put in a more appropriate dress and regretted that she was not at that moment wearing an embroidered blouse she kept locked up in her wardrobe. When the photograph was developed, it was found that it not only produced a phantom by the side of Miss Scatcherd, but that she was actually wearing the greatly desired blouse with its embroidery, which appeared somewhat diaphanous, but nevertheless clearly distinguishable and indubitable.' (Liverziani)

"*The experience of Mr. Bradrook*" – This gentleman had sent to the review '*Light*' the photograph of a soldier in which by the side of the seated soldier one could note another figure, attenuated and transparent of the same soldier on his feet. When the latter was questioned about this, he limited himself to saying that at the moment the photograph was taken, he had thought with a certain regret that he should have had himself photographed in a standing position. (Liverziani)

Many experiments of a like nature followed.

Roger's Thought Experiments

Such tests, we are told, have been made by Mr. Inglis Roger, of Plymouth, England. An ardent photographer, he had for some time been trying to produce clear and exact photographs of human thoughts, and at last he claimed to have succeeded.

He produced his results in this way: First, he stood in front of a sheet of white cardboard, on which was drawn a cross surrounded by a circle, and at this cardboard, which was placed under a bright jet of gas, he looked steadily for half an hour. Then he removed the cardboard and put in its place a sensitive plate, at which he gazed steadily for another half an hour, having first taken the precaution to extinguish the gas. Finally, he tried to develop the plate, but with no success whatever.

Not daunted, he resumed work next morning. Again, he looked at a sheet of cardboard, on which was drawn a plain cross without any circle, and again he entered into a long tête-à-tête with the sensitive plate. On this occasion, however, he placed between his eyes and the plate a box, from which all air had been removed. His experiment over, he examined the plate and found on it two images, one representing the simple cross at which he had just been looking and the other representing the cross and circle at which he had looked on the previous evening.

Emboldened by this success, Mr. Roger determined to attempt a more ambitious experiment. He had seen a shipwreck scene in a Plymouth Theatre in which Miss Daisy Wallace played a prominent part and the scene having made a strong impression on him, he determined to try to produce a thought-photograph of the actress. So his wife and he went to see her, and the result was that on the following day Mrs. Roger found herself unable to attend to any work for the reason that the actress seemed to haunt her. She finally complained to her husband, saying "I see Daisy Wallace's figure everywhere."

Then this strange scene occurred:

"When I heard these words," says Mr. Roger, "the pen fell from my hands." "Remain as you are," I cried to my wife, and straightway

I placed a bandage over her eyes and led her into my dark-room. There I took a sensitive plate, and placing it in a proper position I arranged the box in front of it, and then, having removed the bandage from her eyes, I urged my wife to look fixedly at the plate and to think meanwhile of the actress as intently and as earnestly as possible. She did so, but only for the space of four minutes. Under these circumstances, I had little hope of obtaining a satisfactory result; and yet, when the plate was developed, I found thereon a perfect image of Miss Wallace, so perfect, indeed, that it could be recognized by anyone." (1897)

Following the experiment of Prof. Rogers, other physicists tried to photograph the psychical images by the force of imagination. It is evident that such images are distinct from those arising from immediate contact with reality; but their real nature is the same in essence. When Inglis Rogers was gazing at the stamp he saw only an image on the retina, and in reality it was not on the material cells of the retina itself that the image rested was on the tabula rasa of the mind. It was outward from the mind itself, not from the retina, that this was projected through the sensitive and responsive ether to the sensitive plate of photography, an arrangement of unstable cells which is the triumph of the art of the chemist.

It is therefore not necessary for this experiment that one should gaze at an individual stamp. To think of a stamp will serve as well. Recognizing this fact, Mr. Cameron Lee, another English experimenter, attempted to secure the image of a thought. Placing his own eyes in the focus of a lens in absolute darkness, he thought intensely of the face of a certain cat. After a long exposure, necessary on account of the comparative grossness of the photographic materials, a picture was formed. The negative showed a rounded outline evidently that of the enlarged pupil of the eye, and in its centre was a faint image, which could be mistaken for nothing other than a cat. (Jordan, 1896).

Dr Hyppolyte Baraduc

Back in May 1896, Dr Hyppolyte Baraduc (1850–1902), among the serious researchers, probably startled the Paris Académie de

Médecine with the news that he had photographed thoughts. In his experiments, the person whose thought is to be photographed enters a dark room, places his hands on a photographic plate, and thinks intently on the object, the image of which he wishes to be produced. Further it is contended that such photographs can be produced by will power exercised over a considerable distance of intervening space. He quoted the following interesting case as an example.

"An astonishing feat of telepathic photography is related by a medical practitioner of Bucharest, Dr. Hasdeu. Being interested in telepathic phenomena, he and his friend, Dr. Istrati, determined to put it to a photographic test, so as to prove whether it were possible to project an image at a distance upon a plate already prepared. The evening agreed on for the crucial experiment arrived. Dr. Hasdeu before retiring placed his camera beside his bed.

Dr. Istrati was separated from him by several hundred miles. The latter according to agreement was, just before going to sleep, to concentrate his thoughts in the endeavour to impress his image upon the plate prepared by his friend in Bucharest. The next morning, on awakening, Dr. Istrati was convinced that he had succeeded, being assured of it in a dream. He wrote to a mutual friend, who went to Dr. Hasdeu's residence and who found that gentleman engaged in the development of the plate in question. Upon it there appeared three distinct figures, one of them particularly clear and lifelike. It depicted Dr. Istrati gazing with intensity into the camera, the extremity of the instrument being illuminated by a phosphorescent glow which appeared to emanate from the apparition. When Dr. Istrati returned to Bucharest he was surprised at the resemblance of his fluidic portrait, which revealed his type of face and most marked characteristics with more fidelity than photographs taken by ordinary processes." (Leadbeater, 1930)

In 1901, the book 'Thought Forms' was published by Annie Besant and Charles W.Leadbeater – leading figures of the Theosophical Movement – in which the authors explicitly refer to Dr. Baraduc's experiments.

"Dr. Baraduc obtained various impressions by strongly thinking of an object, the effect produced by the thought-form appearing on a sensitive plate […] He quite rightly says that the creation of an object is the passing out of an image from the mind and its subsequent materialization, and he seeks the chemical effect caused on silver salts by this thought-created picture."

Commandant Louis Darget

The French Commandant Louis Darget (1847-1921) reported to the Academy of Sciences, Paris that after many trials he had succeeded in obtaining photographic impression of thoughts of concrete objects. He produced an evidence of two photographs, one showing a walking stick and the other a bottle, in each case the image being perfectly distinct.

In explanation, he gave the following account of the process:

After staring a long time on the object to be photographed in a strong red light, he fixed his gaze with all the will power at his command, on a photographic plate that had previously been immersed in a weak developer in a dark room. At the end of a quarter of an hour, the image of the object appeared on the negative.

According to the Commandant's theory, these astounding results were due to certain obscure light rays which he called 'V' rays.

According to *'Joire: Psychical and Supernormal Phenomena'*:

"Commandant Darget, of Tours, obtained several good thought photographs. His procedure is to gaze attentively at a simple object for a few moments in order to engrave it firmly on the mind, then go into the dark room and (1) place a photographic plate with the glass side against the forehead for a quarter of an hour, mentally picturing the object decided upon and strongly desiring to make an impression on the plate; (2) Place the hand on a plate (or hold the plate in the hand) for a quarter of an hour, operating as before; (3) Put the plate into a developing bath, placing the fingers of one hand on the edge of the plate for ten minutes. There should always be the desire to imprint on the plate the picture of the object which is very strongly thought of." (*Joire: Psychical and Supernormal Phenomena p.* 380).

This is what Darget himself says:

"The photograph of the walking stick was obtained at vouziers eleven years ago. I was stick with a candle which I generally used. I had put it on my desk where I made my photographs that evening, after closing the windows and taking out my red lantern.

With regard to the eagle, it was produced in this way. Mme. Darget was in my Office, lying on my sofa, about ten o'clock in the evening. I said to her: "I am going to put out the lamp and to try (as I have already done sometimes) to take a fluidic print over my forehead. I will hand you a plate for you to do it as well.

I therefore handed her a plate, which she held with both her hands about an inch in front of her forehead. A short time afterwards, it might be about ten minutes, she said to me: 'I think I have been asleep; I am very tired, I am going to lie down'. And, feeling her way in the darkness she handed me the plate. Then I went to develop it, and was surprised to see this astonishing figure of an eagle. I have called it 'a dream photograph' although my wife does not remember having dreamed of a bird or anything else while she held the plate.'"

For Darget, "thoughts are creative, radiating, almost tangible, forces, [.....] when the human soul produces a thought, it sends vibrations through the brain, the phosphorous it contains starts radiating, and the rays are projected out." (Darget, 1911)

Eusapia Palladino

In the later 1890s, the multi-talented medium Eusapia Palladino (1854–1918), couldn't stretch to creating images on film, but did produce bas-reliefs of herself, and of her 'spirit control' John King, in tubs of wet putty, some of them weighing over 65lb, that had been kept away from anyone's physical contact – but particularly hers – at various sittings.

In 1897, for example, a series of séances was held at the home of one M. Blech, at Montfort l'Amaury in France. Camille Flammarion described part of the proceedings in his *'Mysterious Psychic Forces'* (Small, Maynard: Boston, 1909, pp74–6):

"The medium pants, groans, writhes. The chair in the cabinet comes forward and places itself by the side of the medium, then it is lifted and placed upon the head of Mme. Z Blech, while the tray [containing putty, and weighing some 9lb] is lightly placed in the hands of M. Blech, at the other end of the table. Eusapia cries that she sees before her a head and a bust, and says 'E fatto' (It is done). We do not believe her, because M. Blech has not felt any pressure on the dish. Three violent blows as of a mallet are struck upon the table. The light is turned on, and a human profile is found imprinted in the putty. Mme. Z Blech kisses Eusapia upon both cheeks, for the purpose of finding out whether her face has not some odor (glazier's putty having a very strong odor of linseed oil, which remains for sometime upon the fingers). She discovers nothing abnormal.

"This discovery of a 'spirit head' in the putty is so astonishing, so impossible to admit without sufficient verification, that it is really still more incredible than all the rest. … The imprint has a resemblance to Eusapia's face. If we supposed she produced it herself, that she was able to bury her nose up to the cheeks and up to the eyes in that thick putty, we should still have to explain how that large and heavy tray was transported from the other end of the table and gently placed in the hands of M. Blech. But how?"

Fukurai's Experiments

In Japan, Prof. Fukurai, of the University of Tokyo, published a large book, giving the results of his experiments in psychic photography. For example, on one occasion, Prof. Fukurai, after handing a plate to the entranced psychic, said, "I want you to impress upon that plate, by an effort of your will, the words *'Myo Ho'* – meaning 'marvelous processes.'" The subject then stated that she saw the words before her – in the air as it were – and that she was trying to impress the outlines of these words upon the plate, in Japanese characters. A few moments later she said, "They are taken," and handed the plate to the Professor. Immediately upon the plate being developed in the dark-room, it was examined, and the words "Myo Ho" were found upon it!

More difficult tests were then undertaken. A pile of a dozen wrapped plates was placed upon the lap of the psychic. She was asked to impress a plate several down the pile – that is, not the top or the bottom plate. She made an effort at will, and in a few minutes exclaimed, "I have impressed the word 'Ten' (meaning 'Heaven') on the third plate. I will now try to impress my three fingers of the left hand upon this plate. I will impress the word 'Kin' ('God') upon the sixth plate in the pile." Soon she exclaimed that this had been done and the pile of plates was taken from her. Under development it was found that the word "Ten" and the faint outlines of three fingers were impressed upon the third plate, and the word "Kim" upon the sixth plate. All the rest were blank.

The Thoughtographic Man: Serios

The best-known example of a thought-photographer is the Chicago-based Ted Serios whose efforts have been described in details by Dr. Jule Eisenbud, a Denver psychoanalyst. Serios's thought-photographs have included recognizable pictures of buildings and people, blurred and usually curiously distorted.

Serios could just think of images and make them appear on photographic films. In 1962, Pauline Oehler of the Illinois Society for Psychic Research sent Dr. Eisenbud, a copy of an article about Serios that she had published in *Fate* magazine. Eisenbud initially responded by saying that he had "seen enough of this sort of stuff" to know "there must obviously be something fishy somewhere," but he was eventually prevailed upon to research Serios's talents in depth.

Eisenbud's book, *'The World of Ted Serios,'* (1967) contains over a hundred of these 'mental pictures,' and reproductions of various pictures that he had in mind when trying. There is immense variety. Buildings, cars, people, rockets, and many weird and unidentifiable shapes. The usual method of taking them was as follows: Serios would take a small plastic tube, which he called a 'gismo,' and hold it over the lens of the camera, then concentrate very hard and press the trigger of the camera. Anyone who has used a Polaroid will know that such a procedure would normally produce a blur. The camera and film were produced by Dr. Eisenbud or anyone else present. Serios could produce a 'photograph' whether or not there was a lens in the camera, and whether or not he was blindfolded. He usually had a fairly clear idea of what the picture would be and on occasion, was quite certain that it had been successful. When trying to 'get' the Chicago Hilton, he muttered, "Missed, damn it," and produced the Denver Hilton instead (in colour).

One notable thing is that there were anomalies within the thought photographes produced by Serios, suggesting further proof that they have their psychic origin. One example is the apparent misspelling in his thoughtograph of the Royal Canadian Mounted Police Air Division building in Ottawa. The image was conspicuous for the mis-spelling of the word 'Canadian,' which in Serios' thought-photograph was spelt 'Cainadian' (his own incorrect spelling of the word).

On another occasion, Serios was asked to produce images of something from the distant past. What appeared was astounding; an apparent image of a Neanderthal man leaning over what looked like a fire. Later examination of the photo however revealed that it bore a striking resemblance to an exhibit in the Field Museum of Natural History in Chicago. Dr. Eisenbud describes this as follows:

"... in a session that took place in May 1967 at the Denver Museum of Natural History. The objective of the session was to determine if Ted who had recently come up with images of a building that, several years earlier, had ceased to exist, could go back thousands of years in time as well. To facilitate this Wellsian adventure, an effort was made to try to stimulate and direct his imaging by placing close by him a number of ancient artifacts, including several from the Paleolithic period. The result, as it turned out, could only be described as a "detour de force." Instead of producing images of the distant past itself, Ted came up with merely contemporary representations of the distant past." (Eisenbud, *Visions, Old and New: An Addendum to Paranormal Film Forms and Paleolithic Rock Engravings*, 1985)

Another of Serios's thought photograph features part of a livery stable opposite the old Opera House in Central City, Colorado.

Figure 1 Opera House in Central City, Calorado (Left) **Figure 2** Ted Serios' Thought photograph (Right)

Serios' defender, Jeffrey Mishlove, says:

"The way in which Ted's mind ostensibly shaped the pictures was sometimes quite remarkable. In one session, in front of several witnesses, Ted first tried to reproduce images of the medieval town of Rothenburg. Then the experimenters asked him to try to reproduce an image of the old Opera House in Central City, Colorado. Serios agreed, and then asked the experimenters if they would like a composite of both images. The results are extraordinary. The photograph shows a striking resemblance to the livery stable across from the old Opera House. However, instead of the brick masonry, the image shows a kind of embedded rock characteristic of the buildings in the medieval town." (Eisenbud, *The World of Ted Serios: "Thoughtographic" Studies of an Extraordinary Mind*, 1989)

This is a classic example of photographic reproduction of vivid hallucinations. Professor Gonady Pavlovich Krochatev had successfully obtained thought photographs of this kind in his laboratory in the Ural Mountains for some time by holding a negative film or plate in a sealed container in front of the eye of the hallucinating subject.

Spirit-Photography – A Kind of 'Thought-Photography'

The Spiritualist movement, which began in the 1850s, was founded on the belief that the human spirit exists beyond the body and that the spirits of the dead can, and do, communicate with the living. The first photographer to produce and market spirit photographs was William H. Mumler, who opened a studio in Boston in the early 1860s, where he photographed clients accompanied by ghostly images of deceased friends or relatives. Mumler is perhaps best known for his portrait of Mary Todd Lincoln, who appears with the spirit of her martyred husband, President Abraham Lincoln, hovering just behind her, hands reassuringly on her shoulder.

Figure 3   Mary Todd Lincoln's portrait with the thought-form of her husband, President Abraham Lincoln, photo taken by William H.Mumler

Spirit Photographs, although genuine, were not the photographs of 'spirits' in most of the cases, but represented the projected thoughts or mental portraits emanating from the sitters or from the experimenters. The following instance may testify this.

The wife of Mr. Desmond Fitzgerald, M.I.C.E., an eminent electrical engineer in London, and at one time on the Council of the then National Association of Spiritualists, obtained a fully identified portrait of her own father. The lady went to Hudson with her daughter, for a spirit photograph, but she did not tell the photographer either what she wanted or the special character of the picture she expected to receive. She thought of her father, and longed, naturally to have his photograph. She hoped that if he came he would appear wearing the old black cap which he had been accustomed to wear in his last illness. She neither told her daughter, who was with her, nor the photographer of this test. It was not until the plate was developed and this clear features of her father revealed that she made known the test which was in her mind. This particular spirit photograph was published in the *Daily Graphic* in June 1892 and was reproduced in Glendinning's interesting work *'The Veil Lifted.'* What she thought of came on the photo-sensitive plate.

Persons of high stature like late Mr. Traill Taylor, for years President of the *British Royal Photographical Society*, made statements that 'psychic pictures' can be obtained under the strictest test conditions. Mr. Taylor gave to the society an interesting account of his own experiments in which he detailed the method of operation adopted and the precautions taken by him. But Mr. Taylor argued that such pictures were quite worthless as aids to establish spirit-identity. He called them thought – or mind – or memory pictures or projections and traced them back to the sub-conscious mind of the medium or of the experimenters.

He stated that pictures had been obtained of the conventional angels with wings, on the ordinary mind that had been led to imagine them. It is further confirmed, he stated, by the circumstance that on some of these pictures there appeared, with the spirit form of their departed owners, deceased pet dogs and cats and parrots which are nothing but manifestly images drawn from the memories of the medium or of the sitters. He further cited those photographs on which the materialized spirit appeared as he existed at various ages in his physical body, in one case as a child or youth, in another as a grown-up person, the presentation evidently corresponding with the peculiar mind-image which the experimenter had retained of the deceased, reasoned Mr. Taylor (Raupert, 1920).

Thought Photograph of Abraham Lincoln

In Manhattan, half-dozen experimenters were requested to project a mental image of Abraham Lincoln within a specific area of white wall. Then while they "held the thought" of Lincoln standing there as they conceived of him – each one – in imagination, the shutter of the quartz-lens camera was clicked and the resultant plate developed. Six perfectly discernible figures of Lincoln appeared superimposed on one another against the indicated area of wall, two of them wearing stovepipe silk hats (Pelley).

Other Examples

Willie Schwanbolz, investigated by Professor Uphoff, had the habit of moving his head during the 'taking' of thought-photographs. The instant camera covered with its lens-cap is pointed at his forehead, as is usual in thought-photography; but multiple images are found on the print, just as though a rapid series of mental images was projected.

Dr. Kotikl (*Die Emanation der Psychophysischen Energie-Bergmann, Wiesbaden*, 1908) of Moscow put before a person acting as agent a clear sheet of notepaper, and a picture post-card, with a request to image vividly the picture transferred to the blank sheet and to fix the attention upon the sheet for several minutes with that idea. Then the blank sheet, so treated, was shown to another person acting as the percipient and living in another place.

Blind psychic Margarent Schutlz put images on photo-paper with the power of her mind alone. She then took the process a step further and made the objects materialize in her hand. 'This is more than mind over matter – this is mind over reality,' declared Dr. Phillip Bresler, the paranormal researcher from Chicago.

Dr. Baraduc, of Paris, of whom we have talked about earlier, also conducted a number of very interesting experiments in this connection, with specially sensitized plates, and apparently succeeded in directly photographing thoughts by the aid of a camera. In this case, the swirls or vortices of the ether were directly caught upon the plate and photographed. A number of these have been reproduced in the past – illustrating different types of thoughts or emotions emitted by the sensitive subject – usually in hypnotic trance. Similar experiments have been conducted by other continental investigators.

Dr. Hereward Carrington, in his book *'Modern Psychical Phenomena,'* recounts an interesting case as follows:

"The story was once related to me of a lady who strongly objected to having her photograph taken. One day she died. She was laid to rest in her coffin, where she remained two days. On the second day a photograph of her was taken by the local photographer. Next day she was buried. Two days later the photographer came round in a great state of excitement, saying that, although he had carefully developed his plate, not a mark – not a trace of the face – was to be found on it! Where the face should have been was a blank space! Now the possible explanation is that the still-active will of this person was being exercised in some occult manner, to the end that she interfered with the light-rays coming from her face sufficiently to prevent its image being recorded. I do not for a moment advance either the case or the theory as "scientifically established"; I merely give it as an example – illustrating a possibility which may one day be demonstrated." (Carrington, Modern Psychical Phenomena, 1919)

Another Instance of a Thought Photograph

A German mother who photographed her infant son in 1914 left the film to be developed at a store in Strasbourg. In those days some film plates were sold individually. World War I broke out and unable to return to Strasbourg, the woman gave up the picture for lost. Two years later she bought a film plate in Frankfurt, over 100 miles away, to take a picture of her newborn daughter. When developed the film turned out to be a double exposure, with the picture of her daughter superimposed on the earlier picture of her son.

It was assumed by Carl Jung that through some incredible twist of fate, her original film, never developed, had been mislabeled as unused, and had eventually been resold to her. But it appears to be a case of thought photograph – the persistent thinking of the son by his mother imprinted his image on the photographic plate.

Thoughts Projected into Water

Recently, the researchers at the Mind Science Laboratory of the Shun Shen Tao Temple, Florida, have conducted a curious experiment, projecting the thought form of the albhaphent 'G' into the water and got the thought-image photographed.

Senior Researcher D. P. Meyers stated, "We started this phase of our research work back in October of 2006. Our first letter to be photographed was the capital letter "G". We now have completed over one hundred of these remarkable "mind projected thought into water" experiments, and consistently the letters emerge up out of the water. Completing the first phase of our research, we are now moving into the second phase and our results appear very promising."

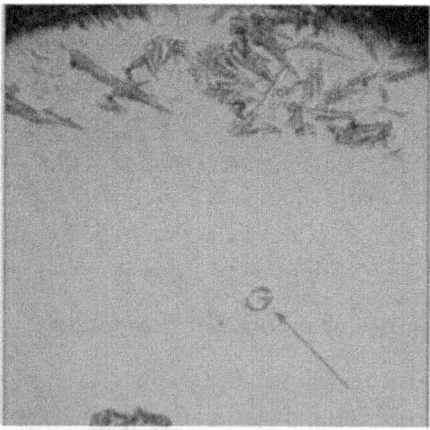

The photograph is of a mind projected capital letter "G" caught emerging up out of water viewed through a microscope.

Figure 4 The phogograph of a mind projected capital letter "G" caught emerging up out of water viewed through a microscope

© Mind Science Laboratory of the Shun Shen Tao Temple in Florida

Astonished researcher Edwin Bickel III declared; "This makes clear that; a specific thought held in mind and directed by intention at physical matter, can indeed affect that physical matter. Further, even be mirrored back in physical matter with that specific thought represented in form.

"This means too that the nutrient rich water, like that of the body, becomes an extremely receptive psycho-responsive (responds to thought) medium, provided that the body has available the nutrients it needs."

Grand Master David Harris, a Qi Gong Master, stated; "From ancient Chinese medical text we are told that; the body forms a crystalline matrix of nutrients within the waters of the body. Our research findings strongly suggest that what may be happening in human bodies with regards to thinking, is the mind also writes and encodes information directly into the body via a crystalline matrix interface of nutrients produced by the human body.

"The upshot of this research is clear "as we think a thought, so we embody that thought."

Thus the problem of accounting for thought-photographs still remains unsolved. How is it possible or conceivable for thought thus to impress a photographic plate, leaving upon it the image in the mind? Are thoughts more real, more objective things than we have been in the habit of supposing? When we "visualize," or construct a mental picture in thought, we form a mental image which is, so far as we know, purely mental, and composed only of "such stuff as dreams are made of." How can such a mental image be projected outwards into space, and actually exist in the material world? How can it affect a photographic plate, or any other instrument which can usually be influenced only by physical forces?

The only rational solution consists in believing that thoughts are in a sense more real, more actual, and more material than we have been in the habit of supposing. Thoughts must possess mental energy; this mental energy probably sets in motion certain vital, nervous currents in the brain and nervous system, which in turn affect the surrounding ether and thus create ether vibrations and other disturbances in the environment of the medium or psychic. These vital radiations, as we have seen, have been photographed; and it also seems probable that the mental image can directly affect the ether, setting-up in it certain strains and swirls and modifications which are direct thought photographs.

Doubtless each human brain is sending out every minute countless etheric vibrations that radiate outward into space. In telepathy these waves operate possibly something like wireless telegraphy. They impress solid objects. They can be reflected by a mirror – just as when we "see" a solid object in a mirror we don't really see it, but only ether vibrations which have been reflected by the glass – the real object being a long distance away!

Vitvan (1946), in his book, *'Clear Thinking,'* remarks that as an image appears on the photographic plate in a camera, so energy wave-lengths and frequencies are formulated as a picture in the mental functions of an individual's psychic nature. When this picture, due to the various neural and brain processes, appears 'out there,' i.e., substantive, it becomes identified with a given configuration of units of energy from which stimuli are received. Then that image-appearing-substantive in the psychic nature becomes designated or labeled a "thing," an "object," etc. (For explanation of why we see this 'thing' as 'having qualities' of 'hardness,' 'smoothness,' 'solidness,' instead of seeing it as a dynamic energy system or configuration of units of energy, also refer to the books, *'Clear Thinking'* and *'Perceptive Insight'.*) In the totality, this formulation of qualities into mental images constitutes what we call "the objective world." This identification and belief therein represents what we called "the error."

5
IDEOPLASTY AND MATERIALIZATION

"Every person has, in addition to this natural body of flesh, bones and blood, a Thought Body, the exact counterpart in every respect of this material frame. It is contained within the material body, as air is contained in the lungs and in the blood. It is of finer matter than the gross fabric of our outward body. It is capable of motion with the rapidity of thought. The laws of space and time do not exist tor the mind and the Thought Envelop of which we are speaking moves with the swiftness of the mind"

— William Thomas Stead

Ectoplasms, spirit materializations, phantasms, etc., are further evidences that the thoughts of the subconscious are capable of embodying themselves in visible form. 'Spirit Materializations' are said to be thought-projections of the subconscious. As Hudson puts it, 'the power resides in the subjective mind of man to create phantasms perceptible to the objective senses of others. Again, it seems to be well established by experiment that some persons have the power not only to create such phantasms but also to endow them with a certain degree of intelligence and power'.

C. W. Leadbeater, in his book *'The Astral Plane: Its Scenery, Inhabitants, and Phenomena,'* classifies materialization into three kinds. First, those which are tangible but not visible; second, those which are visible but not tangible; and third, those which are both visible and tangible.

To the first kind, which Leadbeater refers to as the most common, belong the invisible spirit hands which often strike the faces of the sitters or carry small objects about the room, and the vocal organs from which the 'direct voice' proceeds. In this case, an order of matter is being used which can neither reflect nor obstruct light, but which is capable under certain conditions of setting up vibrations in the atmosphere which affect us as sound. A vibration of this class is that kind of partial materialization which, though incapable of reflecting any light that we can see, is yet able to affect some of the ultra-violet rays, and can therefore make a more or less definite impression upon the camera, and so provide us with what are known as 'spirit photographs'.

When there is not sufficient power available to produce a perfect materialization we sometimes get the vaporous-looking form which constitutes the second class and in such a case the 'spirits' usually warn their sitters that the forms which appear must not be touched. In the rarer case of a full materialization, there is sufficient power to hold together, at least for a few moments, a form which can be both seen and touched. (C.W.Leadbeater, The Astral Plane, 1895)

Again, the medium goes into a trance or hypnotic state and projects the shapes of various persons, generally of the deceased friends of some of those present. A good medium will produce any number of visions, of any number of persons, men and women, large and small. Under certain extreme conditions of the mind, this emanation is enormously increased in volume and may even become an agency for the transmission of kinetic energy to accomplish levitation of tables and other objects.

The greatest advance in the knowledge of the elementary phenomenon of materialization is furnished by the experiment of Professor Ochorowicz with the medium Stanislawa Tomczyk. In the first place, the experiment observed the occurrence of 'rigid organic rays' in 1893, in the case of *Eusapia Paladino*, and subsequently with the above-mentioned medium. These 'rigid rays' are thread-like connections, which are formed between the fingers of the medium when she brings her hands together. These may remain invisible, and yet exert mechanical effects as for instance, by the motion and raising of small objects without contact. When condensed, they are visible and can be photographed.

Similar experiments were carried out scientifically by many – including Imoda, Schrenct-Notzing and Mme. Bisson, by Crookes and Varley, by General and Mme. Noel and numerous other observers such as A.de Rochas, Lombrogo, Finzi, Morsell, Oliver

Lodge, Dariex, Maxwell, Schiaparelli, Bottazzi (who experimented with Eusapia) and Ochorowicz, with Stanislawa Tomczyk.

Little Stasia

Polish psychologist Dr. Julian Ochorowicz (1850-1917), who held professional posts successively in the Universities of Lemberg and Warsaw, was known to all researchers as a careful investigator. Professor Charles Richet of the University of Paris, had spoken him in the highest terms, and regarded him as 'an exceptionally careful and cautious investigator.' Between 1908 and 1909, Ochorowicz experimented with the Polish medium Stanislawa ('Stasia') Tomczyk and published his results in the French magazine *Annales des Sciences Psychiques,* which included on its editorial board persons of high stature like Professor Charles Richet, Sir William Crookes, Professor Camille Flammarion, Dr. Paul Joire, Dr. Joseph Maxwell, Dr. Mangin, Professor Henry Morselli, Baron von Schrenck-Notzing, and others.

Dr. Ochorowicz's experiments were conducted in the realm of 'thought photography' – the photographs of emanations issuing from the human body. In these experiments no camera was used; the plate, wrapped in opaque paper, was placed either between the hands of the subject, or against the forehead or the 'solar plexus' and a definite *thought* was impressed upon the plate at the will of the experimenter. In all these cases, Dr. Ochorowicz supplied and developed his own plates and they were never under control of the subject except for the few moments during which she placed her hands upon them.

These experiments of Dr. Ochorowicz's were conducted in the dark or in feeble red light; and, the subject being in trance, was requested to project an astral form or hand from her own and place this upon the plate held in the air by the experimenter at some distance from her body. The results of some of these experiments are thus described by Dr.Ochorowicz:

"I hold a plate at a distance of about one metre from her right hand, which is held in front of her. The red light is turned slightly low; the somnambule sees a shadowy hand detach itself from hers, which is at the same time also attached to a very long, thin arm, which approaches the plate. The hand is very large, she says, and is a right hand. It places itself over the plate, which I thereupon remove and develop. A large hand is distinctly visible upon it. Finally I hold a plate two and a half metres away from the medium's hand. The somnambule shivers and feels cold in her lower limbs, despite the fact that my laboratory is very warm. She again holds out her right hand, and a left hand, attached to a long thin arm, is seen by her to detach itself and place itself over the plate held in my hand. Upon being developed, the impression of a very large left hand was found upon the plate – so large that only a portion of the hand could be seen (the whole of the medium's hand could easily be placed upon the plate). These are very similar to the enormous hands frequently seen at the Palladino séances, and said to be those of John King."

The next puzzling stage of his discoveries was reached when in several of these "radiographs" the medium's ring appeared on the finger of her etheric hand. This seemed to indicate to him:

1. That there is a kind of link between the organism and the object it wears.
2. That the occult notion that material objects have an astral body is not limited to living bodies.

The ring did not always appear in the radiographs. Dr. Ochorowicz tried to find out whether objects frequently worn by the sensitive were more easily produced on the plate than others. He chose a thimble which she rarely used. The medium suggested that he should himself retain the thimble on the finger of his left hand, holding her with his right hand.

"Perhaps," she added, "the thimble will pass from your body on to my finger."

The experiment appeared absurd, but Dr. Ochorowicz was willing. He took a plate from his box, marked it, and laid it on the medium's knees. She was seated on his right. With his right hand he held up her left hand about sixteen inches above the plate, the thimble being on the middle finger of his left hand which he kept behind his left knee. A red lamp was burning at a distance of about three feet. After a minute had elapsed, the medium said that she felt a sort of tingling in the direction of her forearm, where their hands met. She exclaimed:

"Oh, how strange. Something is being placed on the tip of my finger... I do not know if it is the thimble; I feel something keeps pressing the end of my finger."

When the plate was developed it showed the hand of the medium, and on the middle finger was what she called jokingly the soul of her thimble.

Dr. Ochorowicz asked in some bewilderment: was the image a "double" of the thimble, or was it a photograph of the idea of the thimble?

A close examination of the photograph and comparison with the thimble showed that the two corresponded exactly, the one "was a true copy of the other, precise in details and in dimension". This exactness supports the idea of a direct impression from some object rather than a thought image merely. The finger supporting the thimble is the palest of all the fingers, probably, as Dr. Ochorowicz suggests, because the light by which the radiograph was taken proceeds from it. He leaned to the conclusion that an etheric hand wearing an etheric thimble produced the image, and that mental desire gave the direction to the light which was necessary in order to make the details of the thimble visible on the plate.

When, however, he proceeded to test his conclusion, a strange thing happened. Unknown to the medium he held in his left hand an Austrian five-crown piece. Presently she exclaimed:

"I see behind you a white round object... it is the moon."

"At the same instant," writes Dr. Ochorowicz, "I saw a faint but distinct light pass near my left hand, which held the coin; it was not round, nor a flash, it was like a little meteor, like a thin ray, lighting up the space round my hand on the side away from the medium."

When the plate was developed it showed an image of a full moon.

"The moon floats," he wrote, "on the background of a less luminous cloud, and is of a rather different form from that in the preceding experiment."

The preceding experiment took place on September 7th, 1911. The medium the night before was much impressed by the superb light of the starry heavens, and particularly by the full moon at which she looked for some time with admiration. On the plate, instead of the little hand which was desired, a full moon appeared against a background of white cloud.

There was something very curious about this photograph of the moon. On April 17th, 1912, the moon was in eclipse. Cinematograph pictures disclosed a slight flattening of the image of the moon in the direction of the axis of rotation. This characteristic appears in the radiograph of September 7th. The impression was double and it looked as if the cloud had not been duplicated. In that case the moon alone must have moved. How can we conceive - asked Dr. Ochorowicz - of this apparent movement of a mental image?

Eva Materialization Case

A French physician and Laureate of the French Medical Faculty at the University of Lyons, Dr. Gustave Geley, made research in the field of physical mediumship, especially with the medium Marthe Beraud ("Eva. C").

Geley stressed that the experiments were carried out under strict controls. They were held in his laboratory, to which no one was permitted beforehand. Eva C. was completely undressed in his presence and then dressed in a tight garment, which was sewn up the back and at the wrists. Her hair and the cavity of her mouth were examined by both himself and his collaborators before and after the séances. Eva was walked backwards to the wicker chair in the cabinet and her hands were always held in full sight outside the curtains, the room always quite well lit the whole time. "I do not say merely, 'there was no trickery,' I say, 'there was no possibility of trickery," Geley stressed. "Nearly all the materializations took place under my own eyes, and I have observed the whole of their genesis and development." (Richet, 1923)

Thought-Forms and Hallucinations

Dr. Charles Richet, who was awarded the Nobel Prize in Medicine in 1913, attended many of the séances in Geley's laboratory. "I can say exactly the same," Richet vouched Geley's comment about there being no possibility of fraud (Richet, 1923).

Whatever may be the mode of its formation, the materialization does not always remain in contact with the medium; it may sometimes be observed quite detached; the following example is typical in this respect, Geley wrote:

"A head appears suddenly, about three-fourths of a yard from Eva's head, above, and to her right. It is the head of a man, of normal size, well formed and in the usual relief. The top of the head and the forehead are completely materialized. The forehead is large and high, the hair short and abundant, brown or black. Below the brows the contours shade off; only the top of the head and the forehead are clearly seen.

Figure 5 Medium Eva.C Photograph taken in 1912, apparently showing a light manifestation between her hands and a materialization on her head.

The head disappears for a moment behind the curtain, then reappears as before; but the face, incompletely materialized, is masked by a band of white substance. I put my hand forward and pass my fingers through the tufted hair and feel the bone of the cranium.... an instant later everything has vanished. The forms have, it will be observed, a certain independence, and this independence is both physiological and anatomical.

Geley further noted, "the materialized organs are not inert, but biologically alive. A well-formed hand, for instance, has the functional capacities of a normal hand. I have several times been intentionally touched by a hand or grasped by its fingers. The most remarkable materializations which I have myself observed are those produced by Eva in my laboratory, during three consecutive months of the winter of 1917-1918. In the bi-weekly stances in collaboration with Madame Bisson, the Medical Inspector General, M. Calmette, M. Jules Courtier, and M. Le Cour, we obtained a series of records of the greatest interest. We saw, touched, and photographed representations of heads and faces formed from the original substance. These were formed under our eyes, the curtains being half-drawn. Sometimes they proceeded from a cord of solid substance issuing from the medium, sometimes they were progressively developed in a fog of vaporous substance condensed in front of her, or at her side."

Figure 6   Materialization obtained from the medium Eva C. during an experimental session performed with Prof. Schrenck-Notzing

Thought-Forms and Hallucinations

 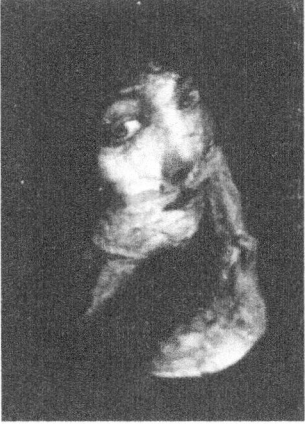

Figure 7   Gustave Geley: Materialization of a Woman's Face Produced by the Medium Eva.C, February 26, 1918.

Geley continued, "In the former case, when the materialization was fully formed, traces more or less marked of the original cord of substance could be seen. The materialized forms, photographs of which were given in my study on so-called supernormal physiology and are reproduced at the end of this volume, were remarkable from several points of view.

1. They were always three-dimensional. During the stances I could convince myself of this by sight and on several occasions by touch. Moreover, the relief is evident in the stereoscopic pictures taken.

2. The different faces in this series presented some similarities together with great differences. Differences in the features; differences in the size of the forms, some less than natural size, but of dimensions variable from one stance to another, and in the course of the same stance; differences in the perfection of the features, these being sometimes quite regular, in other cases defective; differences in the degree of materialization, which was sometimes complete; sometimes incomplete, with rudiments of substance; sometimes merely indicated." (Geley, From the Unconscious to the Conscious, 1920)

Franek Kluski

There are instances on record in which the visitants, who appear to be born into temporary existence through the agency of a materializing medium, were not human beings. They were the "beasts that perish"; animals whose presence inspired fear. To Franek Kluski, a Pole, whom the late Dr. Gustave Geley, Director of the *Institut Metapsychique International of Paris*, called the King of Mediums, we owe the most incredible experiences of this kind which scientists ever had the good fortune to share.

materialized not only solid, speaking human beings, but also birds and a hairy beast christened *pithecanthropus*, who used to lick the sitters' faces in the darkness.

The Bird

For the consideration of those who would accuse them of temporary insanity there are flashlight photographs, which demand an explanation. The best of these pictures [which is reproduced in Dr. Geley's classical *Clairvoyance and Materialization*] was taken in 1919 in Warsaw.

Figure 8   Photography of the materialization of a bird obtained at the session of the Paris Institute of Metaphysics by Franek Kluski

A bird, described by Prof. Pawlowski, of the Massachusetts Institute of Technology, as a hawk or buzzard, was heard to stretch its wings with a whirring sound, accompanied by blasts of wind. It "flew round, beating its wings against the walls and the ceiling; when it finally settled on the shoulder of the medium it was photographed with a magnesium flash, as the camera was accidentally focused on the medium before, and was ready.

"There was no possibility, we are assured, of introducing that bird surreptitiously into the room or hiding it after the manifestation. It appeared and vanished in the way of human phantoms," he said.

'Ape-man' Materialized in Experimental Physical Séance in Warsaw!

There was another, more dangerous customer in charge of a completely luminous old man. Prof. Pawlowski describes the man (an Afghan native who called himself Hirkill) as a column of light. He illuminated all the sitters and even the more distant objects of the room. The light appeared to be focused in his hands and in the region of his heart.

"Accompanying him always was a rapacious beast, the size of a very big dog, of a tawny colour, with slender neck, mouth full of large teeth, eyes which glowed in the darkness like a cat's, and which reminded the company of a maneless lion. It was occasionally wild in its behaviour, especially if persons were afraid of it, and neither the human nor the animal apparition was much welcomed by the sitters. The lion, as we may call him, liked to lick the sitters with a moist and prickly tongue, and gave forth the odour of a great feline, and even after the séance the sitters, and especially the medium, were impregnated with this acrid scent as if they had made a long stay in a menagerie among wild beasts." ("Psychic Science", April, 1926)

The acrid scent was very pronounced with the weirdest of all these apparitions - the Pithecanthropus, which showed itself several times. "One of us," writes Dr. Geley, "at the séance of November 20th, 1920, felt its large shaggy head press hard on his right shoulder and against his cheek. The head was covered with thick, coarse hair; a smell came from it like that of a deer or a wet dog. When one of the sitters put out his hand the Pithecanthropus seized it and licked it slowly three times. Its tongue was large and soft. At other times we all felt our legs touched by what seemed to be frolicsome dogs."

Figure 9 The Materialized "Ape-man"(veiled human form) standing behind Franek Kluski on his right side

According to Col. Norbert Ochorowicz, "this ape was of such great strength that it could easily move a heavy book-case, filled with books, through the room, carry a sofa over the heads of the sitters, or lift the heaviest persons with their chairs into the air to the height of a tall person. Though the ape's behaviour sometimes caused fear, and indicated a low level of intelligence. It was never malignant. Indeed, it often expressed goodwill, gentleness and readiness to obey... It was seen for the last time at the séance of December 26th, 1922, in the same form as in 1919, and making the same sounds of smacking and scratching."

Dr. Ochorowicz later wrote a book on the mediumship of Kluski. He speculated that the figure had its origins in the subconscious mind of a sitter – namely himself – as he had a strong interest in fossil man. (Sources: Zofia Weaver: "The Enigma of Franek Kluski", Journal of the Society for Psychical Research vol.58 1991–92, 289–98; Dr Zofia Weaver pers. comm. 7 April 2011)

Of another small animal, reminding the sitters of a weasel, the following description was quoted by Mrs. Hewat McKenzie, widow of the founder of the British College of Psychic Science:

"It used to run quickly over the table on to the sitters' shoulders, stopping every moment and smelling their hands and faces with a small, cold nose; sometimes, as if frightened, it jumped from the table and rambled through the whole room, turning over small objects, and shuffling papers lying on the table and writing-desk. It appeared at six or seven séances, and was last seen in June, 1923."

Kluski himself discovered that the materialization was as small as only 2/3 or even 1/2 the size of a normal one when he felt weak. It returned to the normal size when he recollected his strength. F. W. Pawlowski, one of Kluski's major researchers, aeronautical engineering professor at the University of Michigan, had also noticed this and made records about this. (Xiong, 2009)

Paraffin moulds of the materialized Hands

With Kluski, however, Geley decided to see if paraffin moulds of the materialized hands could be obtained. This evidence was so concrete that the famous parapsychologist Scott Rogo felt that the most convincing evidence of materialization came from the hand mould experiments done with Franek Kluski in Warsaw.

Geley and his collaborators set a bowl of paraffin wax in the laboratory in which they conducted the experiments. The materialized 'entity' was then asked to plunge a hand, foot or even part of a face into the paraffin several times. A closely fitting envelop was thus formed, which was dipped into another bowl of cold water. They obtained nine molds on their first effort – seven of different hands, one of a foot, and one of a mouth and chin. These were produced in various sizes, including the hand and foot of a child, and so it was clear that there were not Kluski's and that there was no trickery, although other controls completely ruled out this possibility. Photographs of these molds were taken and are shown in Geley's 1927 book, *'Clairvoyance and Materialization: A Record of Experiments.'*

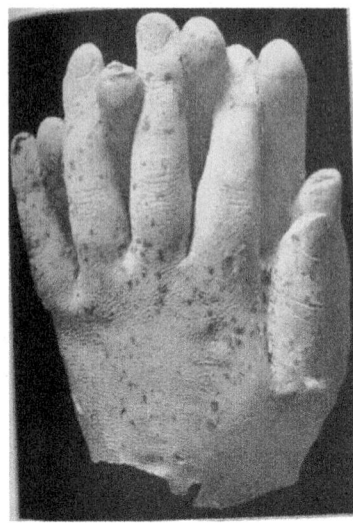

Figure 10 Photograph of the plaster casting of the materialization hand made from the paraffin molding in a séance with Franek Kluski

Geley wrote that there were some manifestations showing mental intelligence, including communicating raps. "One of these asked us to sing," Geley reported. "We sang the 'Marseillaise' softly, and this was applauded by hand-clapping in the dark cabinet, behind the medium." However, Geley concluded that the 'entities' at this particular séance and at subsequent ones "did not seem to me to be of a high order of intelligence." (Geley, 1927)

Many materialistic scientists criticized Geley, claiming that he was duped, but he had many esteemed scientists, including the Nobel laureate Charles Richet, renowned astronomer and author Camille Flammarion and renowned physicist Sir Oliver Lodge, who observed some of his experiments and fully validated his research. Lodge referred to the paraffin casts as "a standing demonstration of something inexplicable by normal science... a permanent material record, which can be examined at leisure, and which …are, as it were, a standing miracle." (Joyce, 1991)

Ethel Post-Parrish and her 'Silver Belle'

Here is an extraordinary case of complete materialization of a thought-form, Silver Belle, photographed by infrared light at 50-seconds intervals, during a séance that took place at a spiritualist summer camp in Ephrata, Pennsylvania in the year 1953. The medium sitting in her curtained cabinet is Ethel Post-Parrish. Silver Belle was her sprit control or guide. During this manifestation, Silver Belle was reportedly witnessed by 81 people, some of whom apparently walked arm-in-arm with her.

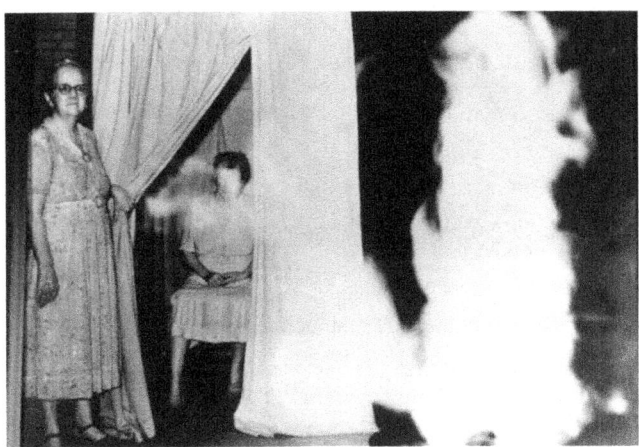

Figure 11 The white smoky ectoplasm is being drawn from the medium- Ethel Post-Parrish, sitting inside the cabinet (the curtained enclosure)

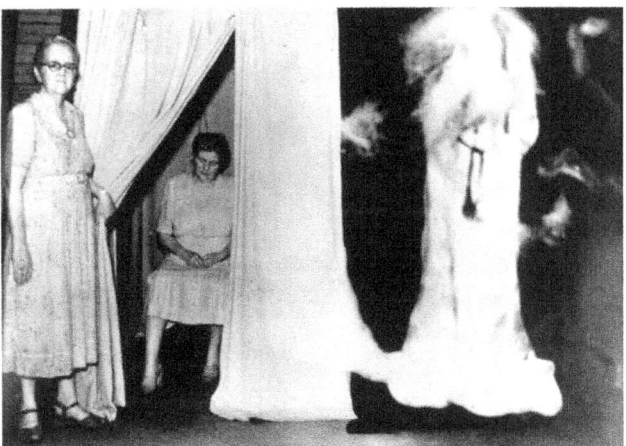

Figure 12 The ectoplasm coming from the medium's body forms a 'pillar of cloud' from the ground upwards

Figure 13 Slowly, Silver Belle, the spirit guide of the medium, sculpts her features into the column of ectoplasm

Figure 14 The fully materialized 'Silver Belle'

Goligher's Table Levitation

Kathleen Goligher (later Lady G. Donaldson), a Belfast, Ireland medium was studied extensively by Dr. William Crawford. Crawford, who taught mechanical engineering at Queen's University in Belfast, began his investigation in 1914 when Goligher was 16 years old.

During December 1915, Crawford invited Sir William Barrett, professor of physics at Royal College in Dublin to join him. At first, he heard knocks, and messages were spelled out as one of the sitters recited the alphabet. Barrett then reported observing a floating trumpet, which he tried unsuccessfully to catch. "Then the table began to rise from the floor some 18 inches and remained suspended and quite level," Barrett wrote. "I was allowed to go up to the table and saw clearly no one was touching it, a clear space separating the sitters from the table." (Barrett, 1917).

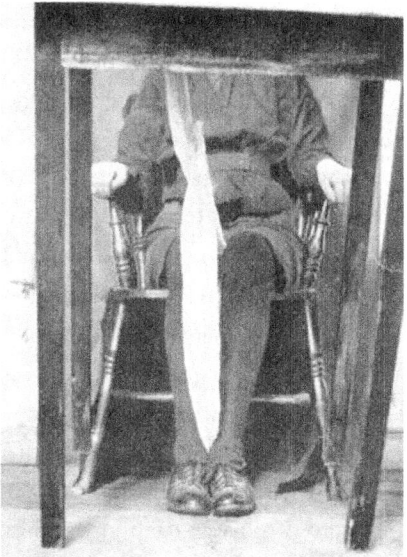

Figure 15 Kathleen Goligher ectoplasm rod is levitating table

On one occasion, a clairvoyant joined in the circle and told Crawford that she could see "a whitish vapory substance, somewhat like smoke," forming under the surface of the table and increasing in density as the table was levitated. She could see it flowing from the medium in sort of a rotary motion."

Hamlin Garland's Observations

A student of Charles Darwin and Herbert Spencer, and the author of 52 books and a Pulitzer Prize winner, Hamlin Garland was noted for his agnosticism and skepticism. He joined the American Society of Psychical Research (ASPR) as an open-minded skeptic.

Once, in the year 1907, Garland was asked by John O'Hara Cosgrave, the editor of 'Everybody's Magazine,' to attend a sitting with Daniel Peters, a young New York medium, and Garland welcomed the opportunity.

"After a few moments' silence, I observed a cloud of glowing vapor slowly forming on the floor just in front of the portieres," Garland recorded. "It resembled, as it rose, a cone of fire-lit steam, like that which rolls from a locomotive smokestack on a winter morning. It expanded as it slowly rose, and at last out of it the dim figure of a man emerged. He spoke in a foreign tongue, and I observed that his voice resembled that of the psychic. The Pole who sat beside me on the couch called out, "it is my brother!" Garland noted that the materialization appeared to be almost an exact twin of the man claiming to be his brother.

When this form faded out, the materialization of 'Evans,' Peters' spirit guide took place. "This dimly seen figure appeared enveloped in a cloud of vapor, but his voice was distinct," Garland further noted. "At his invitation I went forward to shake hands with him. He seemed taller than the psychic, but his manner of speech was distinctly similar to that of Peters. I could not see his face. The hand he offered me was draped in an exceedingly fine, faintly shining material, cobwebby in texture, which appeared to melt away between my fingers and his. The hand was narrow and pointed. I felt its bones for a moment. When I released it, the figure vanished like a bubble. It made no sound when it appeared and none as it disappeared. One instant it was there, the next instant it was not." (Garland, 1936).

When Peters emerged from the Cabinet, Garland noted that he appeared distraught. Peter yelled in a commanding tone, "Come out!" Garland then observed the form of a man appearing outside the cabinet. He stood at attention like a soldier and wore a turban of gray-white material and was draped in the same type material. "He gave the impression of a form suspended – unfinished – in the air and yet with bulk," Garland wrote. "Whether the psychic commanded him to greet me or not, I cannot now recall, but the phantom (as if to show he was alive) bowed to me three times gracefully, slowly and solemnly, while the psychic with both his hands outstretched and with bent, trembling legs, crept slowly toward the figure. At the same time the phantom moved toward the psychic as if drawn by some magnetic force. They met in the centre and appeared to coalesce like two drops of mercury. The figure vanished seemingly into the body of the psychic who reeled backward through the curtains and fell like a log on the floor." (Garland, 1936).

Garland considered that his observations were in harmony with similar reports by Sir William Crookes of England and Dr. Charles Richet of France, both world-renowned scientists.

As we have seen, the materialization is only a kind of externalization of thought in a perceptible form and an advancement of thought-photography. As rightly noted by Baron Von Schrenck Notzing in his book *"Phenomena of Materialization,"* the materializations do not offer a rigid demonstration of the inferences from supernatural things. The analysis of their psychological contents shows that they are merely creations of the medium's imagination, creations of his subliminal consciousness.

In Imada's work *'Phantasmal Photography,'* numerous teleplastic portraits taken by flash-light were produced. Among these there was a photograph taken at Professor Charles Richet's house, by De Fontenay on the 29th of April 1909, representing a rather distorted masculine face, with eyes directed upwards. Long after, on the 1st of March 1913, the newspaper, Le Matin, proved that this picture was strikingly similar to an angel head painted by Rubens. Comparing the two pictures, there can be no doubt that this picture was the model for the mediumistic reproductions. Baron Von Schrenck Notzing later observed the medium's great interest in painting and already had seen the Rubens Angel head picture. It left a vivid remembrance in her subliminal consciousness. In the state of trance, the dream memory of this head was translated into a reality. The image gives the impression more of an artistic recollection than that of a true copy. Apart from the distorted expression in comparison with the original, the right eye was entirely covered with a black substance which may be regarded as a veil or hair which was not found in the original painting. (Notzing, 1923)

Schrenck Notzing asserts his materializations were "materialized thought forms" of the medium, and he presented even some interesting evidence for it. He writes, "the teleplastic creations are so closely connected with the psychic condition of the medium that Morselli compared them with materialized dream images. This view regards the products as ephemeral, externalized precipitates of the medium's psychic impressions and reminiscences. That the phenomena in many cases realize the thoughts of the medium may be considered as established. I need only recall the repeated occurrences of hands as suggested by the sitters, and other fulfillments of their wishes. Such a process may also account for the projection of memory images of deceased persons, such as M.Alexandre Bisson and Mme.Bisson's nephew; also the production of an image resembling Leonardo da Vinci's "Mona Lisa," which was so greatly talked about when it was stolen from the Louvre. Here, again, we have no slavish replica, but an impressionistic representation of the style in which the picture was painted. The results of this process, which may be called ideo-plastics, are closely connected with the psychic life of the medium, with her storage of memories, and with the intensity of dominant ideas." (Notzing, 1923)

There are many other evidences that suggest that the materialized forms are true revelations of the subconscious mind of the medium. For instance, in many of the cases, the materialized forms are either larger or smaller than the actual object or being thought of. Madame Bisson experienced the materialization of an eight inch naked female figure who did gymnastics and danced. It is said that she materialized several times with different hair styles and stood in the hands of Eva.C., the medium and Mme.Bisson. Similarly, small walnut sized heads materialized in glasses of water at the sittings of Mme.Ignath. The spirit control, Nona, gave the opinion that they were materialized plastic thought forms. (Long, 1948)

6
PAST LIFE MEMORIES

The experiences gained in one life may not be remembered in their details in the next, but the impressions which they produce will remain.

-H. Hartmann

Death is the inevitable condition to which all living bodies must, sooner or later, be reduced. Different religions and cultures view death differently. Thinkers see death even as a necessity – a law of Nature to provide a safety valve to adjust with the perpetuation of species. Thinkers of Western realism however say death is just death – rotting of the corpses and returning to dust. Then there are those who say death is just like going off to sleep – as sleep is temporary, so is death. If death is thought of as temporary, it involves some sort of continued life elsewhere. It is here the concept of rebirth comes into play.

The theory of rebirth is as old as the human race itself and its origin is unknown. Even Plato the Greek philosopher shares his opinion on death and reincarnation when he says, '*Soul is older than body.*' Rene Descartes told as early as in 1641 that 'the extinction of mind does not follow from the corruption of the body,' and gave the hope of another life after death. Souls are continuously born over again into this life. This is what Lord Krishna preaches in the *Bhagavat Gita*, 'this body is destructible, but the *Atma*, the inner soul that governs the body, is indestructible.'

Does death terminate our existence altogether, or open the doors to our next life? This is a question that always engages the human mind. But there is another side to this question which must by no means be overlooked. What happens to human consciousness and memory when the biological body dies?

Another stupendous fact, which the phenomena we are going to deal with in this chapter discloses, is that *memory is non-local and imperishable*. The term 'non-local' connotes that mind has no definite or permanent locality – indeed it has very little relation to any locality, and it is independent of time as of space. All our thoughts and actions leave their eternal impressions and form an ineffaceable record in the cosmic library. We may forget the past, but it is a mistake to suppose that we are doing with it forever. Scientific investigation of cases of alleged spontaneous recall of past-lives among children have revealed beyond the shadow of a reasonable doubt that bodily deformities of previous life personality are carried over as birthmarks in the next birth in many cases.

Skeptics may ask a deserved question, "If reincarnation is true, why can't all the people in their present birth remember their past lives?"

Perhaps, the answer lies in another question. "Why do they not remember everything in detail in the present life itself?" To understand the science of past-life memory, to know what lies before us after death and what lay behind us before birth, we must begin by a better understanding of human body, mind and consciousness. So long as we do not carefully analyze the difference between brain, mind and consciousness, we remain under the wrong impression that the mind (or memory) gets obliterated with the decay of the brain and it is not our mistake.

Current science sees the brain as a complex organ of electro-chemical network full of neuron excitation, and as a storehouse of information, a kind of memory disc of a computer. If the memory disc is destroyed, the entire information stored in the computer goes with it, with no possibility of its recovery. But the fact is different. As someone said, it functions like an internet connected to a universal server, archiving all information and facilitating access to them under appropriate circumstances – for instance, by providing a correct internet protocol (IP) address.

Consciousness is *non-local*. It is not located in the individual physical body nor bounded by time. In other words, consciousness is not limited by spatial and temporal dimensions, and it transcends space and time. If the mind is non-local, it must in some sense be independent of the strictly local brain and body. And if the mind is non-local, unconfined to brains and bodies and thus not entirely dependent on the physical organism, the possibility of survival of bodily death is opened. (L.Dossey, 1989). It is also non-objective. It is quantum pocket of energy that is not localized but extends *ad infinitum* in space.

This fact we find in the ancient Hindu philosophy of transmigration which presupposes the existence of the soul as an entity which can live even when the gross material body is dead or decayed. For Samkhya philosophers, the subtle body – necessary as the physical support of an individual's mind during the transformation between death and rebirth – travels from life to life, becoming associated with the mind 'like an odor is attached to a cloth' until the mind disassociates from it by attaining true knowledge.

Dr. Ian Stevenson proposed to call the vehicle that carries a person's mental elements between incarnations a *psychophore* (which means mind-carrying). Paul Von Word in his 'The Soul Genome: Science and Reincarnation', has preferred the word *'psychoplasm'* to *psychophore* to suggest both the container and its contents. *Psychoplasm* must be capable of encompassing a non-material template that carries forward energetic fields of physical, cognitive, and behavioral patterns. When it is connected with a body, it is called 'mind' and when it leaves the body on its death, it is called 'soul'.

Birthmarks/Birth Defects in Cases of Alleged Re-births

Past-life spontaneous memory recall is a widely reported phenomenon transgressing religious and cultural boundaries. All the world religions, including Christianity, has held on to this great theory of rebirth, and all the world has run against this fascinating and exasperating question of lost memory and its recall. It has been thought upon and widely discussed in India, Egypt, Greece and Italy. How does so universal an opinion get established? If false, nothing can force it to live. If true, there must be some confirmation of it so as to impress itself upon any candid mind.

However, it is not the purpose of this chapter to argue either for or against reincarnation; but simply to present some fascinating evidence to suggest that memory lives and bodily deformities encountered in the previous life get manifested in the present life in certain circumstances.

Let us revert to the subject of birthmarks/ birth defects in cases of alleged rebirths. Any attempt to explain the theory of rebirth should necessarily record all forms of memory manifestations relating to the previous personality. Our objective here is somewhat different inasmuch as we limit our discussion to the nature of deformities/birth defects in the present birth having exact correspondence to some physical injury sustained in the previous birth.

James G. Matlock, an American parapsychologist and anthropologist, divides the past-life memories into four categories:

1. *Verbal or informational memory* – the ability to remember names, dates and events connected to the previous life

2. *Imaged Memory* – the ability to remember or identify people, places and objected associated with a prior living person

3. *Behavioural Memory* – existence of great similarity between the deceased and a living person in mannerisms, habits, likes and dislikes, especially philias and phobias, skills, etc., that would have been carried over from the past

4. *Physical Memory* – involves such traits as birthmarks, scars, or deformities of one person that are the same or very similar to those of a second person who died previously.

According to Matlock, in many cases only one or two of these four categories is present in the presumed reincarnated person. Rarely, if ever, are all four fully present. Cases in which the subjects have birthmarks corresponding to injuries or physical defects/ characteristics they bore in the previous life form an important class of the rebirth case histories and they belong to the category of *physical memory*. If we could have physical memory of past lives, the theory of rebirth would be considered better proved than ever before. Past-life memory recall cases may again be categories into two major kinds: spontaneous recall and those by Past Life Regression analysis.

In the case of spontaneous memory recall, as soon as the child is able to talk he starts mentioning things relating to his previous life. Past Life Regression analysis is a method of taping into the subconscious mind, through hypnosis, to visualize the subject's previous lives. We are concerned with the cases of spontaneous memory recall.

The transference of physical marks from one body to another in the process of rebirth – or rather their reproduction in a new body – is a recurring feature of many of these cases. According to Francis Story, author of 'Rebirth as doctrine and experience: essays and case studies,' such birthmarks can be explained only on the assumption that there is a psychosomatic interaction brought about by a strong mental impression during the previous life or at the time of death.

We are going to discuss many of such cases of birthmarks/birth defects relating to the previous birth. Most of these cases were brought to light by the tireless efforts made by Dr. Ian Stevenson (October 31, 1918–February 8, 2007), a Canadian bio-chemist who worked as the head of the Department of Psychiatric Medicine at the University Of Virginia School Of Medicine, Charlottesville, Virginia. He devoted the last 40 years of his life to the scientific exploration and documentation of past life memories of children across the world and collected over 3000 cases in his files.

Stevenson's research into the possibility of reincarnation began in 1960 when he heard of a case in Sri Lanka where a child claimed to remember a past life. He thoroughly questioned the child, his parents, as well as the people whom the child claimed were his parents in his previous life. This led to Dr. Stevenson's conviction that re-incarnation was possibly a reality.

The more cases he pursued, the greater became his drive to scientifically open up and conquer an unknown territory among the world's mysteries, which until now had been excluded from proper scientific observation and research. He compared birthmarks of living persons with wounds or scars of a deceased person and suggested that these marks are physical manifestations that connect to the two lives and that reincarnation was the transfer 'agent' of the appearance of birthmarks and birth defects on the reincarnated body from a previous body.

Stevenson's findings disproved the popular assumption that reincarnation cases are peculiar to Hindu and Buddhist countries of the Indian sub-continent, which have strongly believed in reincarnation since ancient times. Of 1,300 cases in his files in 1974, the Unites States led with 324, followed by Burma (139), India (135), Turkey (114), Great Britain (111), and so on – showing a large number of such cases from among the modern Western nations. (Becker, 1993)

According to Dr. Ian Stevenson, birthmarks nearly always occur on subjects who claim to remember that in the previous life they were killed or murdered in circumstances which led to wounds corresponding in location and appearance to the birthmarks. It is the murderee rather than the murderer who on the hypothesis of rebirth usually carries the birthmarks when he is reborn. Among all the birthmark cases from anywhere in the world, known to him, only in one instance did he find that the birthmark occurred on a subject for whom the related previous personality was a person who inflicted (instead of received) a wound. This exceptional case relates to Wijeratne of Ceylon (now known as Sri Lanka). He claimed to remember a previous life in which he stabbed his fiancée when she would not complete marriage ceremonies with him. He was born with a small and seriously deformed right arm and hand. When he was a very small child, his mother heard him saying to himself that he had been born with a deformed arm because in his previous life he had killed his wife. (Stevenson, Characteristics of Cases of the Reincarnation Type in Ceylon, 1973)

At the close of this chapter, we will see a detailed analysis of the holographic storage and transfer of information, which may possibly offer an explanation to the phenomenon of reincarnation, and mainly to the occurrences of birth defects/deformities corresponding to the injuries sustained in the previous life.

Let us turn now to presenting some brief reports of cases investigated by Dr. Stevenson, Dr. Erlendur Haraldsson and Dr. Satwant K. Pasricha – all previously published in the *Journal of Society for Scientific Exploration*.

The Case of Thiang San Kla – Fatal Wound on the Head

The case of the Siamese Sergeant Thiang San Kla belongs to a most interesting category, that in which birthmarks or congenital deformities correspond to injuries remembered to have been sustained in the previous life. Briefly, this is his story:

Thiang San Kla was born in the village of Ban Rasai, near Surin, in Surin Province, Thailand on October 9, 1924. His parents were Charon and Puen San Kla. Phoh San Kla, brother of Puen San Kla, had been a notorious cattle thief, and was killed by his enemies. He was hit on the back of the head with a heavy knife of the kind that Thai villagers use for opening coconuts or chopping wood. The blow probably killed Phoh instantly. This occurred in October 1923, exactly one year before the birth of Thiang San Kla.

After this incident, Charon and Puen had both dreamed before Thiang's birth that Puen's deceased brother Phoh had appeared to them and said that he wished to be reborn as their child. Thiang, born to the couple in the year 1924, claimed that he was Phoh in the previous birth. He was less than 4 years old when he began to speak about the life of Phoh. As a young child Thiang said his name was Phoh and he would sometimes become angry if he was called Thiang instead of Phoh. Sometimes, he called his father "brother" and called his paternal aunt "sister" instead of "aunt."

A policeman who had investigated both Phoh's cattle thieving and his murder learned that Thiang was claimed to be Phoh reborn and went to see him. He said that Thiang at once recognized him and called him by name. Thiang also correctly stated to him the names of the persons who had killed Phoh.

Phoh's wife, Pai, also visited Thiang and tried to test his knowledge of Phoh. She brought with her a number of articles that had belonged to Phoh as well as some that had not. Thiang easily sorted out the articles that had belonged to Phoh and he also narrated to Pai incidents of their married life. Phoh's daughter, who visited Thiang, said that Thiang had spontaneously recognized her and called her "daughter." (For a detailed reading of the case, readers are requested to refer 'Where Reincarnation and Biology Intersect' by Ian Stevenson).

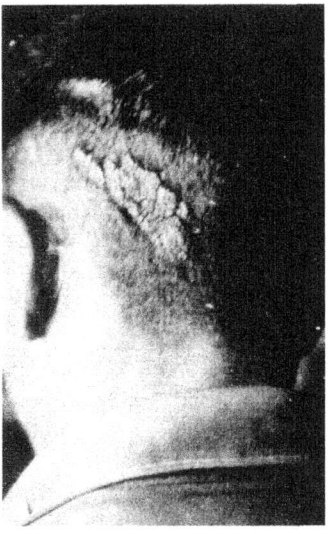

Figure 16 Large verrucous epidermal nevus on Thiang San Kla's head, who as a child remembered the life of his paternal uncle Phoh, who was killed with a blow on the head from a heavy knife. The photograph was taken in January 1962 when Thiang was 38 years old
© 1998 Society for Scientific Exploration

Coming to the point, Thiang's two major birth defects corresponded respectively to the fatal wound on Phoh's head and the chronic infection of his right great toe. On the back of the left side of his head, Thiang had an extensive lesion that in medical terms was a *verrucous epidermal nevus*. When Dr. Stevenson examined it in 1969, it was lightly raised above the surrounding skin, hairless, heavily pigmented, and much wrinkled. It was irregular in shape and measured about 5-6 centimeters long and 1-1.5 centimeters wide.

The defect of Thiang's right great toe consisted of a partially detached portion of the nail of that toe, and this nail or the tissue beneath it was darkly pigmented. (Stevenson, Birthmarks and Birth Defects Corresponding to wounds on Deceased Persons, 1993)

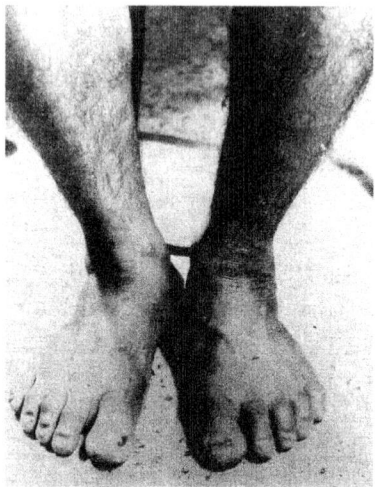

Figure 17 Congenital malformation of nail on right great toe of Thiang. This malformation corresponds to a chronic ulcer of the right great toe from which Phoh (the previous life personality) had suffered
© 1998 Society for Scientific Exploration

The second witness to the case was a man of 72, Nai Pramaun, of the Municipality Office, Surin. He had been formerly Assistant District Officer, and was a young man at the time of Phoh's murder. He had known the late Phoh and had known Thiang from childhood. He told the investigator Francis Story[1] that Phoh actually was a cattle-thief and a notorious character in his lifetime. Nai Pramaun had investigated the case of the cattle theft and the murder in the course of his duties. On hearing the news concerning the rebirth of Phoh, he had gone to see the child who was then between four and five years old. Thiang had recognized him and had addressed him by his name. He also had given correctly the names of all the people concerned in the affair. Nai Pramaun had

---

1   This case was originally investigated by Francis Story and published in his books "The Buddhist Outlook: collected writings"(1975) and "Rebirth as doctrine and experience: essays and case studies" (2000)

examined the birthmarks and found they correspond exactly with Phoh's death wound and with other marks he had had on his body.

The transference of physical marks from one body to another in the process of rebirth – or rather their reproduction in a new body – is a recurring feature of many of these cases.

According to Francis Story, there is a psychosomatic interaction brought about by a strong mental impression during the previous life or at the time of death.

'It seems to belong to the same order of mind-body relationship that can cause a weal to appear on the arm of a hypnotized person, who being told he is going to be burned, then is touched with a cold object.' (Story, 2000)

The Case of Krishnan Chaudhri – Sutured Wound on the Face

Krishnan Chaudhri was born on November 16, 1985 in the village of Palwan, State of Haryana, India. He had a birthmark of longish, purple-red color on his face near the right ear. His parents, Jai Singh and Parameshwari, first thought perhaps he had scratched himself, but when they saw it in the daylight, it looked like a sutured wound and the 'stitches' appeared to be filled with blood.

At the age of about 15 months, Krishnan began referring to a previous life. He used to sit on a suitcase and bang his feet on the ground as if he were kick-starting a motorcycle. He also protested against being in his present family. He said that his parents were different, that his mother and father used to dress differently; his mother used to wear saris and his father used to wear trousers (His parents in the present life did not wear trousers or saris. Jai Singh wore the loose fitting Indian dhoti, and Parameshwari did not wear saris).

Around the age of 3, Krishnan gave more details about his previous life, including the details about a vehicular accident which ended his previous life.

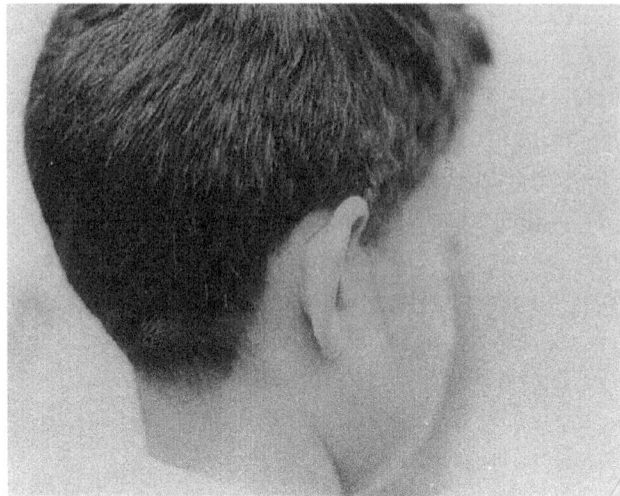

Figure 18 Birthmark on the right cheek of Krishnan Chaudhri as it appeared in March 1997 when he was 13 years old. The mark was 0.2 centimeters wide, irregular in shape, slightly raised, and dark brown in color, beginning about 2 centimeters behind the right ear, continuing upward, encircling its upper part and then extending downward about 4 centimeters along the front of the ear on the right cheek.
© 1998 Society for Scientific Exploration

Krishnan's statements were later found to correspond with events in the life of a young man, Vinod Goyal, who had been involved in a vehicular accident on November 26, 1980 and died almost instantly.

Further investigations by Dr. Satwant K Pasricha revealed that Vinod had lived in a town named Narwana, 15 km north of Palwan. On November 20, 1980, Vinod was driving a motorcycle along with a friend, Mihan Singh, when they collided with a cart in front of them. Vinod was struck in the face by a wooden beam loaded on the cart. He fell down and was rushed to hospital, where he was declared dead. The accident occurred about 17 kilometer away from his home and about 2 kilometer from Palwan.

On examining Krishna's face the investigator saw a mark about 6 centimeters long, and 0.2 centimeters wide, beginning about 2 centimeters behind the right ear, continuing upward (encircling the upper half of the pinna) and then extending about 4 centimeters along the front of the ear on the right cheek. It was somewhat irregular in shape, slightly raised, and dark brown in color.

The investigator says, though she could not obtain a medical report in this case, she understood from the description of the informants that Vinod had not suffered any major external injury. Vinod's father Ram Prasad Goyal stated that his son had a minor injury of his right ear, which seemed to correspond to the birthmark of Krishnan. No medical treatment was given to Vinod who died before arriving at the hospital. No stitches were made on the injured parts. If the visible external injury of the ear was itself insufficient to cause death, we have to conjecture that Vinod died of severe brain injury although this remains unverified. (Pasricha, 1998)

The Case of Chatura Karunaratne – Reminiscence of an accident

Dr. Erlendur Haraldsson studied the case of a young boy Chatura Karunaratne in Sri Lanka, who made several statements regarding a previous life, among them where he had lived and how he was killed when travelling in a truck through a forest. The boy associated two birthmarks with his claimed memories. The details of the case are as follows:

Chatura Buddika Karunaratne was born on 20 April 1989, in the rural area of Metiyagane in the Karunagala district of Sri Lanka. At the age of three, Chatura started to speak about a previous life in the nearby Narammala area. This incident was widely published in the newspapers across the country.

M.P.Martin, a retired farmer and mason in Henegedara, a rural area near the town of Narammala overheard in a shop some people talking about this news report. Martin, after reading the report, believed that the story of Chatura Karunaratne fitted his son M.P.Dayananda, who had joined the army in August 1985 and died on 18 April 1986, as a result of injuries suffered in a bomb blast. Dayananda's family had lived 12 Km away by road from Narammala in a house with a tiled roof. Close by, there had been a hut with a shop which he owned and where his son used to sell groceries until he joined the army. Near their house was a small lake with tortoises living in it. Interestingly, all these corresponded with what Chatura had been describing as having happened in his previous life.

Later, Chatura, the three-and-a-half year boy, was brought to the house of Dayananda and was given a warm reception by Dayananda's parents, who believed him to be their son. Dayananda's mother brought some old clothes that had belonged to her son. According to a news report, the boy complained somewhat angrily that only his long trousers were there and that they had been torn and worn by someone else.

Dayananda's mother asked the boy if he could remember the house where they used to live. Chatura said he had not lived in that house but in another one somewhere else, which was true of Dayananda. They had only recently moved to the present house, which is located on the same premises about 100 yards away. They went to the house where they used to live. There an old woman walked up to the boy and asked him if he could remember her. He looked at her for a while and then said she was his grandmother.

Dayananda had lived longer with his grandmother than with his parents. Inside the house the boy made the comment: "Now you have electricity", something they had not had when Dayananda lived there. Hanging on the wall he saw the scales that had been used in the shop. He made the comment: "These are the scales we used to weigh things with. Don't you have the store now?"

He then asked the late Dayananda's mother to take him to the store. It had been torn down, and he asked why. According to the newspaper report, Chatura also identified one of his old friends (his brother-in-law), who was in the crowd.

Our main point of concern in the case was the match between Chatura's birthmarks and Dayananda's wounds. Chatura has two birthmarks close to his left ear, each about a centimeter in diameter. They have darker pigmentation than the surrounding skin. One is on the lower part of the jawbone and the other is on the neck/throat below the jaw. The closest edges of the two birthmarks are about two centimeters apart. Another birthmark, also darker than the surrounding skin, is on the inside of his right upper arm.

According to his mother, when Chatura started to talk about a previous life, he stated that he had been shot in two places and pointed towards the birthmarks in the two locations near the neck and ear.

An autopsy report for Dayananda would have given greater certainty about the location and nature of his wounds, but none is available. The military document regarding Dayananda's death states only that the patrol commander found Dayananda near the overturned vehicle, which was completely wrecked. He was unconscious but no external injuries were to be seen, although when Dayananda's parents visited him in the Polunnaruwa hospital he had a bandage around his head and neck. The physicians told them that he had injuries to "the nerves of the smaller brain". This is the cerebellum, which lies beneath and behind the cerebrum. Bandages covered his left ear. They were told that he had broken his left arm, and that was covered with bandages. A photograph of Dayananda's body at his funeral shows his face bare, but his head and neck are covered with bandages, and also his left ear, which suggests that he suffered injuries to this area of his body.

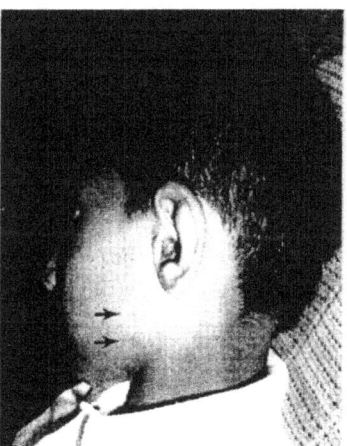

Figure 19 Chatura's birthmarks on the rear of his jaw and on his throat, both close to the left ear, are close to the location of the internal head injury that brought Dayananda to death.
© Dr. Erlendur Haraldsson

The Case of Ranbir Singh – Missing Hand Mangled in a Machine

Ranbir Singh was born on December 23, 1990 in the village of Basai, Uttar Pradesh, India. His parents were Shiv Singh and Mithilesh. Ranbir was born without his right hand and the distal fourth of his right forearm. At the age of about two, Ranbir claimed to have remembered the life of one Idrish and mentioned the name of the village where Idrish had lived.

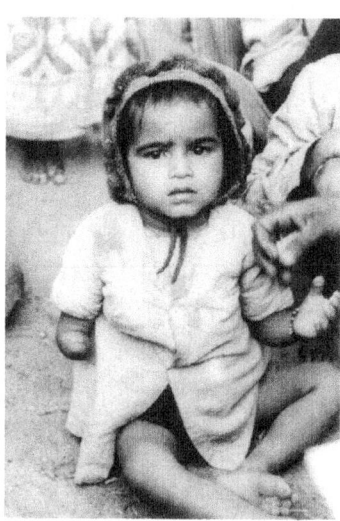

Figure 20 Ranbir Singh at his home in February 1994. His right hand and distal fourth of his right forearm was missing. His left hand was normal.
© 1998 Society for Scientific Exploration

Idrish was a Muslim who lived in the village of Gadka, about 2 km from Basai. He was a farmer-cum-labour, and on an occasion when he was working with a fodder-cutting machine, his right hand was caught in the machinery and was badly mangled. As a result, he lost a major part of that hand. He recovered however, and later died of unrelated causes on June 15, 1983.

As a mark of behavioural memory, Ranbir asked for meat whereas other members of the family did not eat meat; they ate eggs only. Ranbir could recognize the Moslem prayers and also assumed the posture of saying Namaz. In addition, he did not mind eating leftover food from another person's plate or drinking tea left over in a cup. His family considered this a Moslem characteristic.

Idrish' right hand was mangled in the machine; only a part of his palm and thumb remained intact. But Ranbir, who claimed himself to be the rebirth of Idrish, was born without his right hand and the distal part of the right arm. Thus the extent of damage was far greater than Idrish's deformity. According to Ian Stevenson, 'a disturbance of a morphogenetic field may account for cases in which the birth defect is more extensive…' (Pasricha, 1998).

The Case of Semih Tutusmus – Rebirth of a Man who came in the dream

Semih Tutusmus was born in Sarkonak, Turkey. Two days before his birth, her mother Karanfil had dreamed that a man with his face covered with blood came to her. He said that he was Selim Fesli, that he had been shot in the ear, and that he wished to stay with her. Karanfil had never met Selim Fesli but she knew a little about him and particularly that he had died from a shotgun wound some months earlier.

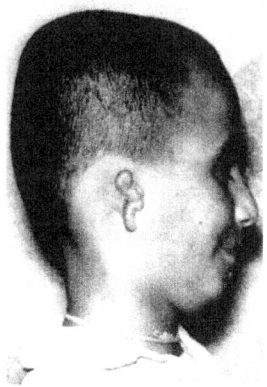

Figure 21 Severely malformed ear (microtia) in a Turkish boy who said that he remembered the life of a man who was fatally wounded on the right side of the head by a shotgun discharged at close range.
© 1998 Society for Scientific Exploration

Semih Tutusmus in his childhood said that he remembered the life of a man who had been shot (with a shotgun) at point-blank range. The wounded man was taken to a hospital where he died six days later – of injuries to the brain caused by the shot that had penetrated the right side of the skull. Curiously, Semih was born with a diminished and malformed ear (*unilateral microtia*). He had also underdevelopment of the right side of his face (*hemifacial microsomia*). Dr. Stevenson had obtained a copy of the hospital record, in this case. (Stevenson, Birthmarks and Birth Defects Corresponding to wounds on Deceased Persons, 1993)

The Case of Hanumant Sexena – Impressions of an accidental gunshot

Another case from Stevenson's files was very astonishing as well. A little boy Hanumant Saxena in Uttar Pradesh, India claimed that he was a man named *Maha Ram* and that he had been shot in the chest which caused his birthmark in his chest, which was clearly discernible. Later investigations showed that one Maha Ram, an innocent man, was killed in an accidental gunshot when he was standing by a tea shop on September 28, 1954.

Eventually, Hanumant went back to Ram's neighbourhood and amazingly identified many people known to him in his previous life. One remarkable feature of the study of this case is that the investigator Dr. Stevenson was able to obtain the medical postmortem report of Ram, which showed that the gunshot bullets had struck him in the lower chest in a pattern almost exactly matching the location of Hanumant's birthmarks. (Stevenson, Birthmarks and Birth Defects Corresponding to wounds on Deceased Persons, 1993)

Thought-Forms and Hallucinations

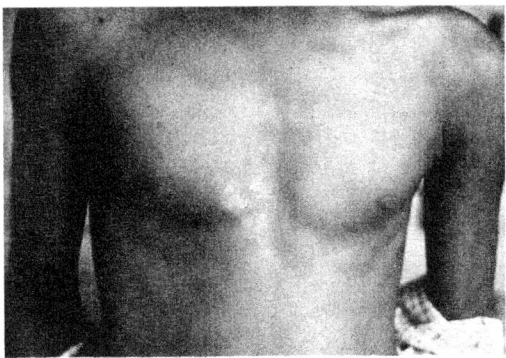

Figure 22 Hypopigmented macule on the chest of Hanumant Saxena's chest as it appeared in 1971 when he was 16 years old. The birthmark was an area of lessened pigmentation

© 1998 Society for Scientific Exploration

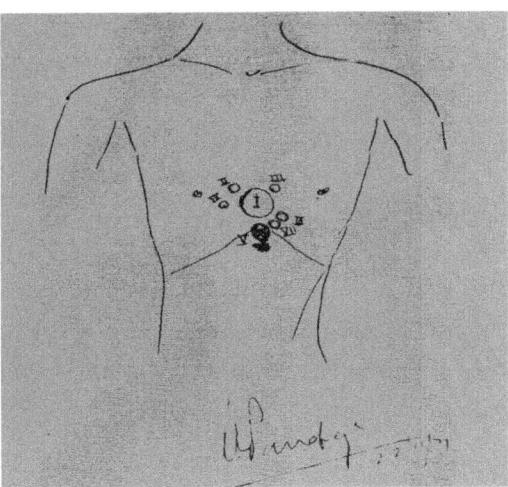

Figure 23 Sketch showing location of fatal wounds on Maha Ram Singh, Dr. S.C.Pandeya (Civil Surgeon, Fatehgarh, UP., India) drew the circles on the lower chest and upper abdomen. The Roman numerals correspond to the different wounds described in the postmortem report. Number 1 marked in the largest circle indicates the largest wound. Note the characteristic smaller wounds on the periphery of the large central wound. This is due to the scattering of the shot after they leave the barrel of the gun

© 1998 Society for Scientific Exploration

The Case of Rajani – Indelible Scars of self-immolation

Rajani Singh was born on November 16, 1991 in the village of Bhalaul in Etah district, Uttar Pradesh (India) to Virender Singh and Bimla. Previously, Mithilesh, one of Virender Singh's cousins, came to stay with his family to pursue her higher studies. There, Mithilesh became involved with a boy of a different caste[2], and her family did not approve of this. She became depressed about the situation and committed suicide on October 6, 1991 by immolating herself.

Rajani was born without any medical complications of pregnancy, about one and a half months after Mithilesh's death. She had red marks all over her body, but they were more prominent on her head. Her mother and paternal grandmother noticed the marks on her head within a few days of her birth. They noticed the marks on the rest of her body within a month after her birth, when Mithilesh's mother, Rajwati Devi, came to see her. Notably, Rajwati Devi had dreamed within one month of her daughter Mithilesh's death that she was coming back to their family. At this time Rajani was thought to be Mithilesh reborn. When Rajani grew up and could speak, she asked for Mithilesh's younger sister, Meena. When Rajani came to stay with Mithilesh's family in 1995, she showed a familiarity with the place and with persons there. Also, she addressed Mithilesh's parents as "Papa" and "Mummy" and insisted a few occasions that she be called "Mithilesh."

---

[2] A caste system is a social structure that divides people on the basis of an inherited social status.

Thought-Forms and Hallucinations

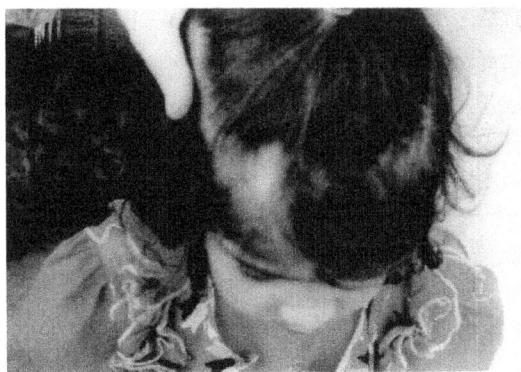

Figure 24 Birthmark on Rajani Singh's head as it appeared in November 1995 when she was 4 years old. The birthmark was a hairless hypopigmented area on the right frontal region of her head
© 1998 Society for Scientific Exploration

Rajani had several birthmarks. Two of these were areas of erythema (increased redness) of the skin on her back and shoulder that were still visible in 1992, when Dr. Pasricha made a personal investigation of the case. In addition, she had a prominent area on the right frontal region of her head that was hairless and hypopigmented. This was clearly visible as late as 1995. (Pasricha, 1998)

The Case of Yashbir Yadav – Birthmark of Bullet Wound

Dr. Satwant K Pasricha investigated this case between February 1995 and March 1997.

Yashbir Yadav was born in the village of Mastipur in the Etah district in Uttar Pradesh (India) in October 1987. His parents were Rajinder Singh Yadav and Kusum Yadav. Yashbir's parents noticed two marks on his neck within a few days of his birth. However, they did not pay much attention to these until Yashbir spoke about a previous life and pointed to the marks, saying that he had been shot there. His statements mainly included the name of a sister in the previous life, names of the persons who had killed him, and how they killed them.

The flashback goes like this: A man called Durga Lal had been murdered in the village of Ranipur Gaur on July 7, 1985, a little over two years before the birth of Yashbir. He was present during a quarrel being settled by the then headman, Jamadar Singh. Durga Lal indulged in an altercation with Jamadar Singh, which was taken as an insult by the headman's supporters; consequently, they had Durga Lal shot on July 7, 1985 at his neck and abdomen.

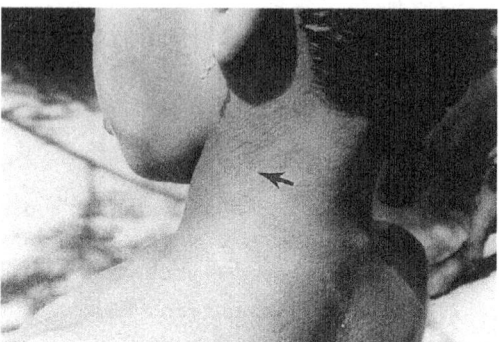

Figure 25 Birthmark on the neck of Yashbir Yadav as it appeared in March 1997 when he was 9 ½ years old. The arrow mark points to an area of approximately 1 cm x 1 cm which corresponded in location to a gunshot wound of entry on the neck of Durga Lal
© 1998 Society for Scientific Exploration

The birthmarks of Yashbir included a hyper-pigmented area 6 centimeters below the left ear. It was about 1 cm x 1 cm area. It corresponded in location to the gunshot wound of entry on the left side of the upper neck; the postmortem report of Durga Lal gave its dimensions as 4 cm x 3 cm.

A second mark on the lower abdomen was a round, slightly elevated hyper-pigmented area about 1 cm in diameter. It corresponded in location to a gunshot wound of entry (which also finds mention in the postmortem report) that was on the right side of the abdomen 2 centimeters above the right iliac crest. Its dimensions were given as 4.5 cm by 3 cm. According to Dr. Pasricha, there was a third hyper-pigmented area 5 centimeter below the right ear. It was about 1 cm x 1 cm in area. No wound corresponding to this mark was mentioned in the postmortem report. (Pasricha, 1998)

The Case of Khin Mar Htoo – Congenital absence of lower leg

Ma Khim Mar Htoo was born in Upper Burma in 1967. Before she was born, her mother dreamed that a girl called Ma Thein Nwe (nicknamed 'Kalamagyi') was going to be reborn as her daughter. Htoo was born missing her right leg (below the knee) and when she could speak, she expressed many memories of the life and death of Kalamagyi.

A year ago, in August 1966, Kalamagyi (Nwe) had died under the following circumstances:

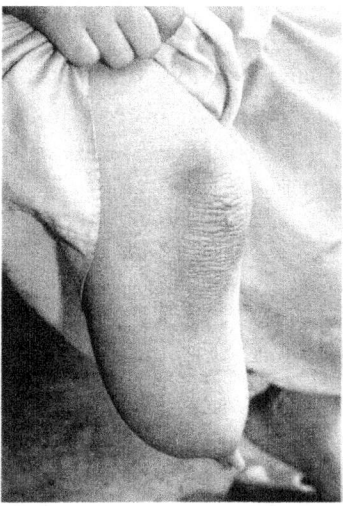

Figure 26 Khin Mar Htoo's right leg as it appeared in 1980 when she was 12 years old. It shows congenital absence of the lower right leg (unilateral hemimelia). She said that she remembered the life of a girl who was run over by a train. Eye witnesses said that the train severed the girl's right leg first, before running over the trunk. (Stevenson 1993)
© 1998 Society for Scientific Exploration

Kalamagyi and her mother earned a living by selling food, water and other items to train passengers. On the day of her death, Kalamagyi was walking on the central line, confidently expecting the train to be switched onto the line next to the platform. On that day, however, a switch failed to function properly, and the train, instead of moving to the side line beside the platform, continued on the central line. Horrified, the switchman saw that it would run down Kalamagyi. The engine driver sounded his horn and braked the train. It was too late, and the train ran over Kalamagyi.

As ascertained by Dr. Stevenson, Kalamagyi's right leg was found at a considerable distance behind the rest of her body, which the train had sliced in two as it ran over her. Thus it seemed likely that as Kalamgyi fell under the train, she thrust her right leg out under the wheels, and it was cut off before other parts of her body were injured. (Stevenson, Birthmarks and Birth Defects Corresponding to wounds on Deceased Persons, 1993)

The Case of Lekh Pal – Amputated fingers

Lekh Pal was born in December 1971 in the village of Nagla Devi in Uttar Pradesh (India). He was born without the fingers (phalanges) of his right hand, which were represented by mere stubs; his left hand was normal.

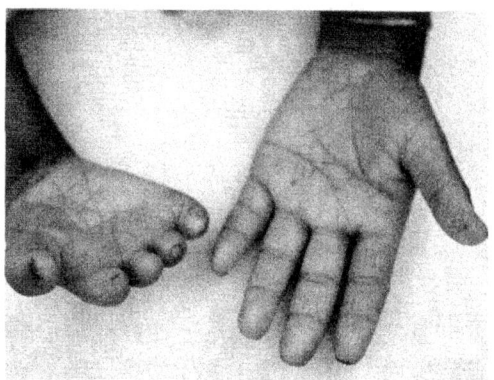

Figure 27 Almost absent fingers (*brachydactyly*) of one hand in a boy of India who said he remembered the life of a boy of another village who had put his hand into the blades of a fodder-chopping machine and had his fingers amputated
© 1998 Society for Scientific Exploration

When he was able to talk, he claimed he remembered his previous life in which his right-hand fingers were cut off in a fodder-chopping machine. He kept repeating the word 'Tal, Tal" (which was later identified to mean a nearby village Nagla Tal). He said Nagla Devi was not his home and he would not stay there.

He said that he had a mother and father in "Tal" and also an older sister and a younger brother. He did not give his father's name. He indirectly identified him as the person operating the fodder-chopping machine when his fingers were cut off.

Later, it was learnt that a child in Nagla Tal called Hukum Singh had had his fingers cut off when he inadvertently put them into the blades of a fodder-chopping machine, which his father was operating without noticing that his little son, who was about 3 ½ years old, had approached the machine. Hukum Singh survived this accident, but he died the following year of some unrelated illness.

In this case, Dr. Stevenson made an important remark that the thumb of Hukum Singh was not cut off when the other four fingers of his right hand were (as confirmed by his family). Yet Lekh Pal's thumb was as much affected in his birth defect as other fingers of his right hand. This, the investigator relates, is caused by the change in the psychical field and that the new body may show an influence from the previous body that exceeds the area involved in the previous body's wounds. (Stevenson, Birthmarks and Birth Defects Corresponding to wounds on Deceased Persons, 1993)

The findings of Stevenson have been published in such distinguished scientific periodicals as the *American Journal of Psychiatry*, the *Journal of Nervous and Mental Disease*, and the *International Journal of Comparative Sociology*. And in a review of one of his works, the prestigious *Journal of the American Medical Association* stated that, "he has painstakingly and unemotionally collected a detailed series of cases in which the evidence for reincarnation is difficult to understand on any other grounds… He has placed on record a large amount of data that cannot be ignored."

The transference of physical marks from one body to another in the process of rebirth – or rather their reproduction in a new body, is a recurring feature of many of the aforesaid cases.

It can be explained, only with the assumption that there is psycho-somatic interaction brought about by a strong mental impression during the previous life or at the time of death – so strong as to make an impression on the subtle body and the consciousness.

Further research in this interesting field of spontaneous past-life memory recall cases should be continued to facilitate improved understanding of the various aspects of the phenomenon of rebirth, because of its proven ability to contribute to the proper understanding of human biology itself.

Bio-Holographic Model

Although critics have argued there is no physical explanation for the survival of personality, Tucker suggests that quantum mechanics may offer a mechanism by which memories and emotions could carry over from one life to another.

He argues that since the act of observation collapses wave equations, consciousness may not be merely a by-product of the physical brain but rather a separate entity in the universe that impinges on the physical. Tucker argues that viewing consciousness as a fundamental, non-physical part of the universe makes it possible to conceive of it continuing to exist after the death of the physical brain. He provides the analogy of a television set and the television transmission; the television is required to decode the signal, but it does not create the signal. In a similar way the brain may be required for consciousness to express itself, but may not be the source of consciousness.

Dr. Ian Stevenson theorized *template body* analogous to the *human energy field* of Tiller. It is a holographic template that guides the form and structure of the physical body. Stevenson's findings regarding birthmarks add further support to the idea that we are holographic energy constructs.

Matti Pitkänen, in his paper, '*A Model for Remote Mental Interactions,*' contends that the field body does not die though the material body dies and decays. According to him, there is the electromagnetic body serving as a template around which ordinary matter self-organizes by phase transition and at the same time modifies this template. The phase transition front proceeds from the moment of birth to the geometric future in a manner analogous to the polymerization process or to the gradual build-up of a protein in mRNA-protein translation process.

Electromagnetic body could correspond to the electromagnetic part of the genetic information hypothesized to be coded by transversal magnetic mirror structures (massless externals parallel to magnetic flux tubes) and the 4-dimensional body becomes mature and could survive at least for some time in a state in which conscious experience does not contain the dominating input from the phase transition zone. He further surmises that these 4-D bodies can in principle communicate with the living ones and long term memories about the deceased might represent one form of this communication. The communications would be based on the same mechanism as long term memories in general: by looking at magnetic mirror with length of order light-life or more, one can see not only 'he' of the past, but also his fellow human beings (not only human beings). At quantum level, this means time-like quantum entanglement making it possible to share experiences (Pitkanen).

Dr. Ervin Laszlo, in his work, *'An Unexplored Domain of Non-locality: Toward a Scientific Explanation of Instrumental Trans-communication'*, asserts that the holographic transfer of information is realistic and can explain trans-communication with the deceased persons. He says, a vacuum-hologram does not have sensory organs. How then does such a hologram access information from a flesh-and-blood individual?

We should note that the evidence from trans-communication does not suggest that the vacuum-based hologram has sensory types of perceptions, such as seeing sights in three dimension and hearing ordinary sounds. It does indicate, on the other hand, that such an entity can perceive questions and comments from living persons, according to Laszlo.

How this may be possible calls for reference to the theory of holographic information transfer. The hologram that represents the consciousness of the deceased access the utterances of the living interlocutor through interaction with the hologram created in the vacuum by the living individual's brain. The latter does not carry the living individual's voice, only the information that his or her voice would articulate. Trans-communication is an exchange of information between the two vacuum-based holograms. This is a realistic possibility. Trans-communication can be assumed to take place when the hologram created by the living interlocutor and the hologram that carries the consciousness of the deceased resonate at the same frequency. Then the hologram that carries the consciousness of the deceased person can access the information carried by the hologram of the living person. (Laszlo, 2008)

Michael Talbot cites the proposal made by the University of Connecticut psychologist Dr. Kenneth Ring that near-death experiences could be explained by the hologrpahic model. Ring believes such experiences as well as death itslef, are really nothing more than the shifting of a person's consciousness from one level of the hologram of reality to another.

In particular, Stanislav Grof feels the holographic paradigm offers a model for understanding many of the baffling phenomena experienced by individuals during altered states of consciousness. In the 1950s, while conducting research into the beliefs of LSD as a psychotherapeutic tool, Grof had one female patient who suddenly became convinced she had assumed the identity of a female of a species of prehistoric reptile.

During the course of her hallucination, she not only gave a richly detailed description of what it felt like to be encapsuled in such a form, but noted that the portion of the male of the species's anatomy was a patch of colored scales on the side of its head. What was startling to Grof was that although the woman had no prior knowledge about such things, a conversation with a zoologist later confirmed that in certain species of reptiles colored areas on the head do indeed play an important role as triggers of sexual arousal.

The woman's experience was not unique. During the course of his research, Grof encountered examples of patients regressing and identifying with virtually every species on the evolutionary tree (research findings which helped influence the man-into-ape scene in the movie Altered States). Moreover, he found that such experiences frequently contained obscure zoological details which turned out to be accurate (Talbot, The Holographic Universe, 1996).

Filippo Liverziani, in his interesting book, "*Reincarnation? The phenomena which seem to suggest it,*" contends that the entire personality of the deceased person is not reborn, but only the psychic residues in the life of the previous personality are reflected in the next life. According to him, "no personality ever flows into any other. Nevertheless, each individual personality can become enriched by what other personalities have made of themselves: every personality models itself and its own psyche, models of its own astral shell; and once the astral residues of a disincarnate personality have become separated and attached to another personality, the latter incorporates within itself also the fruit of the actions of the former, which can be either positive or negative; and there can be no doubt that the transmitted positive psychic residues of the disincarnate personality cannot but enrich the living personality, while the transmission of negative actions must have the opposite effect and act as ballast. Given the law of affinity, that governs the mental universe, one may also assume that the psychic residues abandoned during the ascent of a disincarnate soul are transmitted to an incarnate soul that is bound to it by some affinity."

7
MATERNAL IMPRESSIONS

> *The sensitive paper in the camera of the photographist repeats not more certainly the lines thrown upon it by the graphic pencils of light, than does the unconscious embryo the images, whether of beauty or deformity, reflected from the maternal soul.*
>
> —The Water-Cure Journal (1857)

The belief in the reality of the transference of strong mental impressions on the mother into corresponding physical changes, including stamping of images pictographically in the child, is very ancient and widespread.

Commonly referred to as 'Maternal Impressions,' *imagination maternelle* or *das Versehen* (a German noun meaning *accident* or as a verb *to provide*), it is the belief that a sudden fear of some object or animal or even mental cravings in a pregnant woman can cause her child to bear the mark of it. Perhaps the first and most famous instance of this is that of Jacob in the *Book of Genesis*.

As the story goes, Jacob served his uncle (and father-in-law) Laban for seven years for the sake of his wife Rachel. Being deceived by her father, he served for her yet another seven long years; at the end of that period, Laban offered him no wages. Jacob being desirous of returning his home in Canaan and setting up an independent household, requested Laban to send him, his wife and children away. But knowing the fact that much of the prosperity he earned was due to the faithful service of his son-in-law, Laban did not like this, as he would lose a very good worker. He entreated him to remain and Jacob consented on certain strange conditions.

An agreement was made between them whereby Jacob would be paid for his work with any of the cattle or sheep or goats that had *spots or ring marks on their hides*. In order to understand what follows, one must know that majority of the sheep and goats were then unicolored and spotted or striped animals were much rarer. Here Jacob seemed to be playing a risky game because the uni-colored female animals seldom give birth to striped or spotted offspring.

But Jacob followed a local custom which people believed would change the colour of herds. He took fresh rods of poplar, almond and plane, and peeled white streaks in them, exposing the white of the rods. He set these peeled-off rods in front of the flocks in the runnels, that is, the watering troughs where the flocks came to drink. Since they bred when they came to drink, the flocks bred in front of the rods, and so the flocks brought forth were striped, speckled and spotted. Thus over time, Jacob built up strong herds of striped, speckled and spotted animals and his flock increased exceedingly, bringing him all wealth and prosperity.

Such belief existed among people even more primitive than the early Hebrews, and in all parts of the world.

Among the Greeks there is a trace of the belief in the theory of maternal impressions. For example, the Greek physician Galen believed that a pregnant woman need only look at an image of someone and her child might resemble that individual. Plato wrote of it, and, beggars and cripples were forbidden to walk the streets in Sparta, in case their disabilities imprinted themselves on the unborn children of innocent passers-by. Plutarch states that Empedocles had remarked that women produced children resembling statues which they found pleasure in regarding during pregnancy. The law of Lycurgus mandated Spartan wives to look upon representation of the strong and beautiful, e.g., statues of Castor and Pollux.

The belief continued to persist unquestioned throughout the Middle Ages. Ballantyne thinks that up to the end of the 15th century, belief in the efficacy of maternal impression seem to have been confined to what was seen at the moment of conception.

In the 16th century, the idea was so common that physician Ambroise Pare suggested that a mother's imagination affected her unborn child and wrote that maternal impression was one of the thirteen causes of prenatal birth defects. Della Porta, the famous Italian philosopher in the 16th century attempted to formulate a first theory of maternal impressions. At about the same time, Leonardo da Vinci, referring to pregnancy, wrote in his *Quaderni d'Ana-tomia* (ca 1490) 'the same soul governs the two bodies…the things desired by the mother are often found impressed on the members of the child which the mother carries at the time of the desire.'

In the 17th century, there was blind credulity and the idea of maternal impression was even recognized in a court of law. Geoffroy Saint-Hilaire in his *Histoire des Anomalies* (1832, page 332) records that in the third year of the French Republic an infant was born with the representation of a Phrygian cap of liberty on the left breast and the French government gave the mother 400 francs per annum as an award for her patriotic thoughts! Dr. Samel Turner, in the eighteenth century, published a work on diseases of the skin, in which there was a dissertation on the congenital marks contained in the 12th chapter, and in which he attributed them to the influence of the mother's imagination. In 1731, Schurig, in his *Syllepsilogia* devoted more than a hundred pages to summarizing a vast number of curious cases of maternal impressions.

In China, Wang Kentang's widely read work on childbirth suggested that people with deformed features or misshapen appearance should be avoided because the shape (*xing*) of the foetus remained malleable during the first three months of pregnancy (Kentang 1602). *'The Essentials of Childbirth'*, a popular eighteenth century manual compiled by Ke Jia went so far as to prohibit women from looking at wild animals, in particular tortoises, snakes and rabbits, for fear of producing offspring with bestial features. The popular *Dashengbian* (Boon on successful childbirth), reprinted more than eighty times, added "murderous and evil" scenes (*Zaisha Xiongwu*) to its list of ominous occurrences from which pregnant women should avert their eyes.

Thus, the belief in maternal imprinting has a long recorded history. But antiquity alone cannot be a sufficient argument for any doctrine which is not rationally accounted for by any known scientific principle. Since there is no direct connection between the mother and her unborn baby, the maternal impression theory failed to have a rational explanation in those times.

There are many authentic records from the time of Hippocrates down which demonstrate the transmission of pre-natal mental influence from the mother to the child.

Darwin cites the case of a cow that lost a horn by accident, with consequent suppuration; and who gave birth to three calves, hornless on the same side of the head; and on the authority of Bluemenbach another case of a man, "who had the little finger of the right hand almost cut off, and which in consequence grew crooked; and his sons had the same finger in the same hand similarly crooked." Similar incidents have occurred within the observation of most families and are extremely puzzling.

Robert Boyle, whose mind conceived the well-known law concerning the relation between the volume and pressure, conformed sufficiently to contemporary thought to repeat a tale about a speckled child whose mother had gazed long and earnestly at some red pebble-stones at St.Winifred's Well.

The story is reproduced here.

"A very ingenious physician has diverse times related to me that being called to a young Lady, he found that though she much complained of health, yet here appeared so little cause either in her body, or her condition, to guess that she did any more than fancy herself sick that scrupling to give her physic, he persuaded her friends rather to divert her mind by little journeys of pleasures: in one of which going to St.Winifred's Well, this lady, who was a catholic, and devout in her religion, remained a pretty while in the water to perform some devotions, and fixed her eyes very attentively upon the red pebble-stones, which, in a scattered order, made up a good part of those that appeared through the water; and a while after growing big, she was delivered of a child whose white skin was copiously speckled with spots of color and bigness of those stones." (Turner, 2007)

There are thousands of curious clinical cases of mental impressions on record. From the myriad of facts relating to this phenomenon, I have limited myself to choosing those that seemed to me the most essential or the most interesting. The phenomenal illustrations of this part of the subject are as significant and forcible as they are numerous and diversified. Though it is difficult to make a rational classification of these phenomena, attention has mainly been paid on transfer of 'pictographical' information to the child, especially resemblance to animals due to fright caused by them, etc., in order to facilitate a better understanding of their operational principles and mechanisms.

Resemblance to Animals due to Fright caused by them

It has been supposed that a sudden fright will cause a resemblance to the animal or object producing it. Instances undoubtedly have occurred of such maternal impressions to suggest that frights caused by animals, the seeing of accidents, bodily deformities, scars and other painful or shocking happenings may lead to corresponding malformations in the unborn child. Indeed, in early modern Europe women were warned that the fright caused by animals, and specifically rats, – would set the maternal imagination into motion with grave consequences for the infant.

The following cases relating to maternal impressions are so serious as to suggest that nothing is more likely to cause malformations than being frightened.

A lizard falling from the ceiling on the bare breast of a sleeping pregnant woman, at dead of night, caused sudden fright and, temporarily, great mental disturbance. The child was born shortly afterwards, and as the mother predicted, had a red mark on its chest which was like the imprint of a lizard's body and extended limbs, and of similar size. According to Walter Heape, this incident happened in China and Captain Whithers, husband of the woman and a friend of Heape vouched for the truth of the story (Heape 1913).

Dr. W. J. Tubbs, in his article, *'Influence of Mental Impressions on the Foetus in Utero,'* published in the *'Provincial Medical and Surgical Journal,'* (1842), recounts the following case:

In the early part of August 1841, I was requested to attend the wife of an innkeeper, in labour with her eighth child. She was a strong, healthy woman, aged about forty-seven. The *os uteri* was dilated to the size of half a crown (the Crown was a silver coin measuring 39 mm in diameter and worth 5 Shilling), membranes unruptured; vertex presentation. The labor being tedious, it was necessary to rupture the membranes, which, from their toughness, and not yielding to the fingernail, was effected by a quill. There was much mental excitement during the greater part of the labor. Fearing cerebral congestion, and from the rigid state of the *os uteri* and the perineum, it was almost decided that venesection (phlebotomy) should be had recourse to. Though repeatedly told all was right, she persisted in a contrary opinion. As her pains increased, so did her ideas, that her child was like the spotted dog by which she had been frightened in the kitchen; as it was always before her eyes, night and day. (These were the words of the patient). She had scarcely uttered those words, when, by a powerful contraction of the uterus, a fine full-grown female child was expelled. Before the child was taken from under the bedclothes, the patient distinctly said these words in the presence of the nurse and a second attendance, "My child is marked like Troughton's dog (the spotted), and at the back of the neck where the black one held it."

On bringing the child to the light, such was the fact; only three or four spots about the size of a sixpence on the face, the rest of the body beautifully marked with black spots varying from the size of a pea to that of a sixpence, with the exception of the back of the neck, which had a brown black appearance covered with hairs, extending about two inches and a half across the neck and shoulders, and one inch and a half down the back. It appears from the patient's statement, that about the period of her third month of pregnancy, she was crossing the kitchen with a pint of beer, when a black dog and a spotted terrier, then lying under the table, began to fight close to her feet; and in the fright turning round, she saw the black dog seize the other by the back of the neck; a chillness came over her, and she felt ill all the day.

What is singular, her last two children were born marked from mental impressions made (as she believed) about the third month of each pregnancy; therefore, she was more convinced that she was to have a spotted child this time. The child is living, and very much admired. The spotted dog frequently passes my house; many persons call at the inn for a pint of beer as an excuse to see the rare spotted lass." (W.J.Tubbs, 1842)

It is a striking illustration of the power which the mind can exercise by constantly (consequently morbidly) dwelling on a fixed subject, and the influence which that mental power eventually effects upon the distant organ.

John Merrick, better known as the 'Elephant Man' claimed that his condition was due to his pregnant mother having been knocked down by a circus elephant. In a similar vein, and in common with many other freak-show performers, Kionel the lion-faced man– a famous exhibit of P.T. Barnum, assured audiences that his mother had witnessed a terrible sight, specifically his father being torn apart by lions.

The journal *Tomorrow,* (Vol 1-2) carries the following case on the authority of Van Swieten in Commenar Zu Boerhave, III, Page 406:

A pregnant woman was frightened when a caterpillar fell on the back of her neck and she had difficulty in catching it and throwing it away. A daughter, born some time later, had a birth mark on her neck resembling a clearly defined caterpillar. Even the color of the mark suggested the insect. (Tomorrow, 1952)

Another author recounts the case of a child with so exact likeness of a leech full of blood and hanging down with its point highest, on the leg of the child of a lithographic printer, that at a little distance any one would suppose a leech was there. The mother told him that in her fourth month of pregnancy she had occasion to apply some leeches; that one remained longer than the rest and hung down full of blood. This rather frightened her and she dreamt about it.

Here is another case. When the pregnant mother was working in a hayfield her husband threw at her a young hare he had found in the hay; it struck her on the cheek and neck. Her daughter had on the left cheek an oblong patch of soft dark hair, in color and character clearly resembling the fur of a very young hare. (A. Mackay, Port Appin, N. B., *Lancet*, December 19, 1891.) The writer records also four other cases which had happened in his experience.

'*The American Journal Obstetrics*,'(1898) carried the following story:

"A healthy woman with no skin blemish had, during her third pregnancy, a violent appetite for sunfish. During or after the fourth month, her husband, as a surprise, brought her some sunfish alive, placing them in a pail of water in the porch. She stumbled against the pail and the shock caused the fish to flap over the pail and come in violent contact with her leg. The cold wriggling fish produced a nervous shock, but she attached no importance to this.

The child (a girl) had at birth a mark of bronze pigment resembling a fish with the head uppermost on the corresponding part of the same leg. Daughter's health good; throughout life she has had a strong craving for sunfish, which she has sometimes eaten till she has vomited from repletion." (C. F. Gardiner, Colorado Springs, *American Journal Obstetrics*, February, 1898.)

Monstrous Births due to Maternal Mental Influence

Teratology is the study of malformations and monstrosities in animal and human newborns. There was considerable debate over how these travesties of human form came into being. Ambroise Pare, in his *Deux livres de chirurgie* (Paris, 1573), listed a number of supposed causes of monstrous births, including maternal imagination.

Paré presents classical and Biblical sources for his diagnosis. The classical sources are Aristotle, Hippocrates, and Empedocles, "who sought out the secrets of Nature." He also cites Genesis 30, recounting how Jacob deceived his father-in-law Laban. What Paré asserted with this Biblical citation is that animals, like humans, have imagination. "[W]hen the goats and ewes looked at these rods of various colors, they might form their young spotted in various colors."³ Maternal impression afflicts both the human and animal realms.

Hartmann describes the birth and anatomical structure of a double monster (*cephalothora copagus*) and notes that the mother was alarmed, when pregnant, by seeing in the forest a new-born fawn which was a double monstrosity (Hartmann, *Münchener Medicinisches Wochenschrift*, No. 9, 1895.)

A large number of cases might be quoted in support of this. It appears important, however, to note that in majority of the cases of this kind, which are sufficiently authenticated to deserve our attention, the mental impact of the mother is not slight and soon-forgotten but deep and morbid enough to induce a settled conviction of what the result to the child would be.

Fright by Opossum[4]

Under the title, '*Influence of the Mind on the Foetus*,' an article appeared in the '*Memphis Journal of Medicine and Surgery*' in August 1856, containing an account of three cases of deformity in infants due to maternal impressions.

The first case is so extraordinary that it deserves a mention here. A lady in Habersham county, was delivered, at the end of the seventh month, of a child whose left leg was destitute of a foot and ankle, the stump appearing as if the limb had been amputated by a dull instrument a short time previously; the bone protruded about an inch and a half and appeared to have been broken off obliquely. The right leg 'resembled in shape the foreleg of the opossum.' The foot was turned inwards, and the toes were grown together to near their extremities, and were destitute of natural nails, but had claws precisely like those of the opossum. The right finger of the right hand was off at the first phalangeal articulation, and very much resembled the toe of the above-named animal, and on the extremity was a claw, like those on the toes.

At an early period of her pregnancy, the mother had witnessed

---

[3] Gen. 30: 38.

[4] A native American marsupial

the killing of an opossum, one of whose forelegs was cut off with an old, dull axe, leaving the bone protruding. She was very much frightened at the time, but she thought no more of it, or very little, until the birth of her child, which died two weeks afterwards. (Henry Goadby, 1856)

A Child Half-Fish

Orson Squire Fowler, Editor of the *American Phrenological Journal*, in his *"Maternity, or, The bearing and nursing of children: including Female Education and Beauty" (1853)* recounts the following case:

"A woman, about four months pregnant, was on a visit to her native town, on the northern shore of Lake Erie, and stopped at her father's. A fishing excursion, in a row-boat, and in the night, was proposed and which she was persuaded to join. The fish were to be caught with a spear while asleep in the water, and were discovered by means of a torch. The kind of fish caught had a grissly snout that turns upwards and backwards, thus forming a kind of hook, and often weighs twenty pounds. She took a seat in the middle of the boat.

A large fish, probably frightened, leaped from the water, clear over the boat, and right before her face, uttering, as it passed, a kind of snort or wheeze peculiar to the fish when it jumps out of the water, or is captured. This frightened her terribly; so as actually to sicken her for several days. Her progeny, when born, proved to be a monster, half-fish and half-human, without a mouth, but having nasal appendage like that of the fish alluded to above. Its lower extremity resembled that of a fish and every few minutes it would spring and throw itself up a foot or more from its pillow and at the same time utter the same noise made by the kind of fish alluded to.

Having no mouth, of course, it could not be fed, and lived only about twenty-four hours. Being a monster, it was refused a Christian burial, and was interred in the corner of a field." (Fowler, 1844)

Fowler states he had it from Mrs. Fowler of Burford, Canada West, a woman of superior natural abilities and an eye-witness of the fact so that no doubt about its authenticity needs to be entertained.

A Snake Man

'The Family Magazine' published in the Savannah Georgia carries the following curious case of a man resembling a snake. The editor of the magazine says a correspondent in the country had furnished them the account of an individual by the name of Robert H. Copeland and that the facts were vouched for by a number of the most respectable physicians and other persons in Henry County.

"This most singular being, perhaps has not a parallel in medical history. He is now about twenty-nine years old, of ordinary stature and intellect. His deformities and physical peculiarities are owing to a fright his mother received from a large rattlesnake attempting to bite her, about the sixth month of her pregnancy. For several minutes after the snake struck at her, she believed herself bitten just above the ankle, and so powerfully was her mind affected that when she was delivered, the child's will was found to have no control over his right arm and leg; which are smaller than his left extremities. He can use his right leg now sufficiently to walk in a hobbling manner, but cannot restrain it stationary without the aid of the weight of his body. His right hand has the usual number of fingers but they are smaller than those of his left hand. The wrist joint is looser than usual, and his hands stand at an angle with his arm. His front teeth are somewhat pointed and inclined backward like the fangs of a snake. The right side of his face is affected; his mouth is drawn considerably further on the right than on the left side; his right eye squints, has several deep groves radiating from it, and has a very singular appearance much resembling a snake.

But perhaps the most extraordinary circumstance on record, is that his right arm when not restrained will draw the lower part to about a right angle with the upper, and sometimes two or three, but most commonly only the fore finger will project curved at the first joint, much resembling a snake's head, and neck when in the attitude of striking; and the whole arm will strike at an object with all the venom of a snake, and precisely in the same manner, sometimes for two or three, and sometimes for four or five strokes, and then the arm assumes a vibratory motion, will coil up, and apply itself close against his body. During this period, his right foot and leg become excited, and if not restrained will shake also. His face is also excited; the angle of his mouth is drawn backward, and his eye snaps more or less, in unison with the strokes of his hand, while his lips are always separated, exposing his teeth, which being somewhat pointed like the fangs of a snake, causes his whole visage to assume a peculiar and snaky aspect.

During infancy and childhood, the whole shape of the snake, even to its lungs was printed on the anterior of his legs; but as he grew up it become gradually obliterated, till now there is only a small depression where the snake's head was imprinted" (The Family magazine, 1839) (A Physiological Phenomenon, or the Snake Man: Robert H Copeland, 1839)

A similar case was reported by Fowler in the year 1844. "About 1760, a woman in Brookfield, Mass., on going to a hen's nest in a basket for collecting eggs, as she was putting her hand down into the basket partly before she looked, was shocked and terrified so that she fell back and fainted by seeing a large snake that had curled itself up in the nest and swallowed all the eggs, and which hissed and darted towards her hand as she was putting it down. Two months afterwards, she bore a child the eyes and lower part of the face of which, and especially its mouth, resembled a snake. It made violent motions, and a hissing noise, resembling those of the snake in the basket, on account of which it was bled to death by Dr. Honeywood and Upham." (Fowler, 1844).

A Monstrous Cat-headed Child

The following case was reported by the '*American Phrenological Journal and Miscellany*,' in the year 1843.

"A Mrs._____, living in H.,Vt. loved a cat very much, and the cat reciprocated this attachment. That is, one had magnetized the other.

She lived in a house with an old woman who disliked the cat and would frequently cuff it off the table, and out of the way. Many a family quarrel was occasioned by one's liking the cat, and the other not. At length she moved away, but the poor cat was not taken. Her husband went back for the balance of their things, and his wife charged him over and over again, and with great earnestness, to bring the favorite cat. On going for his things, the cat was sick. The old woman told the husband that the cat was sick and pining, and refused to eat, and advised him to kill it. Finally he took it out behind the barn and beat out it brains.

On going home, his wife, the first thing, accused him of having killed the cat. He denied it repeatedly and positively, and she as positively asserted that he had killed it, and thrown it out back on the barn; for she said, "I felt the blows, and saw the mangled cat thrown out behind the barn," and she took on terribly after her favorite cat, so as to be almost beside herself.

Her child, which she carried at the time, when born, resembled a cat in the looks of its head with its brains knocked out, or head beat in; and died in a short time." (O. S. Fowler, 1843).

The Monkey Girl

Thomas Smith F.R.C.S of St.Bartholomew's Hospital of London, in *Clinical papers on Surgery of Childhood*, says that "there are many well authenticated cases where marks and even deformities in the foetus can be fairly attributed to strong and persistent mental impressions in the mother," and describes the following striking case of a child admitted into St.Bartholomew's Hospital in 1865.

"She was at that time twelve years old. The left upper extremity and the greater part of the corresponding side of the trunk and neck were deeply stained with dark-brown pigment, from which grew an abundant crop of brown, harsh, lank hair, varying in length from one to two inches. The skin was rough and harsh; the arm was long, thin and withered; the scapula was unnaturally prominent. In fact, the upper limb, shoulder and back bore a very strong resemblance to the corresponding part of a monkey.

The mother stated that when she was three months pregnant with the child, she was much terrified by a monkey attached to a

street organ, which jumped on her back as she was passing by."
(Surgeons, 1867).

Children Resembling a Frog

"In the spring time of the year 1868, a woman was passing through a meadow where a number of schoolboys were at play. She had advanced to the sixth week, she considered, of pregnancy, when one of the boys, taking up a frog, threatened to throw it at her; she begged of him not to do so, but he persisted and struck her face with the frog. This produced an immediate feeling of sickness. She was obliged to sit down, and upon her return home compelled to go to bed and send for a doctor. She informed the doctor who visited her that her child would resemble a frog.

She appeared to suffer very much throughout her pregnancy; during the latter months she was unable to lie down, as she said she experienced something swimming in her inside; assuredly she was a great size.

At the full period labour begun and upon the rupture of the membranes the room-floor was literally deluged with the waters which escaped, the head presented and the child was quickly born. It gasped, as a fish drawn out of the water will for a few minutes, and died. The head in every particular resembled that of a frog, and the fingers were webbed, otherwise the monster was well formed. The woman had borne three children previously and seemed a sensible person. (Curran, 1869)

This is similar to a case related by Ambrose Pare as follows:

In the year 1517, in the Parish of Boiste-Roy, in the Forest of Bievre, on the road to Fontainebleau, a child was born having the face of a frog. He was seen and visited by Maistre Jean Bellanger, surgeon to the king's artillery in the presence of gentlemen from the court of Harmois. The aforementioned Bellanger, a man of good sense, wanting to know the cause of this monster, inquired of the father what could have been the cause of it. The father replied that he thought it was because of his wife, who was suffering from fever, had followed a neighbour's advice that she should hold a live frog in her hand until it was dead. That night, she went to bed with her husband, still having the frog in her hand; her husband and she embraced and she conceived; and by the power of imagination, this monster had then been produced (Dr. Truck, 1859).

Frightened by a Cow

Lambeth, another believer in maternal impressions, describes a male child whose every feature resembled that of a much excited, but harmless cow. In this case, the mother remembered that in her third month of pregnancy, she was frightened at an encounter between her husband and a cow.

There is mention of another similar case. "At the beginning of pregnancy a woman was greatly scared by being kicked over by a frightened cow she was milking; she hung on to the animal's teats, but thought she would be trampled to death, and was ill and nervous for weeks afterwards. The child was a monster, with a fleshy substance—seeming to be prolonged from the spinal cord and to represent the brain—projecting from the floor of the skull. Both doctor and nurse were struck by the resemblance to a cow's teats before they knew the woman's story, and this was told by the woman immediately after delivery and before she knew to what she had given birth."(A.Ross Paterson, Reversby, Lincolnshire, *Lancet*, September 29, 1889.)

There are many such instances.

"A pregnant woman was frightened by two bulls fighting; her child was born with a head closely resembling a bull's." ('The Chicago Medical Times,' 1888).

"During the second month of pregnancy the mother was terrified by a bullock as she was returning from market. The child reached full term and was a well-developed male, stillborn. Its head "exactly resembled a miniature cow's head;" the occipital bone was absent, the parietals only slightly developed, the eyes were placed at the top of the frontal bone, which was quite flat, with each of its superior angles twisted into a rudimentary horn." (J. T. Hislop, Tavistock, Devon, *Lancet*, November 1, 1890)

Turtle Man

'The American Journal of Clinical Medicine' (Volume 19) recounts the following case:

A young man went fishing and brought home a small turtle, placed the turtle on the ground in the yard, and called his sister, who was pregnant, saying that he had something pretty to show her. He had his foot on the turtle's back, and as she approached, removed it. The woman screamed and was very much frightened. At the expiration of five months she gave birth to a child very much deformed, approximating the shape of the turtle and was of idiotic type. It lived ten months. (1912)

Resembling a Rabbit

In the *'Lancet'* of November 7th 1868, Mr. Child late, House-Surgeon of Charing Cross Hospital, recorded a case illustrating the influence of maternal impressions.

The child was born on August 26th, 1868, and was naturally formed, as regards the baby, except the nails on the thumbs, which were like those of a rabbit. "The parietal, frontal, and part of the occipital bones were wanting; and at the space corresponding to, but larger than the anterior fontanelle, was the brain, entirely denuded of skin or membrane, not even being covered with arachnoid. There was a little hair over the eyes, none elsewhere. The eyes, palate, and tongue were similar to those of a rabbit."

Mr. Child then found that during the second month of pregnancy the mother went to a penny show, in which she saw a trained horse pull the trigger of a pistol, pretending to shoot a rabbit. A dummy was then thrown out; the back of its head was bleeding having to all appearance been shot off. This corresponded, as the mother-in-law declared, to the mark on the child's head. The patient seemed never to have forgotten the circumstance during the reminder of her pregnancy, and was considerably frightened at the time.

Cases have occurred in which the mother, when a few months advanced in pregnancy, has been shocked by the sight of a person who had lost a hand, and the child has been born with the same defect. These are samples of the thousands of cases that have been recorded or that have occurred to different individuals.

Dr. Russegger reports that a woman, who had already borne four healthy children, was, in the seventh month of her pregnancy, bitten in the right calf by a dog. The author saw the wound made by the animal's teeth, which wound consisted of three small triangular depressions, by two of which the skin was only slightly ruffled; a slight appearance of blood was perceptible in the third. The woman was at the moment of the accident somewhat alarmed, but neither then nor afterwards had any fear that her foetus would be affected by the occurrence.

Ten weeks after she was bitten, the woman bore a healthy child, which, however, to the surprise of every person, had three marks corresponding in size and appearance to those caused by the dog's teeth in the mother's leg, and consisting, like those, of one large and two smaller impressions. The two latter, which were pale, disappeared in five weeks; the larger one had also become less, and was not so deep colored as it was at birth.

In page 174, chapter xii, in Dr. Turner's book, speaking of a man greatly deformed, he says:

"But of this kind we have a sad instance at home (I mean in this city) in a child of Sir J.B.'s. His lady, when advanced five or six months in her pregnancy, was so frightened at the unexpected view of a beggar's stump-arm upon the coach door, that the child, of which she was afterwards delivered, was born wanting one of its hands, the stump resembling that of the beggar."

Dr. Turner adds, "How these strange alterations should be wrought, or the child cut, wounded or maimed, as if the same was really done with a weapon, whilst the mother is unhurt and merely by the force of the imagination, is I must confess, above my understanding; but it is a fact undeniable." (Bull, 1837)

Birthmarks due to Mother's Craving and Fantasy

According to the popular belief, if a pregnant woman look at a particular object, is disgusted or frightened by it, and above all, if she 'longs' for it, it very frequently happens that the resemblance, both in shape and colour of that object, will be imprinted upon the body of the foetus, and hence the popular rule that a woman with child must have all her longings gratified, lest the child should be marked.

There has been a frequent tendency, more especially among the folklore, to regard a pregnant woman's longings as something sacred. In the Black Forest, according to Ploss and Bartels, a pregnant woman may go freely into other people's gardens and take fruit, provided she eats it on the spot, and similar privileges are accorded to her almost everywhere. In France, at the Revolution, a law of the 28th Germinal, in the year III, it was enacted that a woman could not be brought before a court of justice so long as she was pregnant.

Even now, there is a customary rule in the Indian villages that a woman with child must have all her longings gratified, lest the child should be marked. They strongly believe if a pregnant woman forms an image in her mind and projects it by her desire, it will impress itself on the body of the child. If, for instance, a woman in her imagination strongly conceives of a certain thing, and then puts her hand upon her knee, the image of the thing will appear upon the knee of the child. Her will (although unconsciously) acts in this way like a master bidding a painter to paint him a picture. Whenever the touch of the hand goes, there will be the image (Laurence 2007).

Dated Kitten

In May 1921, a cat belonging to Madame Davico, a baker in Nice, France, gave birth to four kittens, two gray, one white and one black. One gray kitten had the figure '*1921*' on its chest. The other had the same imprint, though not as distinct, on the abdomen. The figures, formed in dark gray hair, were plainly visible on the light gray background. In both cases three spots, similar to three stars, were visible just above the figures. Madame Davico related that some time before the birth of the kittens, the mother was chasing a mouse and jumped on a sack of flour. Thinking that the animal's claws might tear a hole in the sack, Madame Davico threw an empty sack over the full one. The disappointed cat waited several hours for the mouse to reappear, all the while staring the date 1921 with three stars above the figure. The kittens, born a few weeks later, had in their chest the number 1921! ('Tomorrow,' 1952).

The 'Napoleon Eyed' Child

Countess de Boigne, in her interesting 'Memoires', relates that she once saw a little girl, *Josephine Louis,* born in 1824, with the words *"Napoleon Empereur"* in little letters on the iris around the pupils of her eyes. The mother told the Countess how, while she was pregnant, she had lost and recovered a twenty-*sols* (shillings) coin. She was very fond of this coin because it was a parting gift from a beloved brother who had gone into the army; the coin was the model for the letters imprinted in the child's eyes.

An anecdote titled 'THE 'NAPOLEON' CHILD' appeared in the *Mirror*, and is reproduced below:

"On Friday the 8th inst. [1828], we paid a visit to the Bazaar in Oxford Street, to witness this extraordinary sport of Nature, about which the French and English newspapers have lately been so communicative.

The child is an engaging little girl, about three years old. The colour of her eyes is pale blue, and on the iris, or circle round their pupils, the inscriptions on

Left eye	Right eye
NAPOLEON	EMPEREUR
EMPEREUR	NAPOLEO

may be traced in the above sized letters[5], although all the letters are not equally visible, the commencement "NAP" and "EMP" being the most distinct. The colour of the letters is almost white, and at first sight of the child they appear like rays, which make the eyes

---

5   Size of the texts here is not an exact reproduction of the original.

appear vivacious and sparkling. The accuracy of the inscriptions is much assisted by the stillness of the eye, on its being directed upwards, as to an object on the ceiling of the room & c; and with this aid the several letters may be traced with the naked eye.

This effect is accounted for by the child's mother earnestly looking at a franc-piece of Napoleon's, which was given to her by her brother previous to a long absence; and this operating during her pregnancy, has produced the appearance in question. It was visible at the child's birth, and has increased with her growth. She has been seen by Sir Astley Cooper and other leading members of the profession, and probably before our Number is published, she will have been shown to the King." (*Reuben Percy*, 1828).

Alleged Father's Name Appears in Infant's Eyes

A similar instance was reported about 1825 by Dr. Munro of Edinburg who frequently exhibited a child in whose eyes many persons imagined they could read the name and age of his father.

"A young woman in Galloway [Scotland] having proved with a child, laid the same to a respectable man of the name John Woods, and persisted in his denial saying that he would never acknowledge the child unless his name was written at full length on its face; and he accordingly gave his solemn oath before the court to that effect. This made so much impression on the mind of the young woman, who was present, that his name and person remained constantly in her mind's eye, and when the child was born, the name of the father appeared in legible letters in the child's eye, the name of "JOHN WOODS", on the right eye, and 'BORN 1817" on the left eye. When John Woods, the alleged father, came to know this circumstance, he instantly absconded and has not since been heard of. This wonderful child has now arrived in this city [Edinburgh] and has been inspected by the Professors and other learned Faculties of this city, and pronounced to be a most wonderful phenomenon of nature, and an astonishing dispensation of Providence in pointing out the truth against the wicked and perjured ways of men."
(*T.E.C. Jr. M.D* 1976)

The 'Elohim Eyed Boy'

There are many other curious examples which altogether tend to prove the maternal impressions do sometimes affect the gestating babies.

In April 1701, John Evelyn, the famous English diarist, recorded the following phenomenon which he had observed at a fair in London:

"A Dutch boy of about eight or nine years old was carried about by his parents to show, who had about the iris of one eye, the letters of *DEUS MEUS*, and of the other *ELOHIM* in the Hebrew character. How this was done by artifice none could imagine; the parents affirming that he was so born. It did not prejudice his sight, and he seemed to be a lively playing boy. Everybody went to see him; physicians and philosophers examined it with great accuracy, some considered it as artificial, others as almost supernatural."
(*Evelyn*, 1906).

Deus Meus translates into "My God" and *Elohim* is the Hebrew name for God.

Ace of Spades in the Eye

Here is a curious case. A pregnant woman was engaged in a card party, and only wanted the ace of spades to win all that was staked and, as it happened, in the change of cards, the so such an effect upon her imagination that the child she was expecting at the time, when born, had the ace of spades depicted in the eye, and without injury to the organ of sight. (*Johann Caspar Lavater*, 1804).

Verses from the Quran on an Infant's Body

In 2009, in Dagestan, a small Russian village, text in Arabic from religious book started appearing on a nine-month-old child Ali Yakubov's back, arms, legs and stomach. Ali's parents were left stunned when the word *'Allah'* appeared on Ali Yakubov's chin soon after his birth. Since then, scores of writings in the Arabic script have appeared almost all over his body. Doctors say the markings are a medical mystery, but deny the possibilities of someone writing

Thought-Forms and Hallucinations

on the child's skin. The Telegraph reported pinkish in color and several centimeters high, the Quranic verse *"Be grateful to Allah"* was printed on the infant's right leg in clearly legible Arabic script.

There is an enormous body of evidence for this kind of occurrence of unusual images or letters in the eye, skin and other parts of the body.

Mike Foster of *Weekly World News* (21, November 2000) reports of an infant born with the spitting image of Jesus in its chest. Shawn Gelfand, son of Karen Gelfond, was born with a birthmark that looked uncannily like the face of Jesus Christ. The doctors who have examined the child have confirmed that the bizarre marking is indeed a genuine skin anomaly, not a tattoo or anything else fabricated by human hands.

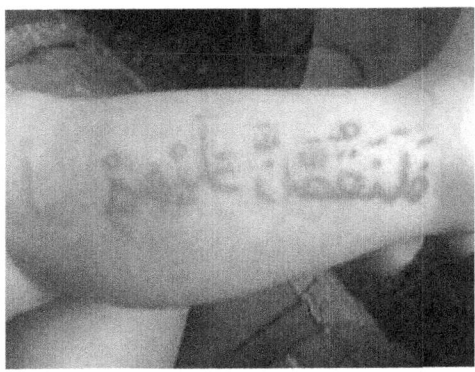

Figure 28 Birthmarks in form of Arabic scripts have been appearing on the baby's body since his birth.
Courtesy: AhlulBayt News Agency (www.abna.ir)

Similarly, in an article in the *International Journal of Parapsychology*, Professor Chari refers to the case of a female infant who was born with the curious birthmarks of the 'bangles' and 'necklaces' of the Hindu goddess *Kali*.

'*The Recreative Magazine*,' Volume 1, reprinted by Monroe and Francis in 1822, carried the following curious cases:

At a place called Buch, near Versailles, lives a woman, the iris of whose eyes is divided into twelve sections, forming an exact dial, the figures resembling those found on the small watches that are included in rings worn on the finger. She was born with this peculiarity, and yet has the perfect use of her sight. ('The Eyes-Long Sight-Squinting', 1821).

Again, on 4th January 1725, there was born at Blois a child named Marthurin Voiret. He had in each eye, a dial-plate of a watch, accurately painted; the hours were easily distinguished in Roman characters. His mother declared that while pregnant of this child, she had an ardent desire to see a watch. ('The Eyes-Long Sight-Squinting', 1821)

There was also a man, who had a pair of the most pious peepers ever known: for in his eyes were these words distinct and legible, *sit nomen Domine benedictum* (a Latin phrase which means, 'Blessed in the name of the Lord'). Delafand is our authority for this account of one who not only had the fear of God before his eyes, but in his eyes!

The above cases, were they not clearly explainable on scientific grounds would almost appear to be incredible; but they are not even one-half so difficult to believe as that alleged marvelous discovery by Dr. Conyers who, it is said, on anatomizing a gentleman who died for love, found an impression of the lady's face upon his heart! (Photographic Effects of Lightning)

Dr. S. P. Crawford of Greenville, Tennessee, reports in the *Nashville Journal of Medicine,* the following sad case: A lady, in the last stage of pregnancy, was burned by the explosion of a kerosene-oil can. She lived twelve hours after the accident. The face, legs, arms, and abdomen were badly burned. The movements of the child were felt three or four hours after the accident. A short time before her death, she gave birth to the child at full maturity, but still-born. It bore the mark of the fire corresponding to that of the mother. Its legs, arms, and abdomen were completely blistered, having all the appearance of a recent burn.

Here is another fascinating incident which Bill Jay, in his '*Animal Knickknacks – odd items from the 19th century photographic press,* recounts.

"It seems that Mr. J. J. Davis of Findlay, Ohio, went out to feed his cow last year. When he left the house, he had a photograph in his pocket, but when he returned he discovered that it had disappeared. He made a long and anxious search for it, but could not find it. Recently the cow gave birth to a calf, and on the left side of the calf's neck was a hairless spot about six inches square. In the centre of the spot was a capital likeness of Mr. Davis, and that gentleman is of opinion that he must have dropped the photograph into the food that he gave the cow on the occasion above mentioned, and she had eaten it. In some way, known only to the mysterious laws of nature, the photograph made an impression on the unborn calf. A number of Mr. J. J. Davis's friends have seen the calf in question, and they all corroborate his story."

Paternal Effects Transmitted to Foetus through Mother

D. Amaury Talbot, in his book, *'Woman's Mysteries of a Primitive People: the Ibibios of Southern Nigeria,'* narrates the following case:

A man named Osim Essiet married a wife, and a little while before the birth of their first child he was attacked by an enemy and left lying in the bush with his head severed from his body. When he did not return, friends set out to look for him. After some time they found the corpse, bore it home and laid it upon a native bed. When the young wife saw this horrible sight, she cried out and flung herself down by the side of the body, calling upon the name of her husband and entreating him not to leave her.

Some weeks afterwards the child was born. Round his neck was the mark as of a line at the place where his father's head has been severed, and indeed, his neck is still shorter than that of most people. The town-folk noticed this peculiarity and felt sure, because of it, that the boy was really Osim Essiet himself come back to life again because he loved his wife very dearly and in answer to her entreaties that she might not be left alone. They therefore gave him, in his new incarnation, the same name as he had borne before. (Talbot 1968)

The next case is taken form an article entitled *'Maternal Impressions and their Influence upon the Foetus in Utero'* by Claudius

Henry Maston, MD of Mobile, Ala, in the *Medical News*, vol.lxxii, January 1898 (New York). It is best reproduced in his own words.

"…..[I here] present a brief history of a case of very great interest, and since it has occurred under my own immediate observation, I can vouch for its truth.

"William Y., aged twenty-two years, was shot on the morning of September 24th 1894. The ball, a 38-calibre, was fired from a Winchester rifle, and entered the rear of the chest on the left side, just below and to the outer side of the angle on the scapula; at this point it penetrated the chest between the seventh and eighth ribs, and passing through the entire chest, emerged from the inter-costal space between the fourth and fifth ribs, two and a quarter inches from the left nipple on the inner side. The exact measurement of the man's chest shows that the distance from the midsternal line in a transverse direction to the centre of the left nipple is four and quarter inches; a line drawn from the wound of entrance to that of exit passes directly through the location of the right ventricle; and it is upon this anatomic fact that I diagnosed the case to be one of direct heart penetration.

I shall not consume time with detail of the case, which has been the subject of a paper upon "Gunshot wounds of the Heart" which was read before the *American Surgical Association* at its New York meeting in 1895, and published in vol.xiii of its *Transactions*. At the time when this man was shot, his wife was nearby, and reached him very soon afterwards. In attempting to render what assistance was in her power, her hands were stained with blood, and she also had her face covered with blood. When I saw the patient late that afternoon, I found her very much agitated, and seemingly as much exercised on account of her condition as she was for her husband's safety. She then informed me that she was pregnant, and felt certain that her child would be born with a bloody face. She was an ignorant country woman, and filled with superstitious notions. I calmed her fears as much as I possibly could, and dismissed the subject from my mind. After a long and tedious convalescence her husband was able to be taken home in the country, and I thought no more of the case beyond the remarkable recovery from a severe wound.

During the succeeding spring, 1895, the man and his wife came to the city and called at my office, bringing with them a new-born infant. She said to me – "Doctor, my baby has not got a bloody face, but it has got the holes where the ball went through Bill's breast." Upon examination of the child I did not find 'the holes' which she said were there, but in place of them I discovered bright red marks, clearly shown upon the chest of the child; they were not simply discoloured spots, but elevated naevi, and bright carmine-coloured spots easily to be seen at a distance of a hundred feet. There they were on the left side of the chest, and although not in the exact anatomic location of the wound on the father's chest, still so near the spot that they are easily recognized as resulting therefrom. The mother had seen the wounds in her husband's chest, and had told me during his illness that they made her sick every time she looked at them.

Interested now in the condition of the case, I made accurate inquiries as to her pregnancy and the date of her delivery. She informed me that her pregnancy had passed as usual in former ones, with the exception that she had been very nervous, and that the motions of the child had been more violent, and were brought on by any noise or excitement. Her labour took place on May 10th, 1895; was about as previous deliveries. Assuming the term of gestation to be 280 days, and this child being born on May 10th, 1895, it is fair to calculate that her conception took place about August 3rd 1894, and from that date to September 24th the date on which the father was shot, gives us 52 days. The question is – was the maternal excitement at the sight of the wound in her husband's chest the cause of the marks upon the child with which she was then pregnant?"

Dr. Maston leaves the question to the readers to answer.

The British Medical Journal, of 4th May 1912, published a statement made by Dr. T.H.Harris (Mildenhall) as follows:

"About forty years ago I attended at Holywell Row, Mildenhall, a single woman in her confinement, and the child when born had an amputated arm above the elbow, and also the appearance of the insertion of five stitches. The scar simulated a circular amputation, and the stump appeared somewhat conical. Parentage was not denied by a retired soldier, who had an amputation done on the same arm (the left) at the same site and in the same manner a short time previously. I examined the soldier's stump and can vouch for its exact resemblance to the baby's." (Heape 1913)

Here is another case of the same kind.

An Officer was severely wounded in battle, he had eleven wounds; two were parallel sword-cuts, across the back of his neck, high up, dividing all structures down to the *ligamentum nuchae* which was notched. These wounds resulted in two broad, indented scars. He also had a sword-cut which split his nose longitudinally from the forehead. The other eight wounds were hidden by his clothing.

He was engaged to be married, and was an invalid at home, which his fiancée first saw him, and she was greatly shocked at the scars on his neck and face. He married shortly afterwards and the first child was born with two red lines across the back of its neck exactly corresponding to the position of the scars on its father's neck, and a red line down the nose following even the same irregular course of the scar on its father's nose. The marks were broad and livid at birth but gradually faded and disappeared altogether in a few months.

Heape reported that the truth of this story was vouched for by the medical man who attended the wounded officer and who saw the marks on the child (Heape 1913).

The Deposit Courier (New York) is responsible for the following story.

"In the vicinity of Spoon river, in Illinois, is a child that was born and has lived five years without a head. Mrs.___, the mother, is a widow of a soldier, formerly living in Marshall County, who enlisted in the 65th Scotch regiment and was killed at the battle of Devington, Mo. She was standing beside her husband during the engagement, when a canon ball carried his head completely away, his body falling into the arms and covering her with blood. The shock affected her greatly. When her child was born there was not a semblance of a head about it. The limbs are perfectly developed, the arms long, and the shoulders, where the head and neck should be, smoothly rounded off."

Dr. R. Lee Fearn related the following very remarkable particulars of a case where the impressions received by a mother during pregnancy, affected her child in utero.

A gentleman, while shooting, shot through the metacarpal bone of his index finger. The wound was a bad one, and piece after piece of the bone came away. A few months after the accident here mentioned, and in due season, his wife bore him a child perfectly formed in all respects. When about four months advanced in her second pregnancy, an operation was deemed necessary to remove the last remaining portion of the bone in her husband's finger. She witnessed the operation and was much shocked and alarmed at the sight. When her child was born, it was found to be deficient in this very bone, though in all other particulars it was a well-formed child. The doctor thought this was by no means the result of chance, but a very conclusive instance of cause and effect. (Samuel Parkman 1853)

Impact of Dreams

Professor Dalton of New York states that the wife of the janitor of the College of Physicians and Surgeons of that city, during her pregnancy, dreamed that she saw a man who had lost a part of the ear. The dream made a great impression upon her mind, and she mentioned it to her husband. When her child was born, a portion of one ear was deficient, and the organ was exactly like the defective ear she had seen in her dream. When Professor Dalton was lecturing upon the development of the foetus as affected by the mind of the mother, the janitor called his attention to the foregoing instance. The ear looks exactly as if a portion had been cut off with a sharp knife. (Hammond, 1868)

Impact of Paintings

The effect of the attentive contemplation of pictures, statues etc by pregnant woman is worthy of notice. A woman gave birth to a child covered with hair and having the claws of a bear, from her constantly beholding the images and pictures of bears hung up everywhere in the dwelling of the Ursini family, to which she belonged.

A woman contemplating too earnestly as it appears a picture of St.Pius has afterwards a child bearing a striking resemblance to an old man. The tyrant Dionysius was aware of the effect of pictures; for he hung a beautiful picture in his wife's chamber, in order to improve his children's looks. (Todd, 1839)

A man had the misfortune to have two or three children born to him, in succession, with great bodily deformities, such as wanting an arm or leg, or even both. This was a great calamity, and the poor man, of course, lamented it. He was advised to consult the Prophet and he did so. The unfortunate parent, in this instance, it was known, had the walls of his bedroom studded over with a great many hideous pictures, representing human beings of very distorted appearances.

The response of the Prophet of Bethelnie, when consulted was short and gruff: "Take down your pictures", were his words. It was done – the pictures were removed, and several children were afterwards born of the same couple, sound in every joint and member of the body.

In the recent past, Dr. Ian Stevenson studied the reports of approximately 300 cases of maternal impressions published in medical journals, books and other publications of the United States, Great Britain, France, Germany, Italy, Holland, and Belgium. From these, he selected 50 cases, in which the correspondence between the stimuli to the pregnant women and the baby's defect had close resemblance, for a detailed analysis. As an example, he cited the case of a woman whose brother had to have his penis amputated for removal of a cancer. While she was pregnant, her curiosity impelled her to have a look at the site of her brother's amputation; she afterward gave birth to a male baby without a penis (Stevenson, Birthmarks and Birth Defects Corresponding to wounds on Deceased Persons, 1993).

We have seen sufficient number cases to believe that the mother's intensive thinking during pregnancy has a corresponding impact on her child. As someone put it, it is a matter of the force of the imagination being conjoined with the conformational power, the softness of the embryo–ready like soft wax to receive any form. The brain of the mother and that of the baby in one body are quantum units that can interact non-locally. Thus whatever occupies the mind of the mother with a certain degree of intensity, at particular times during the period of gestation, will be sure to make an impression upon the physical and mental sub-system of the child. This is exactly what the quantum holographic model teaches.

According to this model, the physical constitution of all organisms is guided by a subtle field body. As a current or an external magnet affects a magnetic field, the mental images (formed out the mother's perception, thinking, or imagination) affect the subtle body (this more susceptible body can be called a 'sub-system') of the child she bears. As we have seen in the clinical cases relating to maternal impressions, the mental effect of the mother on the child is so prevalent and apparent that it cannot be a mere coincidence; it must be seen as indicating a 'latent connection' between the mother's thinking and transmission of such thoughts to her child.

But to move further in this direction, it is necessary to establish that human perception, thinking or imagination, by itself, is able to create a force-field, that correspond to in shape and size (size may sometimes vary) to the object perceived, thought of, or imagined as the case may be, and which is capable of affecting the subtle body of the child (sub-system).

We have already discussed this in a previous chapter entitled *"Thought Photography,"* where it is unequivocally established that images of objects upon which the subject thinks deeply for some time get imprinted on photographic plates without any intervening material kind.

Scientific men are slow to accept the truth of any phenomena which seem to be outside the laws of mainstream science. Many of the things we learn and accept as fact regarding maternal impressions and telegony cannot be proved by experimentation in a laboratory immediately, but the information available is so overwhelming that we are compelled to accept it because there is no other explanation which suffices. As technology advances, this may be possible but at present we are limited to mere observance of these mind-related phenomena.

8

MENTAL STIGMATA AND BODILY IMPRINTS

An object making a violent impression on the mother's mind, its image is instantly projected into the astral light, or the universal ether, which Jevons and Babbage, as well as the authors of the Unseen Universe, tell us is the repository of the spiritual images of all forms and even human thoughts

– H.P.Blavatsky

Strange as are the foregoing cases of maternal impressions, those of mental imprint of images and letters on the skin, eclipse them. There are various instances on record in which individuals have been said to have words (generally a name) pictorially marked upon the iris or on the surface of the skin. These manifestations usually witnessed on a person's skin are scientifically known as 'stigmata' or dermographism. Their importance for the present discussion lies mainly in their demonstration of the body's malleability and susceptibility to imprint of images on skin, and so as to make a basic understanding and acceptance of holographic nature of body and mind.

These phenomena attest the holographic nature of human body and of course, the entire universe. As per the holographic brain theory, the brain projects an image outside of itself. Russian psychologists Dr. Alexander P.Dubrov and Dr. Veniamin N.Pushkin have written extensively on the idea. To use their own words, "Records of ejection of psychophysical structures outside the brain would provide direct evidence of brain holograms."

In the following cases, the human mind, in some extreme conditions, create hologram-like field patterns of the thought-forms, which in turn get impressed on the body. These cases will demonstrate in clear terms that the field patterns created by the mind can accordingly modify the body-field and re-orient the molecules. Readers may, for easy understanding, compare the magnetic field created by a bar magnet which orients the iron-fillings placed near the magnetic field.

Some of the curious cases where the thought-forms or mental images got imprinted on the body of the persons are discussed here.

Dr. Charles Baudouin of the Jean Jacques Roussequ Institute, Geneva, in his *'Suggestion and Auto-Suggestion'* (English translation, 1920), speaks of dermographism as a process of an image existing in the subject's mind that becomes outlined on the skin. He proceeds to cite from Dr.Charles Richet of Paris a well-known instance of dermographism.

A child, playing about the room idly loosens the catch which fastens a chimney draw-plate, and narrowly escapes being guillotined by the quick fall of the heavy steel-edged mechanism. The mother receives such a shock on seeing the danger that a flushing erythematous circle forms round her neck – the corresponding part was threatened in the case of the child and this remains swollen for several hours. Here we have a striking instance of the power of emotion. There is an enormous body of evidence for this kind of occurrence of unusual images or letters in the eye, skin and other parts of the body.

In the *'Medical and Surgical Journal,'* May, 1835, a case is recorded, as having happened in France, in the practice of M Diez, a French surgeon.

"A lady, who is designated as Madame G__, aged 24 years, whose lips and mouth became suddenly enormously swollen, from having seen a child of a few years old pass the sharp blade of a knife between its lips without even cutting itself, which intumescence it required the usual application to subdue, and which is represented to have had an appearance similar to that produced by the sting of a wasp, or some other poisonous insect, which there was no possibility of having occurred. This case is curious, as the organ affected was the same as the one for the apprehension for which, in the child, the nervous horror was experienced. How nature acted in this case it is, of course, impossible to suppose."

Likewise, Carter quotes a case in which a lady saw three fingers cut from the hand of a child, in an accident. She was so affected that her hand began to pain her, and swelling resulted. The three fingers of her hand, corresponding to those cut from the hand of the child, became badly inflamed; an incision becoming necessary to evacuate the pus that had formed.

Cross Mark on a Girl's Arm

The New York Times, Dublin edition dated November 14, 1910 carried an extraordinary story on what is described as mysterious markings appearing upon the arm of a child boarding in the Kiltimargh Convent.

"According to the report in the news, the girl is thirteen, and has been a boarder at the Convent for three or four years. About three weeks ago, she was heard screaming loudly in her sleep. When interrogated she said she had had a fearful dream, in which she had seen the crucifixion. On the following morning she found her arm and wrist sore, and it was seen that her forearm was marked with a cross as were the letters "I.H.S."Some days later there appeared below the letters something that resembled a crown of thorns, and a little later above the cross the letters in scroll "I.N.R.I". Other markings are said to have appeared at a later period, extending from the wrist to the forearm. It is reported that the markings were examined by several people in the town."

A similar instance was reported in the London-based *Sunday News* (Aug. 3, 1926). Dorothy Parrot, 4-year-old child of R. S. Parrot, of Winget Mill, Georgia, was marked by a red spot on her body. Out of this spot formed three letters, *R. I. C.* Doctors could not explain this. (Fort, Wild Talents, 2004)

Another story appeared in *London Daily Express*, Nov. 17, 1913 related to the phenomena of a girl, aged 12, of the village of Bussus-Bus-Suel, near Abbeville, France. If asked questions, answers appeared in bold red letters on her arms, legs and shoulders. Also upon her body appeared pictures, such as of a ladder, a dog, a horse. (Fort, Wild Talents, 2004)

Therese Neumann's Stigmatization

Therese Neumann's stigmatization started on March 4, 1926, first with a wound near her heart. In the following Friday-sufferings during Lent 1926, not only the range of her vision enlarged, but with each suffering more bleeding Stigmata appeared. Pastor Joseph Naber from Konnersreuth reported about Therese's condition on Good Friday 1926:

"When I together with another Priest visited her on Good Friday after lunch, we found her lying in great torture, the eyes clogged with blood, two streamlets of blood running down her cheeks, pale like a dying person. Until 3 o'clock, the Hour of Death of the Saviour, she struggled in terrible agony of death....During this death agony on Good Friday, she had viewed all the sufferings of the Saviour, beginning on the Mount of Olives down to Calvary, and had shared it in a very intense way, even his abandonment on the Cross. At that time, she had felt severe pain on the upper side of her hands and feet. Now both hands and feet show kind of round, open wounds, out of them runs pure blood. Already several weeks before Easter, suddenly a longish wound broke open in the area of her heart. At times, a lot of pure blood came out of this wound. The Medical Doctor had scrutinized all these wounds." (Gerlich, p. 114, *Waldsassener Grenzzeitung*, 21.04.1926)

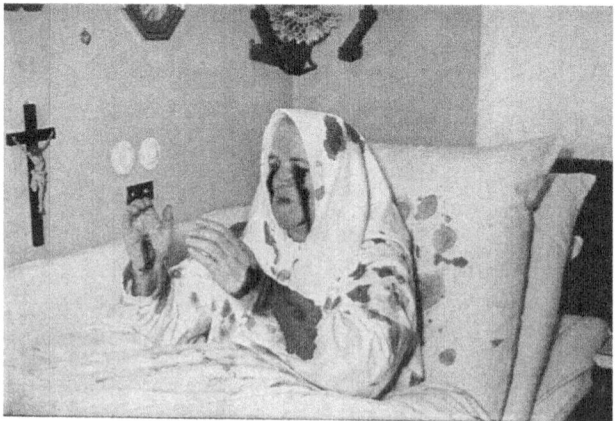

Figure 29 Therese Neumann with stigmata
© Marie Therese Neumann

Girl with Stigmatic Biting

"*Girl with spirit of mischief*" published in the *London Evening Standard* (October 1, 1926) reported that in September, 1926, a Rumanian girl, Eleanore Zugun, was taken to London for observation by the National Laboratory for Psychical Research. Countess Wassilko-Serecki, who had taken the girl to London, said, in an interview (London *Evening Standard*, Oct. 1, 1926), that she had seen the word *Dracu* form upon the girl's arm. This word is the Rumanian word for the Devil.

As the story goes, when she was 11 years old, Eleanore Zugun visited her grandmother's house at Buhai, a few miles away from her village Talpa. On the way she found some money by the side of the road, and when she arrived at Buhai, she spent it on sweets and ate them all. Zugun's 105-year-old grandmother, who had the reputation of being a witch, overheard Eleanore and her cousin arguing about the sweets and warned her that the devil (Dracu in Rumanian) had left the money to tempt her, and from then on she would never be free of him. The next day stigmatic biting and scratches started appearing on her body.

Reproduction of Target Images on Skin

Olga Kahl, a Russian-born clairvoyant living in Paris during the 1920s, provided some of the most impressive evidence of the representation of mental images in one person by bodily changes in another. On one occasion she misplaced a string of pearls; the loss pre-occupied her, and while the pearls were missing, she developed round areas of redness on the skin of her arms which suggested the form of the missing pearls. On another occasion, when living in Istanbul, she watched a group of dervishes, one of whom pushed a skewer through his cheek; the next day she developed an abscess of the cheek at the corresponding site where the dervish had pushed the skewer through.

Olga Kahl's experimental routine provided for a visitor or experimenter to write (hidden from her) a name or perhaps a design on a small piece of paper. The visitor rolled the piece of paper into a ball, which he kept in his hand without showing it to Olga Kahl. After a short interval, the name or design would appear on the skin of Olga Kahl's arm (sometimes on her upper chest). The letters would stand out in red, evidently from extremely localized changes in the superficial blood vessels. Sometimes a letter of a name was omitted, but then a space would be left for it, as if at some level Olga Kahl was aware of the entire word. Olga Kahl sometimes facilitated the process of her kind of dermographism by rubbing the part of her body where the letters were to appear; but such rubbing covered the entire area affected, and no one ever observed Olga Kahl in any endeavour to scratch the words on her skin.

Ian Stevenson, former head of the Department of Psychiatry at the University of Virginia, and a pioneer in reincarnation research, asserted that the mental image in the mind of the experimenter (who wrote the word or design on a piece of paper) had not directly influenced Olga Kahl's skin, and perhaps her mind obtained a copy, so to speak, of the experimenter's mental image and reproduced that on her skin. For example, when the target was the name 'Rene', the letter "N" came out resembling an "H" as in the alphabet of Olga's native Russian. (*Stevenson*, 1997)

Another case is that of a little girl upon whose skin appeared the answer to the sum she was trying to do!

As early as the 13th century, Jacobus de Voragine assigned of the causes of these phenomena to mind and body interactions, thus taking them out of the category of the supernatural. And Joseph Ennemoser (1787-1854), a South Tyrolean physician said, in reference to all such cases, "these appearances are not artificially produced deceptions, nor yet are they to be explained by the mere physical circumstances of the body. To spirits, or to any immediate divine operation, we will hardly ascribe them. Far from being miraculous, it is in every case a purely physiological process, grounded in a psychic cause."

Professor H. Bernheim, in his famous work '*Suggestive Therapeutics*' states that he has been able to produce a blister on the back of a patient by applying a postage-stamp and suggesting to the patient that it was a fly-plaster. On this subject, Bernheim makes the following observation: "Finally, hemorrhages and bloody stigmata may be induced in certain subjects by means of suggestion."

MM. Bourru and Burot of Rochefort have experimented on the subject with a young marine, a case of hysteron-epilepsy. Dr. M. Bourru put a subject into the somnambulistic condition and gave him the following suggestion: "At four o'clock this afternoon, after the hypnosis, you will come into my office, sit down in the armchair, cross your arms upon your breast, and your nose will begin to bleed." At the hour appointed the young man did as directed. Several drops of blood came from the left nostril.

On another occasion, the same investigator traced the patient's name on both his forearms with the dull point of an instrument. Then, when the patient was in the somnambulistic condition, he said, "At four o'clock this afternoon, you will go to sleep, and your arms will bleed along the lines which I have traced, and your name will appear written on your arms in letters of blood." He was watched at four o'clock and seen to fall asleep. On the left-arm the letters stood out in bright relief and in several places there were drops of blood. The letters were still visible three months afterwards, although they had gradually grown faint. (*Hudson*, 1892).

These instances *per se* make it clear that the human body is susceptible to the imprint of photograph-like images on it. If one understands and believes in this phenomenon of nature, then the intriguing question would arise – how are the exact images transferred to the skin or body? How does the human skin become susceptible to such impressions? These questions are so complicated that they cannot be answered in a single word or line. This phenomenon of pictorial impressions is related to various factors under various circumstances; but the underlying science should be the same for all cases.

Dr. Ian Stevenson's investigations into the cases of stigmata revealed that they are manifestations of emotional contents recorded in the subconscious mind of the subjects. He investigated a few cases where the chest wounds similar to those experienced by Jesus Christ during the crucifixion appeared. Some of them had the chest wound on the left side and some had it on the right. According to Stevenson, the Bible does not say into which side of Jesus a Roman solider thrust his spear; and because there was only one appear thrust recorded, right or left may be correct, but both cannot be. Such variations strongly suggest that stigmata were bodily changes produced by the mental images of the stigmatist. Some of the stigmata, according to Stevenson, bore a close relationship to the wounds on the representation – for example, a statuette of Jesus before which the stigmatist was accustomed to worship. An early 19th century stigmatist had on her chest a Y-shaped lesion that matched an unusual Y-shaped crucifix in the church where she used to worship. (Stevenson, Where Reincarnation and Biology Intersect, 1997)

More than a century ago, Prof.Barrett succinctly explained the causes of stigmata in the following words:

"It is not so well known, but it is nevertheless a fact, that utterly startling physiological changes can be produced in a hypnotized subject merely by conscious or unconscious mental suggestion. Thus a red scar or a painful burn, or even a figure of definite shape, such as a cross or an initial, can be caused to appear on the body of an entranced subject solely by suggesting the idea. By creating some local disturbance of the blood-vessels in the skin, the unconscious self has done what it would be impossible for the conscious self to perform. And so in the well-attested cases of stigmata where a close resemblance to the wounds on the body of the crucified Saviour appear on the body of the ecstatic. This is a case of unconscious self-suggestion, arising from the intent and adoring gaze of the ecstatic upon the bleeding figure on the crucifix. With the abeyance of the conscious self, the hidden powers emerge, whilst the trance and mimicry of the wounds are strictly parallel to the experimental cases previously referred to. May not some of the well-known cases of mimicry in animal life originate, like the stigmata, in a reflect action, as physiologists would say, below the level of consciousness, created by a predominant impression analogous to those producing the stigmata? That is to say, to reflex actions excited by an unconscious suggestion derived from the environment; in other words, the dynamic, externalizing power of thought, if the action of that intellectuation or ideation – these are special acts of thought, for the direction of functional activity of our subliminal life has also the attributes of thought though we may be unconscious of its thinking." (Atkinson, 1909)

Dr. Ian Stevenson studied these kinds of mental stigmata extensively. He even attempted to arrive at a formula that might represent the principal factors of such phenomenon.

$CA + DI + PF = CS$

CA – Concentrated Attention or Absorbtion

DI – Duration of the Imagery

PF – Physiological Factor or Factors

CS – Resultant changes in the skin

Arthur E.Powell, in his *'The Mental Body,'* wrote that the emotional and mental life is having profound effects upon the physical body. For, while it is true that the mental and physical bodies are obviously, in the very nature of things, more amenable to the power of thought than is the physical body, yet the matter of even the physical body may be moulded by the power of emotion and thought." As the most striking proof of influence of the mind over body, Powell cites the cases of stigmata.

Thus, there is strong evidence that some kind of psycho-somatic process is involved and this has led to experimental attempts to produce stigmata by hypnotic suggestion. In the year 1933, Dr. Alfred Lechler recreated the full range of stigmatic markings on Elisabeth K, a 29-year-old German peasant girl, after she had seen a film of Christ's crucifixion. After several sessions, the girl produced the markings of a crown of thorns on her forehead, an inflamed shoulder condition related to her imaginary carrying of the Cross, and bloody tears similar to those shed by the celebrated Theresa Neumann.

Ian Wilson comments, "A really reveting feature is the extraordinary precision of the mechanism's conformity to the visualization that triggered it. Stigmata have been precisely positioned to conform with the wounds of a stigmatic's favourite crucifix. Or a wound may have taken on an exact shape such as a Cross. Most dramatic of all, the mechanism seems able to mould the flesh into a feature resembling the head and bent-over point of an iron nail. It is as if something within the body has re-programmed it into a new form." (Wilson, 1989)

9
HOLOGRAPHIC MIND

"My mind works just like an internet search engine that has been set to access only images; the more pictures I have stored in the internet inside my brain the more templates I have of how to act in a new situation... I think in pictures. Words are like a second language to me. I translate both spoken and written words into full-color movies, complete with sound, which run like a VCR tape in my head. When somebody speaks to me, his words are instantly translated into pictures..."

-Temple Grandin, famous autistic writer in her book
"Thinking in Pictures"

We have thus far seen various mental phenomena – all suggestive of the limitations of classical theories to explain brain process. Today, most scientists believe that mind generates from dynamic molecular interactions, processes regulated by physio-chemicals and by gene's expressions in brain cells. During our discussions on the thought photography, we are provided with ample evidence to show that human mind, when it focuses on a photographic film, can record the impression of the thought on the film. There can be no inherent absurdity in the idea as many might suspect. We have seen how the intensive thoughts of some persons take form. Recent experiments in quantum physics have proved that the mere act of observation can affect changes in the real object, affected by the act of being observed. The classical thought that the brain secretes thought just as the liver secretes bile is a blunder. It is important therefore to realize the basic fact that the mind and brain, though closely connected, are not identical. Brain is an organ. Mind is a process, not a physical entity that can be seen and touched. It is processing of information; a function or a phenomenon.

In the recent years, a number of experimental as well theoretical evidences have been developed to support the holographic model of the real world actions. In a study reported in the February 26 issue of *Nature* (Vol. 391, pp. 871-874), researchers at the Weizmann Institute of Science have conducted a highly controlled experiment demonstrating how a beam of electrons is affected by the act of being observed. The experiment revealed that the greater the amount of 'watching,' the greater the observer's influence on what actually takes place.

Quantum physicist Henry Stapp (1997) has argued persuasively that classical physics cannot accommodate the phenomenon of consciousness, because it deals with independent entities that are localized in space-time. In classical physics, one can only conceive of disjointed physical events in various places in the brain, with no experiential unity. Our conscious experience demands a quantum theory of the mind, which allows for instantaneous interaction between the various elements of the brain. The holographic principle is the information theory of such quantum fields.

Holographic Nature of Brain, Mind and Consciousness

This holographic concept of a holistic reality was first given to the world by Eastern philosophy. *Vedavyasa* (13th century BC), the legendary Indian sage who is credited with compiling the great epic Mahabharatha, reflects this wisdom in one of his *shlokas* which reads (in *Sanskrit*) as follows:

Om Poornamadah Poornamidam Poornaad Poornamudachyate; Poornamaadaaya Poornamevaavashiyate which translates into "that (Brahman) is whole. This (creation) is also whole. From that whole (that is Brahman), this whole (creation) has come out. But even though this whole has come out of that whole yet that whole remains whole only." This unique property of fragments having the entire information-content of the whole, and the whole, even after losing its part, retains the whole information, belongs exclusively to holograms. Is it not an astonishing thing that a sage, more than 3000 years ago, unequivocally summoned up the properties of a hologram in just two lines?

Stephen E. Robbins, in his paper, *'Bergson, Perception and Gibson,'* quite rightly points out that French Philosopher Henri Bergon's theory of mental perception was clearly a 'holographic theory' presented to the world half-a-century before Gabor's discovery of holographic principles in the year 1947. Bergon's vision of memory in his book *'Matter and Memory'* (1896) was most profound and well ahead of his time, so much so, in fact that even after three centuries, it is not clearly precise to the most educated and most informed scientific community.

It reads, "......but is it not obvious that the photograph, if photograph there be, is already taken, already developed in the very heart of things and **at all points in space**. No metaphysics, no physics can escape this conclusion. Build up the universe with atoms: Each of them is subject to the action, variable in quantity and quality according to distance, exerted on it by all material atoms. Bring in Faraday's centers of force: The lines of force emitted in every direction from every centre bring to bear upon each the influence of the whole material world. Call up the Leibnizian monads: Each is the mirror of the universe. All philosophers agree on this point. Only if when we consider any other given place in the universe we can regard the action of all matter as passing through it without resistance and without loss, and **the photograph of the whole as translucent**: Here there is wanting behind the plate the black screen on which the image could be shown. Our "zones of indetermination" (organisms) play in some sort the part of that screen. They add nothing to what is there; they effect merely this: That the real action passes through, the virtual action remains."(emphasis supplied)

A complementary of mind-brain was suggested by Neils Bohr (1958) by analogy with his complementary theory in physics, which regards atoms and smaller micro-entities as having dual wave-particle natures. This is related to Heisenberg's uncertainty principle – as particles the entities have precise positions but not precise momentum, whereas as waves they have precise momentum but not precise position. Bohr suggested that the mind may have precise properties such as free will but not precise mechanistic-reductionist properties, whereas the brain has precise mechanist-reductionist properties but not precise free-will properties.

There are many characteristics of brain functioning that makes one believe in the holographic nature of the mind process. Before going into them, let us have an overview of important properties of a hologram.

What is a Hologram?

A common reader may wonder, what is a hologram? A detailed treatment of holography is beyond the scope of this book, but several properties of holograms are of particular interest to our subject and may prove pertinent. Holography is the science of recording the complete wave fronts of objects, intensity as well as phase, to create true three-dimensional images. To create a hologram, a coherent wave (usually laser) is split in two. The first is a beam that stays undisturbed, called the 'reference wave', which strikes the holographic plate directly. The second beam called the 'object wave' strikes the object and then bounces on to the holographic plate. The object's interference with the 'object wave' during its course of travel makes it out of phase with the 'reference wave' though both of them are of same origin initially. This difference in 'phase' is what is actually recorded as moiré patterns in the holographic plate. When this holographic plate is illuminated with the coherent source of the same frequency that created it, a three-dimensional image of the object appears in space.

Viewing a holographic virtual image is physically identical to viewing the original object. Basically, there are two varieties of holograms: one, reflective, which uses normal white light to be viewed. This is common and like a photograph. The other uses highly coherent laser light, and is often used in sci-fi Hollywood movies where ghost-like or semi-transparent figures are projected out into the room. While photography is limited to the recording of the projected image of three-dimensional objects, holography includes depth-information, i.e., a look around the object is possible. But if you try to touch it, your hand will waft right through it and you will discover nothing substantial there.

Thought-Forms and Hallucinations

There are many startling attributes of hologram. First, the image seen by looking through the hologram is complete, three-dimensional. "As the observer changes his viewing position the perspective of the picture changes, just as if the observer were viewing the original scene. Parallax effects are evident between near and far objects in the scene: if an object in the foreground lies in front of something else, the observer can move his head and look around the obstructing object, thereby seeing the previously hidden object. In short, the reconstruction has all the visual properties of the original scene and we know of no visual test one can make to distinguish the two." (Pribram, 1969)

The three-dimensionality of such images is not the only remarkable characteristic of holograms. If a hologram of a rose is cut into fragments and then illuminated by a laser, each fragment will still be found to contain the entire image of the rose. Thus, unlike normal photographs, every part of a hologram contains the information about the whole. The reason for this is that the hologram is not a static photograph, but an energy interference pattern. Within this pattern, every particle, no matter how small it may be, contains the whole.

Second, holograms have the property that "several images can be superimposed on a single plate on successive exposures, and each image can be recovered without being affected by other images. This is done by using a different spatial-frequency carrier for each picture... The grating carriers can be of different frequencies... and there is still another degree of freedom, that of angle." (Upatnieks.J, 1965)

Further, when two or more objects are present in making the hologram, any one of them can serve as a source to reconstruct the others, which appears as 'ghosts' – a simple mechanism for producing associating memory.

Another interesting property of holograms is that they preserve the 'optical properties' such as lenses. For instance, consider making a hologram of a magnifying glass placed in front of a butterfly. When viewing the holographic image of those objects, an observer will find that the portions of the butterfly seen through the holographic image of the magnifying glass will be enlarged (How Products are Made). Likewise, a holographic image of a diamond will reflect glints of light from its facets and these appear and disappear as the viewer moves his head– exactly like a real diamond (Dimensions).

Wave front reconstruction gives rise to real and virtual images of the objects displayed in three-dimension, the magnification of which are determined by the wavelengths of the original and reconstruction waves. Since the basis of holography is interference of waves and wave-front reconstruction, it works in any type of waves, like visible light, infra-red, electromagnetic; but what is required is the waves should be highly coherent like the laser waves.

Thus, another distinguished property of a hologram and which is of importance to our present subject is that holograms can be created even without visible light. Ultraviolet, x-ray, and sound waves can all be used to create them. Acoustical holography can look through solid objects to record images, much as ultrasound is used to generate images of a fetus within a woman's womb. Thus, today holograms can be constructed and reconstructed without the use of lasers.

Last but not the least, holograms – the ghostly, hovering three-dimensional images –have been demonstrated to guide atomic particles in their path. The scientists at the NEC Fundamental Research Laboratories in Tsukuba, Japan have shown that, under certain conditions, they can diffract beams of atoms as if they were rays of light. In theory, a beam of atoms passing through a holographic pattern should spread out in a prescribed pattern and settle neatly onto a surface." (R. *Lipkin*,1996).

"Holographic fields interact and form regular structural patterns. This interaction provides order from chaos. Structured fluxes of waves can affect particles of various substances. Particles move in accordance with wave fluxes, therefore, the whole system of interrelated processes becomes more ordered and complex due to the movement of waves. To sum up, holography is a wonderful phenomenon of wave interference that reconstructs the 3-dimensional image of an object to precision.

It is not necessarily that it works with optical waves; it works with any kind of coherent waves. The difference, however, is that one can view the reconstructed image with the naked eye in the case of optical waves and in other cases, one cannot perceive it without applying some subtle particles which settle on the holographic surface, making it visible. In the human body, the coherent photonic emissions carry with them the entire geometric information of the body in terms of 'phase-change'. Thus, all parts of the body know the entire structure.

Under certain conditions, when they interfere with a reference wave (relating to the frequency of object wave), the exact 3-dimensional image of the body is reconstructed in space. Since the bodily emissions are not visible to the naked eye, their holographic image also is not commonly made visible. Colors, sounds, tastes would correspond to different waveforms at the quantum level in the brain. Once a population of particles is entangled, the collective state of the population can be conceptualized as a 'hologram' that may display isomorphism with the content of conscious experiences." (Pereria, 2003)

Holographic Brain

There are various proven reasons to hold that the human brain and mind functions in a holographic way.

Memories are Disbursed Throughout the Brain

There are a variety of mental functions that are performed by the brain. Whether a specific portion of the brain performs a specific function has been a matter of considerable research and experimentation. Various studies have shown that rather than being confined to a specific location, memories are dispersed throughout the brain.

The relevance of the holographic model to explain human memory is reinforced by the experimental findings of Wilder Penfield who mapped the brain's motor cortex – the area that controls the movement of our body's muscles. He used electrodes to stimulate the temporal lobes (particularly in the area of the hippocampus) of many of his patients, which invariably evoked vivid responses like random flashbacks into a patient's past. In his book, *The Mystery of the Mind* (1975), Penfield described the patients experience as a 'flashback', where the patient actually re-lived the experience. Penfield concluded that this meant that all experiences were stored in specific locations of the brain in memory *engrams*.

In an effort to verify Penfield's experiments, Neurologist Karl Spencer Lashley (1890-1958) began searching for the elusive engrams. Lashley trained rats in maze-running abilities and then he made surgical cuts or lesioned different proportions of the cerebral cortex in the trained rats, searching for the *engram*.

Even a left-out part of a functional area, say visual area of the cortex, can perform the function associated with that area. To destroy the visual function of brain, the entire visual area of the cortex is required to be destroyed. If even a part of the area is left, the function would still be maintained. This second observation, referred to as 'equi-potentiallity' by Lashley, also supported his theory that the brain acted as an integrated whole and not in a mechanistic sense.

Here a reference can be made to a special property of hologram. Each portion of a holographic plate contains information to project the whole three dimensional picture of a given object. Thus the whole is contained in each part, and each part is an expression of the whole. Thus Lashley's theory was reminiscent of the holographic model according to which memories and mental images could be distributed across the entire representational system and a complete image, although of proportionately low resolution, could be reconstructed from a small fragment of the representational system.

Karl H Pribram's Holonomic Mind Process

We have already seen that Lashley, in a series of experiments, demonstrated that perception and memory were unimpaired even though major portions of the brain were removed in rats. These evidences suggested that memory is stored non-locally, i.e., it is distributed throughout the brain so that even when different areas of the brain are damaged or even removed, memory continues to function.

The advent of holographic technology heralded a new departure in the understanding of the relationship between brain, mind, memory and perception. Holography demonstrated that it is possible to convert objects into frequency patterns and again frequency patterns into objects. Karl Pribram, building on the early works of Lashley, Gabor and van Heerden, applied the holographic idea to brain research. According to him, brain seems to be using these same Fourier transformations to analyze frequencies and convert them into visual images.

Pribram raised the question how interference effects can be produced in the brain and he himself offered an explanation. Synaptic events consequent on the arrival of nerve impulses form wave fronts. Such arrival patterns can interact with others and with wave forms produced by the spontaneous potential changes which occur in neural tissue. Immediate cross correlations result and these can be the occasion for the generation of new spatial and temporal patterns of nerve impulses. The assumption made here is that the totality of this process can be conceived as a neural "hologram", an "image" which is perceived. (Pribram 1969).

"Pribram's insight is that there exists a certain yet unknown physical wave in the cerebral cortex, that a hologram is produced by this physical wave, and that this hologram stores memory in the brain. He called this new holographic mechanism a neural holography and anticpated that it might be the nonlocal mechanism of memory." (Jibu, 1995)

According to Pribram, in a paper, *'Four R's of remembering'* (1969) published in *'The Biology of Learning,'* the findings of Lashley that removal of as much as 80 percent of sensory input mechanism fails to impair pattern perception is especially odd since the anatomical arrangement within these systems is such that a topological point-to-point correspondence exists between peripheral sensory receptors and the cortex. On the basis of the evidence of relatively intact perception in the face of removal of as much as 80 to 90 percent of their volume, these anatomical connections cannot conceivably be assumed in the intact individual to produce ordinary isomorphic or iconic images. On the other hand, if these essentially parallel receptor-cortical connections are conceived as constituting a neural reference beam for the construction of a holographic representation, the dilemma is resolved. For holograms have the most unusual property, as already noted, that any small part can be used for reconstruction of the entire image. Any part of the hologram contains all the information necessary to construct the whole (Pribram, 1969).

Shuffle Brain Theory of Paul Pietsch

Paul Pietsch (1981-2009), being skeptic over the Pribram's holographic brain theory, set out to prove him wrong. Interestingly, after performing thousands of operations on salamanders, the results made him fully convinced of the holographic nature of the brain. He discovered that when he removed the brain of a salamander without killing it and then replaced it, the salamander resumed normal feeding behavior. Not only this. When he replaced the brain deliberately upside down or flipped the right and left hemispheres, the salamanders returned to being able to feed themselves. In over 700 operations he sliced, flipped, shuffled, subtracted and even minced the brain of his subjects and found that in all cases the salamanders could still feed normally.

By the 1970's several other researchers had expanded Pribram's theory. British physicist Pieter van Heerden (1970) proposed that our ability to recognize familiar objects is similar to recognition holography. A similar technique known as interference holography could explain our ability to perceive differences in an object that has changed. Harvard researchers Daniel Pollen and Michael Tractenberg (1972) studied individuals with eidetic (photographic) memories and proposed the idea that memory is related to an individual's ability to create holographic images in the brain.

Bohm's Implicate and Explicate Orders

Dr. David Bohm, an eminent theoretical physicist at the University of London and a protégé of Albert Einstein began to view chaos as a misnomer. He believed that "randomness" contains a hidden order, and that we perceive disorder only because of our limited understanding of the complexity of the processes involved. In 1980, Bohm published his first book on the holographic nature of the universe entitled, *'Wholeness and the Implicate Order.'* In it, he theorized that the entire cosmos is made out of a seamless holographic fabric in such a fashion that all things in the universe are no more separate from one another. He identified two orders of existence in our universe. The deeper order of reality Bohm called the 'implicate' (which means enfolded) and he named our level of existence as the 'explicit' or unfolded order. Thomas Germinario has equated the implicate order with the 'unconscious process' and the explicate order with 'conscious process.'

Bohm referred to the universe as a dynamic holomovement. To make his concepts easily understandable, he demonstrated the following experiment. He placed drops of oil in a beaker of glycerin and rotated in one direction using a mechanical stirrer, which dissolved the oil in the glycerin. However, upon reversal of the direction of the mechanical stirrer, the oil droplet was reconstituted as a single entity in the glycerin. According to him, the hologram is a model of such an enfolded reality in that "the form and structure of the entire object may be said to be enfolded within each fragment of the holographic record."

Bohm (1987) concluded that the implications of nonlocal connections are that objective reality itself is entirely a construct of the human brain. The true nature of reality remains hidden from us. Our brains operate as a holographic frequency analyzer, decoding projections from a more fundamental dimension.

Bohm finally concluded that even space and time are constructs of the human brain, and they may not exist as we perceive them.

Michael Talbot, in his renowned book, *'The Holographic Universe'* mentions that the Bohm and Pribram's theories, considered together, "provide a profound new way of looking at the world: Our brain mathematically construct objective reality by interpreting frequencies that are ultimately projections from another dimension, a deeper order of existence that is beyond both space and time. The brain is a hologram enfolded in a holographic universe."

Other Theories that Suggest Holographic Brain Mechanism

New York psychologist Edgar Levenson (1977) believes that the psychoanalytic process is best represented by the holographic model. He points out that the therapeutic process is "capricious and unreliable." When therapy is going well, the therapist is not really saying anything new to the patient, but rather, the therapist somehow resonates with something that the patient already knows. "The change results as a consequence of the expansion of configurational patterns over time." (Ferguson, 1992). The patient's insights (or revelation) can be viewed as a holographic process. All of these ideas have a coincidental connection, and neurophysiologists are beginning to accept that at least some aspects of memory are stored in a holographic way.

Philip R Westlake's Analogy

Philip R. Westlake, a University of California Los Angeles cyberneticist, proved that equations of physical holograms match what the brain does with information. According to him, there are many properties which holography potentially offers to neurophysiology. Chief among these is the property of distributiveness which is displayed only by the holographic process. This obeys Lashley's law of memory distribution in brain. Holography presents the only known way of producing one of the three types of image associability.

Schempp's Quantum Holographic Neuro-Dynamics

Professor Walter Schempp in Germany has carried some of Pribram's work much further by developing more mathematical aspects of these ideas. He has developed what he called 'Quantum Holography.' This is based on the Heisenberg group and 'phase conjugate adoptive resonance.' He used the mathematical formalism of the Weyl-Heisenberg nilpotent Lie group algebra to expand quantum information theory. This quantum hologram with PCAR concept is explained by Dr. Edgar Mitchell as follows:

'Marcer (1997) has proposed that the condition of phase-conjugate-adoptive-resonance (pcar) is a necessary condition for an object in three-dimensional reality to be perceived as it really is. That is, resonance requires a virtual path mathematically equal but opposite to the incoming sensory information about the object. Further, that it is the incoming space/time information (visual, acoustics etc) which decodes the information of the quantum hologram and establishes the condition of pcar so that accurate three-dimensional perception is possible. That is to say, both quantum information and space/time information are used in the act of perception by organisms.' (P J Marcer, 1997)

Universal Holographic Principle – Raphael Bousso

Raphael Bousso (2000) later elaborated on the Holographic Principle as a universal law that holds for all surfaces, open or closed, regardless of location or shape, and demonstrated the Universal Holographic Principle with a wide variety of examples from theoretical physics (Bousso.R, 2002).

He wrote in *Scientific American*: "The world doesn't appear to us like a hologram, but in terms of the information needed to describe it, it is one. The amazing thing is that the holographic principle works for all areas in all space times." According to his theory, the universe is a system of holographic surfaces within surfaces (a nested hierarchy of surfaces like a Russian doll). The most basic order of information is the fundamental quantum of spatial volume, i.e., the Plank's space.

The World as a Hologram – Leonard Susskind

One of the founders of string theory, Leonard Susskind interprets the holographic principle as follows:

'According to 't Hooft, the combination of quantum mechanics and gravity requires the three dimensional world to be an image of data that can be stored on a two dimensional projection much like a holographic image. The two-dimensional description only requires one discrete degree of freedom per Plank area and yet it is rich enough to describe all the three dimensional phenomena.'

In a wider sense, the theory suggests that the entire universe can be seen as a two-dimensional information structure 'painted' on the cosmological horizon such that the three-dimensions we observe are only an effective description at macroscopic scales and at low energies.

Nikolai Bernstein: Movements are Waveforms

Nikolai Bernstein discovered that even our physical movements may be encoded in our brains in a language of Fourier wave forms. He discovered that the wave forms contained hidden patterns that allowed him to predict his subject's next movement to a fraction of an inch. His research contributed to the understanding of how we learn complex physical tasks. During the 1930's, Bernstein painted white dots on the black leotards of dancers. The dots were placed over the joints. When the dancers performed against a black background, moving pictures revealed their motions as a series of dots that formed wave patterns that could be analyzed by Fourier calculus. To Pribram, this indicated that the brain stores movement patterns as wave patterns, a mechanism that could explain our ability to rapidly learn complex physical tasks. It is not by painstakingly memorizing every tiny feature of the process rather by grasping the whole flowing movement.

Pribram also did a series of studies in which he measured the electrical activity in the brains of monkeys as they performed visual tasks. He found that there was no one-to-one correspondence between visual images focused on the retina and neural impulses in the brain. Like memory, vision appears to be a distributed property of the visual cortex. Subsequent work in a number of laboratories has confirmed that cells in the visual cortex respond to the Fourier transforms of visual patterns (DeValois and others). Pribram looked at the older literature and found that other senses, including hearing, smell, touch, and taste seem to employ frequency transforms of the Fourier type. (Oschman, 1995)

Pieter van Heerden's concept of 'Recognition Holography'

How are we able to recognize a familiar face in a huge crowd of people? Physicist Pieter van Heerden proposed in 1970 that this feat is explainable if the brain is capable of 'recognition holography,' in which the optics enable two images to be compared in such a way that the degree of similarity is registered as the brightness of a spot of light. A related method, known as interference holography, enables one to recognize an image such as a familiar face, and, at the same, to highlight those features that have changed since the image was first recorded. Instruments have been constructed that use this principle to detect minute changes or stresses in manufactured objects.

Pieter Van Heerden further points out, if the brain only stored one bit (unit) of information per second for a lifetime it would require an incomprehensible 3×10^{10} elementary binary nerve impulse operations to accomplish this. Amazingly, the brain's capabilities can store many more bits than one per second; again only a holographic model of consciousness appears to explain such a talent.

He showed that holograms can store not only mental images but also such information as similarities and differences between images. This is what allows us to notice how one person's face may resemble another face, but yet be slightly different.

John Eccles – Not Energy but Information

Eccles says that the interaction between brain and mind "can be conceived as a flow of information, not of energy." (*How the Self Controls its Brain*, p. 9.) But information must surely be carried by some form of matter-energy, and if the mind can alter the probability of neural events, it is more likely that it does so by means of subtler, etheric types of force or energy, acting at the quantum or sub-quantum level. Eccles says that his theory can account for ordinary voluntary actions, but that "more direct actions of the will are precluded by the conservation laws." This is significant, for even if there is no measurable violation of energy conservation in ordinary mental phenomena, this may not be the case with certain paranormal phenomena, especially psychokinesis and materializations. Eccles, however, does not take paranormal phenomena seriously. (*'Evolution of the Brain'*, p. 242.)

Collective Consciousness Theory of Carl Jung

The great psychologist Carl Jung has proposed 'the collective unconscious' which represents a vast information store containing the entire religious, spiritual and mythological experiences of the human species. According to Jung, these archetypes have existed since ancient times and are inherited where they exist deep with the human psyche and heavily influence the thinking mind. In a similar manner, Teilhard de Chardin proposed the concept of the 'noosphere' which represents the collective consciousness of the human species that emerges from the interaction of human minds. De Chardin asserted that as individuals and the global society evolve into more complex networks, the noosphere evolves along with it.

Holographic Projection of Mental Images

Professor Sigmund Freud, a century ago, stated that under certain conditions that have not yet been sufficiently determined, even inner perceptions of ideations and emotional processes are projected outwardly, like sense perceptions, and are used to shape the outer world.

As Dr. Geley expressed it: "A certain amount of force, intelligence, and matter of the body may perform work outside of the organism – act, perceive, organize and think, without the collaboration of muscles, organs, senses, and brain. It is nothing less than the uplifted subconscious portion of our being; it constitutes, in truth, an externalizable subconscious nature, existing in the 'Me' with the normal conscious nature." (Carrington, 1909)

In an attempt to explain the holographic nature of mind process, Physicist Fred Alan Wolf points out that a piece of holographic film actually generates two images – a visual image that appears to be in the space behind the film, and a real image that comes into focus in the space in front of the film. One difference between the two is that the light waves that compose a virtual image seem to be diverging from an apparent focus or source. This is an illusion, for the virtual image of a hologram has no more extension in space than does the image in a mirror. But the real image of a hologram is formed by light waves that are coming to a focus, and this is not an illusion. The real image does possess extension in space. Unfortunately, little attention is paid to this real image in the usual application of holography because an image that comes into focus in empty air is invisible and can only be seen when dust particles pass through it, or when someone blows a puff of smoke through it.

Wolf believes that all dreams are internal holograms, and ordinary dreams are less vivid because they are virtual images. However, he thinks the brain also has the ability to generate real images, and that is exactly what it does when we are dreaming lucidly.

Bokkon (2005) explains that 'electrical signals generate visible pictures if electrical signals are converted to electromagnetic waves (EMW) of the visible range (light photons of wavelengths between 350-700 mm).' During dreams our eyes are closed, so the brain is isolated from visible EMWs of the surroundings, yet we can see visible dream pictures. It follows from the foregoing that electrical signals of the brain processes can generate visible pictures of dreams if and only if electrical signals are converted to weak EMWs of the visible range (bio-photons) in the brain. The permanent, ultra-weak electromagnetic light photon emission from living system is called bio-photon emission. However, nobody can explain origin of visible dream pictures if only the laws of physics are being taken into consideration. (Bókkon, 2005). Indeed, latest studies suggest that there is a real possibility that the brain could generate internal images by regulated biophotons during visual dreams and visual imagery (Bókkon I, 2011)

Peter Marcer, Peter Rowlands and Bernard Diaz, in their paper, *"Nilpotent: the Key to a Theory of Everything,"* suggest that the human brain is able to process meaning, i.e., process words not just syntactically but by their semantics, as known from each human beings actual geometric/holographic experience. Furthermore, they say, although such experience will be subjective in part since it takes from the reference frame and viewpoint of that individual, there always remains a fundamental mechanism, the 3D objects of the real world themselves known through their phase conjugate object images, which provide the common medium for all objective human communication.

Some Other Holographic Models of Mind and Consciousness
Pitkanen's TGD inspired Theory of Consciousness

According to Dr. Matti Pitkanen, mental imagery is something which is difficult to understand in the framework of standard neuro-science. There are empirical results suggesting that visual mental images correspond to patterns of activity inside the cortex, which are three-dimensional and continuous so that neural activation provides a concrete recognizable image about object. Also imaginative thought very much resembles visual imagery as is clear from the fact that language is full of visual metaphors. It is also known that imagery uses same regions of the cortex as real sensory experience and the problem is to understand why there is almost sensory experience involved with imagery.

According to Pitkanen, sensory input generates sensory representations based on real space-time sheets possibly accompanied by p-adic cognitive space-time sheets. Field body can share these mental images by quantum entanglement and also receive sensory information as classical signals involving using frequency coding and coding by temporal patterns. These latter representations would correspond to cognitive and emotional aspects associated with the sensory input. One could even say that higher level sensory representations are somato-sensory experiences of field body. The intersection points of real and p-adic space-time sheet would determine the physical cognitive representation and would be always discrete.

Another important fact pointed out by Pitkanen in support of the holographic brain model is that transformations between sensory modalities are easily realized in this. For instance, acoustic holograms can be transformed to optical holograms.

Max Velman's 'Reflexive Model'

Psychologist Max Velmans, in his book, *'Understanding Consciousness'* (2000), proposed a 'reflexive model' of the mind, which he illustrated by this discussion of a subject (S) looking at a cat.

"According to reductionists there seems to be a phenomenal cat in S's mind; but there is really nothing more than a state of her brain. According to the reflexive model, while 'S' is gazing at the cat, her only visual experience of the cat is the cat she sees out in the world. If she is asked to point to this phenomenal cat (her 'cat experience'), she should point not to her brain but to the cat perceived, out in space beyond the body surface." (Velmans, 2009)

Velmans suggested that this image might be like "a kind of neural 'projection hologram.'"

A projection hologram has the interesting quality that the three-dimensional image it encodes is perceived to be out in space, in front of its two-dimensional surface.

But Velmans was ambiguous about the nature of this projection. A hologram is, after all, a field phenomenon. He called it "psycho-logical" rather than "physical" and in the end said he did not know how it happened, but added "not fully understanding how it happens does not alter the fact that it happens."

Rupert Sheldrake's Model of Visual Perception

Rupert Sheldrake proposes that the outward projection of visual images occurs through perceptual fields. These are both psychological, in the sense that they underlie our conscious perceptions, and also in some sense physical, in that they actually exist outside the brain and have detectable effects, as in the sense of being stared at. Human perception is not unique in being extended, and neither are human minds. Of course, the kinds of minds and perceptions in different species differ, but what they have in common is that they depend on extended fields and are not confined to the outside of the body. He further proposes that all animals capable of vision see things through fields projected beyond the surface of their bodies (Sheldrake, 2013).

As Velmans pointed out, perceptual projection is an effect that requires an explanation, and projection requires some 'vehicle' or 'ground'.

Steven Lehar (2003) and Jeffrey Gray (2004) proposed that the entire 3-D phenomenal world is a form of 'virtual reality' located inside the brain, but these internal virtual reality projections also require some vehicle or ground. Both Lehar and Velmans proposed a holographic-type projection process. This is in effect a field model, although neither Lehar nor Velmans regard it literally as an electromagnetic field, as in a real hologram. So the ground of the projection remains obscure. If, as Velmans maintains, the projection process is non-physical, it seems impossible to conceive how it could be related to physical processes in the brain or to the electromagnetic field of light.

According to Steven Lehar:

"There is a third alternative besides the direct and indirect realist views, and that is a projection theory, whereby the brain does indeed process sensory input, but that the results of that processing get somehow projected back out of the brain to be superimposed back on the external world (Ruch 1950 quoted in Smythies 1954, O'Shaughnessy 1980 pp 168- 192, Velmans 1990, Baldwin 1992).

According to this view, the world around us is part real, and part perceptual construction and the two are spatially superimposed. However no physical mechanism has ever been proposed to account for this external projection. The problem with this notion becomes clear when considering how an artificial intelligence could possibly be endowed with this kind of external projection. Although a sensor may record an external quantity in an internal register or variable in a computer, there is no sense in which that internal value can be considered to be external to that register or to the physical machine itself, whether detected externally with an electrical probe, or examined internally by software data access. Unless the principle of external projection can be demonstrated in a simple artificial sensory system, this explanation too remains as mysterious as the property of consciousness it is supposed to explain."

Lehar's model of Gestalt Isomorphism

Steven Lehar's model of vision and consciosuness is based on the Gestalt theory – the central message of which is that the primary function of perceptual processing is the generation of a miniature, virtual-reality replica of the external world inside our head, and that the world we see around us is not the real external world but is exactly that minature internal replica. Lehar presents his model based on the above anology. According to his model,

1. When we veiw a three-dimeantional surface, our subjective experience of that surfance similtanoeulsy encodes every point on that surface in three dimensions at a high resolution; in other words, our subjective experience of the world around us is perceived not as a flatterned "2-D sketch," nor a non-spatial abstraction, but as a solid spatial world that appears to surround us in all directions.

2. Volumes of empty space are perceived with the same geometrical fidelity as volumes of solid matter.

3. Multiple transparent surfaces can be perceived simultaneously as distinct spatial structures with high resolution.

4. The infinity of external space is perceived as a finite, but fully spatial, representation that appears near-Euclidean near the body but becomes progressively flattened with distance from the body, the entire percept beign bounded by a spherical shell representing perceptual infinity.

5. Parallel lines are perceived to meet at perceptual infinity, but at the same time they are perceived as parallel and with uniform separation throughout their entire length.

6. An illusory entity, like the Kanizsa figure or the apparent-motion illusion, is not experienced as a cognitive abstraction but is experienced as an inverseion of a perceptual data structure, changing the perceived depth of every point on the perceived strcutre.

Cowan's Mentaholomorphic field

Dr. Jonathan D Cowan, in his paper, *"Thought and Mind as the Projection of Mentaholomorphic fields by the Brain: A Proposed Mechanism,"* suggests that "mind is not just inherent in the brain, but rather exists in a field that is co-located with it and simultaneouly external to it," – a multifaceted multi-dimensional 'mentaholomorphic field' with dimensions beyond the spatial dimensions of his biohologram.

Cowan proposes a new approach to understanding how the brain can generate a field that may correspond to human thoughts. It suggests that several type of rhythmic activity that travel between the thalamus and the cortex, particularly a 40 Hertz (cycles per second) even scanning thalamacortical rhythm, creates a "brain laser", projecting holographic fields related to mind and thought. Recognising the potential similarities of these fields, says Cowan, to the implicate order in David Bohm's holomovement and to Rupert Sheldrake's morphic fields, he terms them 'mentaholomophic fields.' (Cowan, 2006)

Thought-Forms and Hallucinations

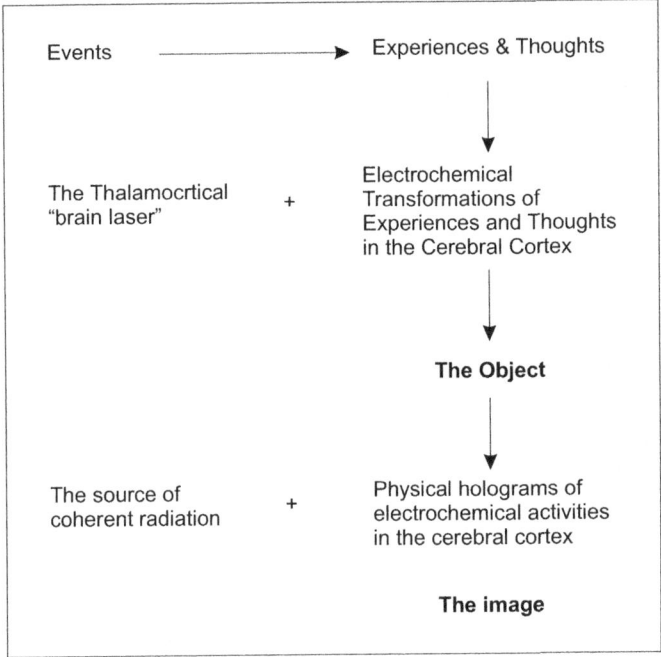

Figure 30 Mentaholomorphic Field Formation according to Dr. Cowan's Model

[Note: The boldface phrases are described in this model. The italicised phrase indicates the corresponding components in the process of forming a traditional holographic image.]

This type of proejction and reception mechanism may also help us to understand the soul, the spirit, and the collective unconscious, as well as to expore the relationships among the brain, the mind, thoughts and states of consciousness, says Dr. Cowan.

Francisco Di Biase' Quantum-Informational Holographic Model

Francisco Di Biase proposes a quantum-informational holographic model of brain-consciousness-universe interactions based in the holonomic neural networks of Karl Pribram, in the holographic quantum theory developed by David Bohm, and in the non-locality property of the quantum field described by Hiroomi Umezawa. He considers this model an extension of the interactive dualism of Sir John Eccles, of an interconnection between brain and spirit by means of quantum microsites named *dendrons* and *psychons*. He views consciousness a holoinformational flux interconnecting the holonomic informational quantum brain dynamics, with the quantum informational holographic nature of the universe. This self-organizing flux, according to Francisco Di Biase, is generated by the holographic mode of treatment of neuronal information and can be optimized through practices of deep meditation, prayer, and other states of higher consciousness that underlie the coherence of cerebral waves (Biase, 2009).

He adds, "experimental studies developed by Pribram and other consciousness researchers like Hamaeroff and Penrose, Jibu and Yassue, confirm the existence of a Quantum Brain Dynamics in nueral microtubules, in synapses and in the molecular organization of the cerebrospinal fluid. This Quantum Brain Dynamics can generate Bose-Einstein condensates and the Fröhlich effect. Bose-Einstein condensates consist of atomic particles, or in the case of Fröhlich effect, of biological molecules, that can assume high level of coherent alignment, functioning as a highly ordered and unified informational state, as seen in lasers and superconductivity."

10
CONCLUSION

The stuff of the Universe is mind stuff... the source and condition of physical reality.

— **Sir Arthur Eddington**

Now, we have reached the end of our investigations about many curious phenomena of human mind. What conclusion shall we say we have reached? One thing that is quite clear is that the mechanistic approach to mind — brain is the mind and mind is located in the brain — is open to serious scientific dispute. Second, the contemporary medical approach to mind is inherently limited. There are hundreds of mind-related activities which our current mental science fails to render any satisfactory explanation to.

We have seen sufficient reasons to convince us that *'human thought takes form.'* Creation of thought-entities is possible with the power of mind. We have seen enough cases to warrant such conclusion. Many authorities have observed this curious power of human mind. In Dr. Hibbert's 'Philosophy of Apparitions,' he rightly concludes that 'apparitions are nothing more than morbid symptoms, which are indicative of intense excitement of the renovated feelings of the mind.' Henry Frank, as early as 1916, had attempted to offer a scientific explanation for the thought-forms. He explained, "Our studies thus far have shown us that thought, as now analyzed, is actually a form of matter; that is, a series of movements in the cells in the brain, instituting a state of consciousness called a thought, become embodied in a form of volatile matter, consisting of electrons or corpuscular elements, possessing radio-active properties. This invisible form of matter is an actual and substantial as everything else in Nature, although it is not amenable to the discernment of the physical senses. However, as there are stars whose vast distance from us renders it impossible for our sense of sight to apprehend them, yet may be grasped by the telescopic eye and indelibly fastened on the photographic plate, thus proving their existence; so, as previously shown, the volatile forms of material objects and of thought may be grasped by the sensitized plate of the camera and presented to our vision."

If the human thoughts are so substantial that they have form and certain fixity, then they must also possess some potential continuity of existence. If they have an existence, such existence must be external to the brain. These characteristics of the thought-form are proved by the thought-photography and materialization experiments. In thought-photography, the mind wave that attains the form of the object thought of, affects the photographic plates and causes the object's image on it. The camera cannot enter the brain and take a picture that is there painted. It can only receive the vibrations that impinge upon it, precisely as it receives the impingement of vibrations of sunlight when it produces the photograph of an external physical object.

The thought-photography experiments demonstrate that thoughts incorporate themselves in invisible matter external to the human brain, and as such are functionally independent of it. It also reveals that the pre-matter or waves that constitute thought-forms have the nature of affecting photographic plates.

We have also seen how a thought-entity acquires its own system of intelligence, and goes out of its creator's control. If thoughts are entities, is it not natural to suppose that the entities which emanate from a distinctive personality would have a disposition to reassemble in the same memory, by the law of association, which caused them to be previously associated? This is proved in the cases of rebirth cases where the birthmarks correspond exactly to physical injuries sustained in the previous life. The spontaneous rebirth memories in children investigated by Dr. Ian Stevenson and others are so convincing that they can hardly be discarded. Free thoughts, emanating from a personality, whose integrating force is its memory, its self-consciousness, these thoughts would have a natural affinity and tend to reassemble in a new personality that would continue after the old personality had relegated to decayed matter.

Let us come to the cases of maternal impressions. We have seen that a man, who dreamed that an enemy threw a stone at him, suffered the pain and scar as if real stone was thrown at him. If an intensive thought can take form, materialize and affect photographic plates (as we have seen in the chapter of 'Thought Photography') or sometimes even the physical body of the person himself, then, what can be the effect of the mother's intensive emotions on her foetus? It is explained by 'maternal impressions.' There is a communication of thought – a kind of thought-transference between the mother and the foetus, and the child in *utero* receives the same impressions of the objects, and are moved by the same passions as their mother.

Since the mind and the body occupied different realms of being, an intermediary agent is needed to communicate the mother's mentality to the malleable body of the foetus. The possibility that mental influence may provide the true explanation of the phenomenon, at once raises a question – what is the latent mechanism within the human brain that operates unpredictably during the course of these phenomena? Unless and until we understand it, we will remain unable to understand these mind-related phenomena too. But to move further in this direction, it is necessary to establish that human perception, thinking or imagination, by itself, is able to create a force-field, that correspond to in shape and size (size may sometimes vary) to the object perceived, thought of, or imagined as the case may be, and which is capable of affecting the subtle body of the child (sub-system).

One instant will shed clear light on the matter. In a Norman farm, a hen and a cat were so affectionate with each other that the cat was frequently seen sitting upon the nest during the absence of her friend. The eggs thus hatched produced a hybrid race of fowl and cat – a fact certified by an eminent Norman naturalist Dr. Vimod at the close of the 18th century (Poyntz, 1845).

Now, let us compare this with a recent experiment conducted by Russian Scientist Dr. Yu V. Dzang Kangeng who has evidentially proved that the transfer of genetic information can be made by electromagnetic means (without biological link).

The successful transfer of genetic information from a donor bio-system (duck) to an acceptor system (hen) was achieved via high-frequency electromagnetic fields fed repeatedly through the optically-active donor bio-system and then delivered over a long period of time to the receiving bio-system in its early developmental stages. Dr. Kangeng was able to use a high-powered electrostatic energy source to generate torsion waves that transferred the wave-DNA code of a duck into a hen. Roughly 80 percent of the eggs hatched were half-duck, half-chicken hybrids.

In the first case, the transfer of genetic information was made through mind waves and in the latter case, it was through high energy laser waves. But the results are almost the same. The biological characteristic information of the donor was transferred to the acceptor through morphogenetic fields.

Bob Toben and Alfred Wolf further stated that these 'bio-gravitational fields' allow human beings to manipulate space-time curvature in a hyper-dimensional manifold to various ends. It is through this manipulation, carried out by consciousness, that paranormal and psi phenomena are manifested.

Peter Marcer and Edgar Mitchell, in their paper, *"What is Consciousness?"* assert that the double helix structure and the flat planes of DNA are the hologram planes for encoding 3 dimensional information about the embryo, such that in the quantum physical world, a complete set of 3 dimensional holographic virtual images of the embryo exists, in the embryo's DNA, from the moment of this DNA's conception. They say, "…This virtual image set, each of which is coincident with the actual embryo/foetus at each step of its development (the meaning of a phase conjugate object image being that it coincides with that of the object itself), would terminate in that of the whole embryo. This whole embryo virtual image, particular to the specific individual organism's DNA in question, can therefore be designated as the organism's Self. For in the quantum mechanics, it can produce actual observable physical effects. That is, DNA is a complete chemically based quantum-hologram 3 dimensional information processing design, which exists for each stage of the DNA's Self (and so phase conjugate adaptively resonant) incremental decoding/development up to and including the completed embryo of the organism." (Mitchell, 2000)

We have thus far seen the amazing powers of human mind. Do we know what happens to it after the death or decay of the physical body? In the case of Past Life Memories, we have seen many cases of innocent children remembering the instances in their past lives, and that they identified their acquaintances and also bore birthmarks corresponding to the physical injuries sustained by them in the previous life. We have seen cases where the scattered markings on a child's chest matched with a shotgun blast to the victim's chest in the previous life, scars on the exact area on the back of the head where the victim was knife in his previous life, and so on. The investigations made by Dr. Ian Stevenson have provided us with amble medical and photographic records to support this.

Then, what is death? Shall we get resuscitated after death with the knowledge that we lived before death and with the remembrance of the events and acquaintances of that previous life? Who is the carrier of the past memories to the present life? Is ours a physical body, or a field of pure consciousness? These are the questions that confound the scientific community.

The popular view of reincarnation is that after a person dies, the soul of that person is reborn in another body. Genetics however firmly rejects the existence of human soul as an entity separate from the gross material body and as a result genetics are not bothered to bestow their attention to the umpteen numbers of cases of rebirths reported worldwide. They however accept that every acquired characteristic of the progeny is the reaction of the organism upon a certain stimulus. Of late, experiments have been conducted under the guise of 'genetic memory' supposing that 'behavioral traits' can be transmitted from one animal to another by mere chemical input.

For example, in the year 1962, University of Michigan psychologist James McConnell found untrained flatworms could acquire knowledge (memory) by feasting on trained worms. He trained a planarian flatworm to respond to a flashing light, causing it to contract its body. If he then crushed trained planarians into pabulum which could be fed to other untrained planarians, the organisms would display the same type of body contracting behavior as the previously conditioned planarians, outperforming the control group. Although the results of this experiment were initially met with considerable skepticism, there have been many similar studies performed on rats since then.

Similar claim was made by Hungarian-born Neuro-chemist Georges Ungar, who has spent years experimenting with memory transfer. In his most notable experiment he jolted rats and mice with an electrical shock whenever they strayed into a blacked-out box, eventually conditioning them to fear the dark. Then, after decapitating his fear-trained animals, he injected a broth made out of their brain tissue into the abdominal cavities of normal mice, which ordinarily prefer the dark. More often than not, he found, the injected rodents—contrary to their nature—also began to shun the dark. (*TIME*, January 11, 1971). Mainstream science is still ignoring these findings. How the acquired characteristics do are transferred from one animal to another in this way? It drives home the message about the true nature of memory. It transcends brain – the neurological apparatus of thought and memory and cognition takes place outside the body.

Dr. Ian Stevenson proposed to call the vehicle that carries a person's mental elements between incarnations a *psychophore* (which means mind-carrying and replaces the common term 'soul'). Similar views are expressed by Dr. John Archibald Wheeler, a Princeton physicist, who believes that memories are stored in the patterns of life and past-life memories come from a universal memory source (similar to the Akashic library) that lies outside the human body.

Dr. Matti Pitkanen theorizes that communications with geometric past using time mirror mechanism in which phase conjugate photons propagating to the geometric past are reflected back as ordinary photons (typically dark photons with energies above the thermal threshold) make possible realization of the declarative memories in the brain of the geometric past. According to him, time-like entanglement explains episodal memories as sharing of mental images with the brain of the geometric past. An essential element, says Dr. Matti, is the notion of magnetic body which serves as an intentional agent 'looking' the brain of the geometric past by allowing phase conjugate dark photons with negative energies from it as ordinary photons.

Thus far, we have seen enough number of cases which convince us that the human thought takes form on certain circumstances and such forms even have their own intelligence and acts as 'independent entities'. We have also seen that such thought-images can be impressed upon photographic plates – solid evidence which can be experimented and tested in any scientific laboratory. Materialization experiments again demonstrated that human thoughts take form and under certain circumstances, they materialize with the aid of some sort of pre-matter called ectoplasm. As the human thoughts affects the photographic plate, or the surroundings, the intensive thoughts of the mother have their own impact on the foetus she carries. Cases of maternal impressions prove this.

But mere anecdotes and observations alone cannot be a sufficient argument for any doctrine which is not rationally accounted for by any known scientific principle. And here comes to our aid the theory of holographic mind.

Both mind and matter are not what they mean to our ordinary perspective. The relationship between mind and matter is also totally different from what the traditional dualistic and the materialistic theories have proposed. This dualistic theory also contended that mind cannot affect matter and there can be no mind-to-mind interactions. But Heinsenberg's uncertainty principle, discovered in 1927, suddenly made it clear that it is mind or consciousness of the scientists which invariably intervenes, affects, and even determines the ultimate findings in the world of sub-atomic particles. Nobel-physicist Eugene Wigner asserts that it is impossible to give a description of quantum mechanical process without explicit reference to consciousness (Jitatmananda, 1993).

Swamy Vivekananda explained this a century earlier: "Mind at a very low rate of vibration is what is known as matter. Matter at a high rate of vibration is what is known as mind. Both are the same substance." (Vivekananda, The Complete Works of Swami Vivekananda, 1978). He further clarified that what we call matter does not exist at all and it is only a certain state of force. Solidity, hardness or any other state of matter can be provided to be the result of motion. Matter is only externalised thought, according to Vivekananda.

Russian psychologists Dr. Alexander P. Dubrov and Dr. Veniamin N. Pushkin have written extensively on the idea. To use their own words, "Records of ejection of psychophysical structures outside the brain would provide direct evidence of brain holograms."

Michael Talbot wrote on David Bohm's Theorem in his book, *"Beyond the Quantum."*

"Perhaps the most intriguing aspect of Bohm's theory is how it might apply to our understanding of the human mind. As he sees it, if every particle of matter interconnects with every other particle, the brain itself must be viewed as infinitely interconnected with the rest of the universe. Bohm believes that such a mind-boggling interconnectedness might even shed light on the phenomenon of consciousness itself.... For example, if the universe is holographic and each human brain interpenetrates every other human brain (indeed, every other particle in the universe) on some level that is beyond ordinary subjective experience, the human race may really be one organism." (Talbot, Beyond the Quantum, 1986)

Thus the theory of holographic universe proves to be intrinsically connected with the theory of holographic brain and mind. Not only the brain, but the body and even the whole universe appear to be a hologram – one participating in another forming a universal fabric of interaction and communication. It is a hierarchical system of "hologram within a hologram" like a Chinese nesting doll. These are not mere theoretical abstractions or philosophical speculations; but something flowing out of pure science based on the empirical observations of natural phenomena.

There are many experimental evidences to prove remote-mental interactions. Of particular, William G.Braud and Marilyn J.Schlitz, in their paper, *'Consciousness Interactions with Remote Biological Systems: Anomalous Intentionality Effects,'* have demonstrated that persons are able to mentally influence remote biological systems, even when those systems are isolated at distant locations and screened from all conventional informational and energetic influences. The effect, according to Braud, appears to occur in a "goal-directed" manner: that is, the influencer need not understand or even be aware of the specific physical or physiological processes which bring about the desired outcome. Maintaining a strong intention of a desired goal event, focusing attention upon the relevant aspect of the target system, and filling oneself with strong imagery of the desired biological activity are, under certain conditions, accompanied by a shift in the target system's activity in the intended direction. (William G. Braud, 1991)

Spyros Papageorgiou has demonstrated that physical forces may cause Hox gene collinearity in the primary and secondary axes of the developing vertebrates. (Papageorgiou, 2011) Remote gene expression based on the use of electromagnetic coding of DNA could give rise to rather exotic phenomena such as maternal impressions, telegony etc., which cannot be understood in terms of standard genetics. Thus, the recent findings in the quantum realm and even in genetics suggest that there is nothing absurd in the notion of subtle field orchestrating the physical body. Concepts like thought-forms, thought-body, subtle body, etc are not mere metaphysical fantasies, but are scientific truths.

To further building the case for a holographic reality, consider the following:

- A holographic universe helps explain all paranormal and mystical experiences and shed light on an increasing number of previously inexplicable phenomena.
- Near-Death Experiences can be explained by a holographic model, in that death is a shifting of a person's consciousness from one level of the hologram of reality to another, as theorized by Dr. Kenneth Ring.
- Current neuro-physiological models of the brain are inadequate and only a holographic model can explain such things as archetypal experiences, encounters with the collective conscious, and other unusual phenomena experienced during altered states of consciousness. In the field of neurophysiology numerous studies have corroborated Pribram's various predictions about the holographic nature of memory and perception.
- Physicist Fred Wolf asserts that the holographic model explains lucid dreams – unusually vivid dreams in which the dreamer believes he or she is awake. Wolf believes such dreams are actually visits to parallel or "shaded" realities. He also states that the holographic model will ultimately allow science to develop a "physics of consciousness" that will enable science to begin to explore more fully these other dimensional levels of existence.
- Synchronicity can be explained by the holographic model. Out thought processes are much more intimately connected to the physical world than has been previously thought.
- Telepathy, precognition, mystical feelings of oneness with the universe, and even psychokinesis can be explained through the holographic model.
- Holography can explain how our brains can store so many memories in so little space and enable face recognition.

I am fully aware of the fact that I am treading a dangerous ground of mind science. Still, what prompted me to venture on, is but a desire to further the importance of the holographic theory of mind, which has the capacity to explain an important number of facts, including facts yet unknown.

I am of the firm belief that the deeper modern research penetrates into the more recondite regions of biology, psychophysiology and psychology, the more readily will reason be inclined to welcome the notion as a fertile working hypothesis to coordinate a considerable number of the mental, vital and physical phenomena of human personality, similar to those narrated in this book, which otherwise remain in our hands as a confused and inexplicable conglomerate.

BIBLIOGRAPHY

(1839). *The Family magazine, 4.* J. A. James & Co.

(1888). *The Chicago Medical Times, 20.*

(1892). *Proceedings of the Society for Psychical Research, 7.*

(1897). *Mind, 1,* 397.

(1912). *The American Journal of Clinical Medicine, 19,* 1137.

(1952). *Tomorrow,* p. 79.

A Physiological Phenomenon, or the Snake Man: Robert H Copeland. (1839). *Boston medical and surgical journal,* 99.

Abercrombie, J. (1875). Intellectual Powers. In J. McCosh, *The Scottish Philosophy* (pp. 406-408). Applewood Books.

Activity of the Brain during Dream. (1885). *Science, VI* (141), 344.

Alberg, A. (1899). *Frost Flowers on the Windows.* Chicago: Fraternal Printing Co.

Atkinson, W. W. (1909). *The Subconscious and the Superconscious Planes of Mind.* Hollister: Yogebooks.

Bakewell, S. (1998). Illustrations from the Wellcome Institute Library: Images of Bodily Transformation. *Medical History,* 503-517.

Barrett, S. W. (1917). *On the Threshold of the Unseen.* E.P.Dutton & Co.

Becker, C. B. (1993). *Paranormal Experience and Survival of Death.* SUNY Press.

Betts, G. H. (1914). *The Mind and Its Education.* Toronto: The Cop Clark Co., Ltd.

Biase, F. D. (2009). Quantum-Holographic Informational. *NeuroQuantology,* 657-664.

Blavatsky, H. P. (2012). *Isis Unveiled: A Master-Key to the Mysteries of Ancient and Modern Science and Theology.* Cambridge University Press.

Bliss, E. L. (1986). *Multiple Personality, Allied Disorders, and Hypnosis.* Oxford University Press.

Bob Toben, F. A. (1982). *Space-time and beyond: toward an explanation of the unexplainable.* Dutton.

Boismont, A. B. (1855). *History of Dreams, Visions, Apparitions, Ecstasy, Magnetism and Somnambulism.* Philadelphia: Lindsay and Blakistan.

Boismont, A.-J.-F. B. (1853). *Hallucinations.* Lindsay and Blakiston.

Boismont, A.-J.-F. B. (1859). *On hallucinations.* H. Renshaw.

Bókkon I, S. V. (2011). Emergence of intrinsic representations of images by feedforward and feedback processes and bioluminescent photons in early retinotopic areas. *Journal of Integrated Neuroscience,* 47-64.

Bókkon, I. (2005). Dreams and Neuroholography: An interdisciplinary interpretation of development of homeotherm state in evolution. *Sleep and Hypnosis,* 61-76.

Bousso.R. (2002). The Holographic Principle. *Reviews in Modern Physics,* 825-874.

Bull, T. (1837). *Hints to mothers for the management of health during the period of pregnancy and in the lying-in room.* London: Longman.

C.W.Leadbeater. (1895). *The Astral Plane.* Adyar: Theosophical Publishing House.

C.W.Leadbeater. (1895). *The Astral Plane.* Madras: The Theosophist Office.

Carlyon, C. (1836). *Early Years and Late Reflections.* Whittaker and Company.

Carrington, H. (1909). *Eusapia Palladino.* New York: B.W.Dodge & Company.

Carrington, H. (1919). *Modern Psychical Phenomena.* London: Kegan Paul, Trench, Tubner & Co., Ltd.

Cater, J. H. (1984). *The Awesome Life Force.* Health Research Books.

Church J, L. (1968). *Childhood and Adolescence.* New York: Random House.

Coates, J. (1906). *Seeing the Invisible.* London: L.N.Flower & Co.

Conscious, F. t. (1920). *Gustave Geley.* London: Harper & Brothers Publishers.

Cowan, J. D. (2006). Thought and Mind as the Projection of Mentaholomorphic fields by the Brain: A Proposed Mechanism. *Subtle Energies & Energy Medicine, 17,* 123-149.

Crowe, C. (1850). *The night-side of nature; or, Ghosts and ghost-seers.* J. S. Redfield.

Bibliography

Cunninghm, R. (1999, March 30). Photos-With. *Weekly World News*, pp. 70-71.

curran, J. (1867). Case of Monstrosity dependent on Mental Shock. *The British Medical Journal*, 468.

Curran, J. W. (1869). On Maternal Impressions. *The Medical Press & Circular*, 320-321.

Darget, L. (1911). *La Photographie Transcendantale.* Paris: Librairie Nationale.

Dolores Ashcroft-Nowicki, J. H. (2001). *Magical Use of Thought Forms: A Proven System of Mental & Spiritual Empowerment.* Llewellyn Worldwide.

Dr. Truck. (1859). Maternal Imagination. In C. (. Institute, *College journal of medical science.*

Eisenbud, J. (1989). *The World of Ted Serios: "Thoughtographic" Studies of an Extraordinary Mind.* McFarland & Company Incorporated Pub.

Eisenbud, J. (1985). Visions, Old and New: An Addendum to Paranormal Film Forms and Paleolithic Rock Engravings. (D. Stillings, Ed.) *Archaeus, 3,* 9-16.

Elam, C. (1869). *Physician's Problems.* London: Macmillan and Co.

Emanuel Swedenborg, G. F. (1985). *A view from within: a compendium of Swedenborg's theological thought.* Swedenborg Foundation.

Estabrooks, G. H. (1943). *Hypnotism.* Dutton.

Evans-Wentz, W. Y. (2000). *The Tibetan Book of the Great Liberation:Or the Method of Realizing Nirvana through Knowing the Mind.* Oxford University Press.

Flammarion, C. (1922). *Death and Its Mystery at the Moment of Death.* (L. C. Eleanor Stimson Brooks, Trans.) Century Company.

Fowler, O. S. (1844). Marks, Deformities and Monstrosities. In O. S. Fowler, *Works* (p. 224).

Garland, H. (1936). *Forty Years of Psychic Research.* The MacMillan Co.

Garrett, E. J. (1949). *Adventures in the Supernormal: A Personal Memoir.* Creative Age Press.

Geley, G. (1927). *Clairvoyance and Materialization: A Record of Experiments.* T.Fisher Unwin Ltd.

Geley, G. (1920). *From the Unconscious to the Conscious.* London: Harper & Brothers Publishers.

Goulet, A. (2011). *Optiques: The Science of the Eye and the Birth of Modern French Fiction.* University of Pennsylvania Press.

Hammond, W. A. (1868). On the Influence of the Maternal Mind Over the Offspring during Pregnancy and Lactation. In *Detroit review of medicine and pharmacy.*

Haraldsson, E. (2000). Birthmakrs and Claim of Previous-life Memories: II The Case of Chatura Karunaratne. *Journal of the Society for Psychical Research,* 82-92.

Henry Goadby, E. K. (1856). Influence of the Mind on the Foetus. *The Medical independent: a monthly review of medicine and surgery.*

Hestlk, W. M. (1899). Four Cases of Monstrosities in the same Family. *British Medical Journal.*

Hudson, T. J. (1969). *The Law of Psychic Phenomena.* Red Wheel/Weiser.

Jibu, M. (1995). *Quantum Brain Dynamics and Consciousness: An Introduction.* John Benjamins Publishing.

Jitatmananda, S. (1993). *Holistic Science and Vedanta.* Bombay: Bharatiya Vidya Bhavan.

Jordan, D. S. (1896, September). The Sympsychograph: A Study in Impressionist Physics. *Popular Science,* p. 597.

Joyce, A. b. (1991). *The Encyclopedia of Parapsychology and Psychical Research.* Paragon House.

Kompanje, E. (2008). 'The devil lay upon her and held her down' - Hypnagogic hallucinations and sleep paralysis described by the Dutch physician Isbrand van Diemerbroeck (1609–1674) in 1664. *Journal of Sleep Research,* 464-467.

L.B.Murphy. (1962). *The Widening World of Children.* New York: Basic Books.

L.Dossey. (1989). *Recoverying the Soul.* New York: Bantam Books.

Laszlo, E. (2008). *Quantum Shift in the Global Brain.* Inner Traditions.

Leadbeater, C. W. (1930, January). Photographying the Unseen. *The International Photographer,* p. 36.

Bibliography

Lehar, S. (n.d.). *The Dimension of Conscious Experience: A Quantitative Phenomenology.* Retrieved December 30, 2013, from http://cns-alumni.bu.edu/~slehar/webstuff/consc/consc.html

Liverziani, F. (n.d.). *The Hope Booklet.* Retrieved August 21, 2013, from http://www.convivium-roma.it/

Long, M. F. (1948). *The Secret Science Behind Miracles.* Retrieved December 1, 2013, from Sacred Texts: http://www.sacred-texts.com/nth/ssbm/ssbm13.htm

Macnish, R. (1835). *The Philosophy of Sleep.* New York: William Pearson & Co.

Maudsley, H. (1878). *Hallucinations of the Senses.*

Mitchell, P. M. (2000). What is Consciousness? In P. V. Loocke, *The Physical Nature of Consciousness* (pp. 145-174). John Benjamins Publishing Company.

Mitchinson, W. (1991). *The nature of their bodies: women and their doctors in Victorian Canada.* University of Toronto Press.

Moll, A. (1890). *Hynotism.* New York: Scribner & Welford.

Newbold, W. R. (1897). Subconscious Reasoning. *Society for Psychical Research*, 11.

Notzing, B. V. (1923). *Phenomena of Materialization.* London: Kegan Paul, Trench, Trubner & Co Ltd.

O.S.Fowler. (1843). Hereditary Descent: Its Laws and Facts. *The American Phrenological Journal and Miscellany*, 619.

Oschman, J. L. (1995). Somatic Recall - Soft Tissue Holography. *Massage Therapy Journal.*

Over, R. V. (1972). *Unfinished Man.* World Pub.

P J Marcer, W. (1997). Model of the Neuron Working by Quantum Hologram. *Informatica*, 519-534.

Panchadasi, S. (1915). *The Astral World: Its Scenes, Dwellers, and Phenomena.* Advanced Thought Publishing Company.

Papageorgiou, S. (2011). Model of Physical Forces Causing the intriguing Hox gene Collinearity. *Development, Growth & Differenciation*, 53, 1-8.

Parish, E. (1897). *Hallucinations and Illusions: A Study of the Fallacies and Perception.* London: Walter Scott Ltd.

Parish, E. (1897). *Hallucinations and Illusions: A Study of the Fallacies of Perception.* W. Scott Limited.

Pasricha, S. K. (1998). Cases of the Reincarnation Type in Northern India with Birthmakrs and Birth Defects. *Journal of Scientific Exploration,* 259-293.

Pelley, W. D. (n.d.). *BEYOND GRANDEUR.* Retrieved August 5, 2013, from http://cdn.preterhuman.net/texts/religion.occult.new_age/William%20Pelley%20-%20Beyond%20Grandeur.pdf

Pereria, A. (2003). The Quantum Mind - Classical Brain Problem. *NeuroQuantology,* 94-118.

Photographic Effects of Lightning. (n.d.). *Recreative Science: A Record and Remembrancer of Intellectual Observation.* London: Groombridge and Sons.

Piaget, J. (1999). *Play, Dreams and Imitation in Childhood.* Routledge.

Pitkanen, M. (n.d.). *A Model for Remote Mental Interactions.* Retrieved December 28, 2013, from Emergent Mind: http://www.emergentmind.org/pitkanenI2a.htm

Poyntz, A. (1845). *A World of Wonders, with Anecdotes and Opinions concerning popular Superstitions.* London.

Pribram, K. H. (1969). The Four R's of Remembering. In K. H. Pribram, *The Biology of Learning* (pp. 191-225). New York: Harcourt, Brace & World.

Raupert, J. G. (1920). *The new black magic and the truth about the ouija-board.* New York: The Devin-Adair company.

Richet, C. (1923). *Thirty Years of Psychical Research.* W.Collins Sons & Co Ltd.

Russell, G. W. (1920). *The Candle of Vision.* London: Macmillan & Co., Ltd.

Sheldrake, R. (2013). *The Sense Of Being Stared At: And Other Aspects of the Extended Mind.* Random House.

Sir Daniel Keyte Sandford, T. T. (1836). *The Popular Encyclopedia.* Blackie & Son.

Stead, W. T. (1921). *Real Ghost Stories.* New York: George H. Doran Company.

Stevenson, I. (1993). Birthmarks and Birth Defects Corresponding to wounds on Deceased Persons. *Journal of Scientific Exploration,* 403-410.

Stevenson, I. (1973). Characteristics of Cases of the Reincarnation Type in Ceylon. In *Contribtuions to Asian Studies: 1973* (pp. 26-39). Brill Academic Publishing.

Stevenson, I. (1997). *Where Reincarnation and Biology Intersect.* Praeger Publishers.

Story, F. (2000). *Rebirth as Doctrine and Experience: Essays and Case Studies.* Buddhist Publication Society.

Talbot, M. (1986). *Beyond the Quantum.* Macmillan.

Talbot, M. (1988). Swedenborg and the Holographic Paradigm. In R. Larsen, *In EmanuelSwedenborg: A Continuing Vision* (pp. 443-448). New York: Swedenborg Foundation.

Talbot, M. (1996). *The Holographic Universe.* HarperCollins.

The Complete Works of Swami Vivekananda. (1978). India.

Todd, R. B. (1839). Generation. *The cyclopaedia of anatomy and physiology,2*.

Tuke, D. H. (1873). *Illustrations of the influence of the mind upon the body in health and disease.* Philadelphia: Henry C. Lea.

Tuke, D. H. (1873). *Illustrations of the influence of the mind upon the body in health and disease.* Henry C. Lea.

Turner. (2007). Of Spots and Marks. *Eighteenth-century British Midwifery*, 225.

Upatnieks.J, L. E. (1965). *Scientific American*, 212:34.

Velmans, M. (2009). *Understanding Consciousness.* Routledge.

Vitvan. (1946). *Clear Thinking.* School of the Natural Order.

Vivekananda, S. (1978). *The Complete Works of Swami Vivekananda.* Calcutta: A.

Vivekananda, S. (1978). *The Complete Works of Swami Vivekananda.* Calcutta: Advaita Ashram.

Walter J. Black, I. (1928). *World's Great Detective Stories.*

William G. Braud, P. &. (1991). Consciousness Internations with Remote Biological Systems: Anomalous Intensionality Effects. *Subtle Energies*, 1-46.

Bibliography

Wilson, I. (1989). *Stigmata: an investigation into the mysterious appearance of Christ's wounds in hundreds of people from Medieval Italy to modern America.* Harper & Row.

Xiong, J. H. (2009). *The Outline of Parapsychology.* University Press of America.

INDEX

A

A Child Half-Fish, 146
A Monstrous Cat-headed Child, 148
A Snake Man, 147-8
Abraham Lincoln, 81
Thought photograph of, 83
Albert Alberg, 53
Alexander P.Dubrov, 168, 109
Alexandra David-Neel, 18-9
Alfred Lechler, 176
Ali Yakubov, 157-8
Annie Besant, 6, 12, 13, 74
Arthur Ladbroke Wigan, 64
August Kekule von Stradonitz, 39

B

Bal masque, 58
Bell's Theorem, 10
Bhagavat Gita, 109
Bio-Holographic, 5, 9
   model 133
Blavatsky, 45, 168
Bose-Einstein condensates, 201

C

Cameron Lee, 73
Captain Walter Carey, 16
Carl Jung, 10, 38, 85
Collective conscious theory of, 193
Central Nervous System, 69
Charles Darwin, 104, 140
Charles Dickens, 36
Charles Richet, 7, 90, 94, 101, 106, 169
Children Resembling a Frog, 150-1
Clairvoyant, 12, 33, 104, 172
Colborn, 42
Collective Consciousness, 193
Commandant Darget, 7, 75-6
Countess de Boigne, 155

D

Daisy Wallace, 72
David Bohm, 10, 188, 199, 200, 209
Dermographism, 168-9, 173
DNA, 9, 205-6, 210
Dr. Hyppolyte Baraduc, 7, 70, 73-5, 84
Dr.Charles Baudouin, 169
Dr.Charles Richet, 7, 90, 94, 101, 106, 169
Dr.Munro, 156
Dream-OBE, 45
Dream-thought transmission, 53-4
Durga Jatav, 48-9

Index

E

Edgar Cayce, 16
Edgar Levenson, 189
Edgar Mitchell, 16, 190, 205
Edmund Gurney, 57, 59
Edward Kelly, 47
Eisenbud, 78-80
Elemental essence, 12-3
Eliphas Levi, 14
Emanuel Swedenborg, 15
Engrams, 185
Erlendur Haraldsson, 115, 120
Eusapia Palladino, 76
Eva.C, 93-4, 96, 107

F

Figures in Imagination, 42
Francisco Di Biase, 200
Franek Kluski, 97-101
Frightened by a Cow, 151
Fröhlich effect, 201
Fukurai, 77

G

George H. Estabrooks, 61, 67
George William Russell, 43
Giuseppe Tartini, 37
Gustave Geley, 93, 96-7

H

H.V.Hilprecht, 41-2
Hanumant Saxena, 125-6
Henri Bergon, 179

Henry Stapp, 179
Herbert Spencer, 104
Hirkill, phantom man 98
Hologram,
  brain, 169
  vacuum, 134-5
  what is, 181-4
Holographic,
  holographic mind, 178, 208
  holographic nature, 9, 168, 179-81
  holographic projection, 10, 193
  holomovement, 188, 199
Honoré de Balzac, 35
Hyacinthe Zanglois, 66
Hypnagogic hallucinations, 6
hypnopompic hallucinations, 6
Hypnotism and Auto-suggestion, 67

I

Ian Stevenson, 7, 48, 111, 113, 114, 124, 133, 165, 173, 174, 176, 203, 206, 207
Ian Wilson, 177
imaginary companions, 24
Impact of Dreams, 164
Impact of Paintings, 164-5
Inglis Roger, 72-3

J

James Coats, 65
James Oxenham, 23

Index

Jean Louis Rodolphe Agassiz, 39-40
Jean Piaget, 24
Jesus Christ, 158, 175
Johannes Brahmns, 34
John Eccles, 192, 200
John Evelyn, 157
John Oxenham, 23
Jonathan D Cowan, 199

K

Karl H Pribram, 185
Karl Spencer Lashley, 185
Kathleen Goligher, 103-4
King Kurigalzu, 41
Krishnan Chaudhri, 118-9

L

Lama, 18, 19
Leadbeater, 6, 12, 13, 19, 23, 74, 88
Leonard Susskind, 190
London Evening Standard, 172

M

Ma Khim Mar Htoo, 130
Malformations, 141, 144
Marcer, Peter 190, 194, 205
Margarent Schutlz, 83
materialization, 7, 11, 75, 88, 89, 93, 94, 95, 96, 97, 100, 101, 105, 106, 107, 193, 203, 208
Maternal impressions, 8, 137, 138, 139, 141, 145, 151, 152, 157, 160, 165, 166, 167, 168, 204, 208, 210

Matryoshka doll, 10
Matti Pitkanen, 133, 195, 207
Max Velman, 196
Mental hallucinations, 6, 55, 62
Mental stigmata, 168, 176
Michael Talbot, 15, 135, 188, 209
Mike Foster, 158
Monstrosities, 144
Montevecchi of Bologna, 51
Moris Klaw, 44

N

Nikolai Bernstein, 191
non-local, 109, 110, 111, 134, 166, 185, 200

O

Object wave, 181, 184
Ochorowicz, 89-93, 99
Olga Kahl, 172-3
Opera House, 80
Optical Laws, 59-60

P

Paraffin moulds, 100
Past-life memories, 112, 207
    types, 112
Past-life spontaneous memory, 111
Paul Greguss, 69
Paul Pietsch, 187
Phantasms, 88
Philip Aylesford, 20
Philip R. Westlake, 189

Index

Photographic memory, 50
   Eidetic memory
Phyllis Atwater, 50
Pieter van Heerden, 187, 192
Portrayals, 15
Previous personality, 7, 8, 112, 114, 136
Psychic humus, 34
Psychophore, 111, 207
Psychoplasm, 111
Psycho-somatic, 4, 132, 176
Psychotherapeutic, 135

Q

Quantum Brain Dynamics, 201

R

Rajani Singh, 127-8
Ranbir Singh, 123
Rebirth, 7, 109, 111, 133, 203, 206
Reference wave, 181, 184
Resembling a Rabbit, 152
Robert Boyle, 140
Robert Dale Owen, 27
Robert Macnish, 66
Rupert Sheldrake, 196, 199

S

Saint-Saens, 36
Samkhya philosophers, 111
Samuel Taylor Coleridge, 37
Satwant K. Pasricha, 7, 115
Schrenct-Notzing, 89, 95, 106

Semih Tutusmus, 124-5
Shuffle Brain Theory, 187
Shun Shen Tao Temple, 85-6
Sigmund Freud, 193
Silver Belle, 101-3
Sir Humphry Davy, 4
Sir Issac Newton, 42
Sir James Mackintosh, 51
Skeleton Spectators, 66
Spirit-Photography, 81
Spontaneous memory recall, 111, 113
Spyros Papageorgiou, 210
Stefan Bolling, 71
Stephen E. Robbins, 179
Steven Lehar, 197-8
Stigmata, 8, 50, 168, 171, 174, 175, 176, 177
Stigmata: Quranic verse, 158
Suggestion and Auto-Suggestion, 169
Suggestive Therapeutics, 173
Swami Panchadasi, 13
Swamy Vivekananda, 209
Synchronicity, 211

T

Ted Serios, 7, 78, 80
Telepathic photography, 74
The 'Napoleon Eyed' Child, 155
The Astral Plane, 13, 14, 19, 88, 89
The Dream Detective, 44

The Monkey Girl, 149
The New York Times, 170
The Philip Experiment, 20-1
The Skippy Experiment, 21
The Telegraph, 158
Therese Neumann, 171
Thiang San Kla, 115-6
Thought form,
  general appearance, 13
  in history, 14
Thought-photography, 6, 11, 54, 70, 81, 83, 106, 203
Tulpa, 17-8
Turtle Man, 152

V

Vedavyasa, 179

Veniamin N.Pushkin, 168, 209
Vern Cameron, 45
Violet Penry Evans, 61
Visual imagery, 194-5

W

Walter Schempp, 189
Wave front reconstruction, 183
Wave-substance, 15
Wilhelm Wundt, 59
William Thomas Stead, 27, 29, 88
Willie Schwanbolz, 83
Wolfgang Amadeus Mozart, 35

Y

Yashbir Yadav, 128
Yu V. Dzang Kangeng, 204

Made in the USA
Monee, IL
05 April 2021